The Culture
and
Politics of Literacy

The Culture and Politics of Literacy

W. Ross Winterowd

42-309

New York   Oxford
OXFORD UNIVERSITY PRESS
1989

Oxford University Press

Oxford New York Toronto
Delhi Bombay Calcutta Madras Karachi
Petaling Jaya Singapore Hong Kong Tokyo
Nairobi Dar es Salaam Cape Town
Melbourne Auckland
and associated companies in
Berlin Ibadan

Copyright © 1989 by Oxford University Press, Inc.

Published by Oxford University Press, Inc.,
200 Madison Avenue, New York, New York 10016

Oxford is a registered trademark of Oxford University Press

All rights reserved. No part of this publication may be reproduced,
stored in a retrieval system, or transmitted, in any form or by any means,
electronic, mechanical, photocopying, recording, or otherwise,
without prior permission of Oxford University Press.

Library of Congress Cataloging-in-Publication Data
Winterowd, W. Ross.
The culture and politics of literacy / W. Ross Winterowd.
p. cm. Includes index.
ISBN 0-19-505708-2
1. Literacy—United States.
2. Reading—United States. 3. Language arts—United States.
4. English language—United States—Rhetoric. I. Title.
LC151.W53 1989 88-22667 428.4—dc19 CIP

All or parts of the following appear in this volume by permission:

"The Library of Babel," in *Ficciones* by Jorge Luis Borges, copyright © 1962 by Grove
Press, Inc. Translated from the Spanish, copyright © 1956 by Emece Editores, S.A., Buenos
Aires.

"St. Maarten's Jaycee Bryson Elected 'Jaycee of the World,' " by Defender. Windward
Islands *Newsday* 4, 491 (November 24, 1980), 12.

"Creature," by Beverly McLoughland. *Language Arts* 63, 5 (September 1986), 481.
Copyright © 1986 by the National Council of Teachers of English. Reprinted by permission.

"The Readability of an Unreadable Text," by Robert M. Gordon. *English Journal* 69, 3
(March 1980), 60–61. Copyright © 1980 by the National Council of Teachers of English.
Reprinted with permission.

Adaptations from *Composition/Rhetoric: A Synthesis,* by W. Ross Winterowd (Carbondale,
Ill.: Southern Illinois University Press, 1986).

Excerpt on p. 105 is reprinted by permission from *IBM Basic,* 2nd ed., © 1982 by
International Business Machines Corporation.

"Composing: A Case Study" from *The Contemporary Writer,* third edition, by W. Ross
Winterowd, copyright © 1989 by Harcourt Brace Jovanovich, Inc., reprinted by permission
of the publisher.

One Writer's Beginnings, by Eudora Welty (Cambridge, Mass.: Harvard University Press,
1983, 1984). Copyright © 1983, 1984 by Eudora Welty. Reprinted by permission.

9 8 7 6 5 4 3 2 1

Printed in the United States of America
on acid-free paper

For Christopher "Topher" Ross
our miracle,
our glowing one

Contents

Introduction

What This Book Can Do For You

If your children, in school or in college, are having difficulty reading and writing, *The Culture and Politics of Literacy* will help you understand the problem and will suggest what you can do to help solve it.

If you are concerned with educational policy at the local, state, or national level, *The Culture and Politics of Literacy* will provide you with the background necessary for making informed decisions.

If you want to understand how written language works as a means of communication and an instrument of thought, you will find this book enlightening.

If you are preparing to be an educator, the book will give you a theoretical background for understanding reading and writing and will help in teaching.

Finally, the book contains a good deal of practical advice. For instance, pages 77–82 will show you simple ways in which you can make your own documents (such as business letters, proposals, and reports) more readable and effective.

The Culture and Politics of Literacy is for everyone who has a child in grade school or high school, acquiring the basics of reading and writing and then moving onward to a "higher" literacy that allows him or her to participate fully in the culture and economy of our society—and particularly for those readers whose children are having difficulties with reading and writing. Chapters 1 through 7 explain reading and writing as psycholinguistic and social processes. The last chapter contains a guide to evaluating the instruction in reading and writing that children receive in the schools.

The book is for anyone who puzzles over the fact that virtually every college and university must provide remedial instruction in reading and, particularly, writing.

It is for anyone interested in the fact that the United States of America is going through a literacy crisis. In the chapters that follow, I will cite data regarding the millions who are unable to read the most basic and essential documents (such as labels on medicine bottles or voting ballots) or complete the simplest writing task (say, filling out an application for a driver's license).

It is for anyone interested in how reading and writing affect the individual's ability to think—and how literacy changes society, culturally and socially.

It is also for anyone who has puzzled over the everyday miracle whereby black squiggles against a white background transmit meaning across time and space.

The "Message" of This Book

Boiled down to its gist, *The Culture and Politics of Literacy* develops this thesis:

> Literacy is a relative term. Its meaning depends on individual needs and values and the norms and expectations of the social group of which the individual is a part.

As an example, consider a teenager who is able to comprehend the instructions on an employment application and fill out that form, but who is unable to read the daily newspaper. This person might consider himself or herself literate and might be so considered by family members and neighborhood peers. But put this youngster in another situation, amid people with other values, and he or she could well be deemed either illiterate or marginally literate.

Later in this book we will discuss cultural literacy: what people need to know in order to function as readers and writers in educated society (for instance, the meaning of such terms as *relativity* and *apartheid*). Everyone who can read (that is, comprehend) articles in news magazines such as *Time,* editorials in the daily paper, books such as this one, and even many advertisements shares with other readers a large body of general information. If a person does not have that "cultural" information, can he or she be considered literate? The U.S. Army has shown that soldiers can gain specific literacy skills very quickly—for instance, the ability to read certain manuals and to fill out reports. Are such individuals literate? These are not easy questions, and we will develop tentative answers as the discussion progresses.

The Same Point from Another Angle

Reading and writing are not so much skills as they are reflections of values and life-styles.

To you, the reader, literacy—the ability to read and write—must seem straightforward and uncomplicated. After all, you undoubtedly grew up with books, and learning to read them was as natural as learning to roller-skate and ride a bicycle. As you became a reader, you also became a writer, penning thank-you notes to relatives; composing book reports, stories, and themes in school; beyond grade school and high school, writing your way through college; and beyond college, in your professional life, writing memos, reports, proposals, and much else.

But change the cultural orientation by a very few degrees, and reading and writing are no longer taken for granted, are not even necessarily valued accomplishments. "Adam," a young man who was in one of my classes at the University of Southern California, is an example. He could not remember ever having read anything (other than the sports section of the newspaper) merely for pleasure, and this college student was not from the ghetto, but from an affluent suburb. He told me that his family was not "book-oriented" and subscribed to only one magazine, *Newsweek.* Although his father was a professional and his mother a college graduate, the young man could not remember having seen either of them read a book for pleasure.

Adam was not totally illiterate, but he was functionally so in the context of the university. His abilities were so minimal that he was unable to do the writing required in his courses (not just English). His reading was excruciatingly slow, and his comprehension was so impaired that he had great difficulty mastering the subject matter in his textbooks. In the middle of his second semester at the university, he dropped out.

I strongly suspect that Adam's problem was simply this: his family and peers did not value literacy, hence neither did he. To "remediate" Adam's weaknesses in reading and writing, one would attempt to change his system of values.

But Everybody Knows That

One problem with literacy is that its processes appear so obvious: a writer gets an idea and makes marks on a surface (clay tablet, papyrus scroll, bond paper, or cathode ray tube) that embody that idea; a reader translates those marks into sounds and from the sounds recaptures the idea that was in the writer's mind. Yet:

- writers often discover meaning in the process of writing;
- good readers do not translate the marks on the page into sound but gain meaning directly from the printed symbols;
- word meanings vary from age to age or even year to year and also from place to place;
- no two readers bring exactly the same background to the text; and
- every reader changes, almost moment by moment, in background knowledge, taste, and attitudes.

The Culture and Politics of Literacy will unpack some of the apparent simplicity of its subject and in the process will reveal the complexity of literacy, which is as fascinating as the human mind itself. In fact, to talk about literacy is unavoidably to talk about mind—and about all that minds are capable of, when properly encouraged.

The Culture
and
Politics of Literacy

1

The Consequences of Literacy

The universe (which others call the Library) is composed of an indefinite, perhaps an infinite, number of hexagonal galleries, with enormous ventilation shafts in the middle, encircled by very low railings. From any hexagon the upper or lower stories are visible, interminably. The distribution of the galleries is invariable. Twenty shelves—five long shelves per side—cover all sides except two; their height, which is that of each floor, scarcely exceeds that of an average librarian. One of the free sides gives upon a narrow entrance way, which leads to another gallery, identical to the first and to all the others. To the left and to the right of the entrance way are two miniature rooms. One allows standing room for sleeping; the other, the satisfaction of fecal necessities. Through this section passes the spiral staircase, which plunges down into the abyss and rises up to the heights. In the entrance way hangs a mirror, which faithfully duplicates appearances. People are in the habit of inferring from this mirror that the Library is not infinite (if it really were, why this illusory duplication?); I prefer to dream that the polished surfaces feign and promise infinity. . . .

JORGE LUIS BORGES
"The Library of Babel"

Reading and writing have profound consequences for the individual and for society.

Whether or not the ability to read and write changes the basic nature of the human mind, literacy clearly enables the individual to accomplish intellectual tasks that would be impossible without writing. At the less exalted end of the scale are documents that serve as adjuncts to memory; for example, the written checklist that an airline pilot goes through before takeoff. At the other end of the scale are the elaborate thought structures in scientific and philosophical writing, such as an article in *The New England Journal of Medicine* or Allan Bloom's influential best seller, *The Closing of the American Mind*. Reading and writing have made Western technology, science, philosophy, literature, and theology possible.

In this chapter we will explore the question, "What are the consequences of literacy for society and for the individual?" For instance, ponder the following: in 1807 a bill for universal elementary education was put before the British Parliament. Responding to that revolutionary development, the president of the Royal Society wrote,

> [G]iving education to the labouring classes of the poor . . . would in effect be found to be prejudicial to their morals and happiness; it would teach them to despise their lot in life, instead of making them good servants in agriculture, and other laborious employment to which their rank in society had destined them; instead of teaching them subordination, it would render them factious and refractory, as was evident in the manufacturing countries; it would enable them to read seditious pamphlets, vicious books, and publications against Christianity; it would render them insolent.[1]

On the one hand, revolutionaries from Lenin through Mao to Castro and beyond have seen literacy as essential to their movements and upheavals; but on the other hand, literacy is clearly an instrument for controlling the masses. The official state press in the Soviet Union and China are only the most commonly cited current examples, but one can think about the theological battles over literacy that were at the heart of the Reformation. If every *man* had not only the right but the duty to interpret the Bible for himself, then literacy was a Christian obligation; but access to the Bible through reading begins to free the individual from the absolute control of a religious hierarchy.

The consequences of literacy depend on any number of factors, not the least of which is the definition of literacy that an individual or a society adopts.

Defining Literacy: A Political Act

Defining literacy is not idle semantic debate or academic hairsplitting but is almost always a consequential political act. The working definition of literacy adopted by a school district, government agency, or any other institution will to a large extent determine educational priorities in general, hence specific allocations of funds. Furthermore, an institution's or society's definition of literacy is also in large part a definition of the culture itself.

For example, the National Health Survey in the late 1970s defined literacy as "reading ability comparable to that of the average child entering fourth grade."[2] As even a minimum national standard, this definition precludes an idea of literacy as an instrument of cognition or of social power and virtually eliminates the cultural value of being able to read and write. If the Survey definition became the policy of, say, an educational district, we could be certain that resources would be diverted away from the courses and community services that were aimed at a more sophisticated level of literacy.

Many agencies adopt a more specific, but equally modest, definition of literacy, such as this one from the National Assessment of Educational Progress: "the ability to perform reading and writing tasks needed to function adequately in everyday life (filling out a driver's license application, reading a train schedule, writing a check, applying for a job, or reading an article in the newspaper."[3] From such a definition a vision emerges—of a citizen who should not aspire beyond the modest rounds of getting a job, going to work, and coming home in the evening to read the newspaper (briefly, before watching television).

We hear a great deal now about "functional literacy," and the key term here is "functional." What does it take to be functional in a society? That, of course, depends on one's point of view. Furthermore, it depends on the society in question. In other words, literacy is a relative concept having to do with what Kenneth Burke would call *scene*. As Exhibit A, I submit an article from Windward Islands *Newsday*, which on the Caribbean island of St. Maarten counts as high literacy:

St. Maarten's Jaycee Bryson
Elected "Jaycee of the World"

by Defender

During the Jaycees International world congress which was held in Osaka in Japan, Mr. Franklin Bryson was nominated as most outstanding Jaycee of the world.

Can you imagine all what you can achieve by being an active and
sincere Jaycee? Well Mr. Franklin Bryson shows you all of it by his
progress in the St. Maarten/St. Martin Jaycees. What Mr. Bryson has
received in Japan this month of November will go down in our history
as the first Antillean to achieve such an honour. I am sure it's like a
dream come true for him in Japan. He is showing all the inhabitants of
this island that idle and careless words and talking get you nowhere, but
to participate and be active, someday you will reap your reward with
joy.

Franklin Bryson is also showing all his fellow Jaycees that you can
reach to the top by being active in your organization and never let up.
Joining the Jaycees as Franklin did, you can move step by step toward
progressive heights, because you are joining a most dynamic training
club that can motivate your whole life. The Jaycee Club teaches you to
think and act positively. How do you feel to see your friends around
you moving step by step towards progress because of their motivation
and you are not even making the slightest progress in life, because you
are not motivated in no way? Sure you'll feel lousy, isn't that a fact?
You can do something about your attitude towards life in general by
following the example of Jaycee Franklin Bryson.

So take up the challenge fellow Jaycees. Now is your chance to move
on to greater heights and progress. The sky is the limit as the saying
goes.

We are too far ahead in world wide recognition to turn back now. It's
onward we go and further yet.

St. Maarten/St. Martin Jaycees is in the foremost to stay and you can
bet your bottom dollar, we are staying there. So to progress in anything, be active. Always lend a hand and you shall surely be rewarded
one way or the other.

All cheers to you, Mr. Franklin Bryson, your fellow Jaycees are
proud of you, and all St. Maarten/St. Martin salutes you with respectful
joy. Long, may your presence be with us.

I say, stay up sir.[4]

In the world of the New York *Times* or the Washington *Post,*
this lively piece of writing would count for very little—indeed,
would be devalued because of its nonstandard language and its
tone. However, the world of St. Maarten is not that of the New
York *Times,* and Defender's writing does count for a great deal in
his own scene.

To account for both the *Times* and the Windward Islands
Newsday, we must have a flexible definition of literacy that takes

scene into account, which is why I think that the following from UNESCO is excellent (in spite of its sexist language):

A person is literate when he has acquired the essential knowledge and skills which enable him to engage in all those activities in which literacy is required for effective functioning in his group and community, and whose attainments in reading, writing and arithmetic make it possible for him to continue to use these skills toward his own and the community's development.[5]

The definition takes account of the reader-writer as an individual with personal goals for development, and as an active participant in the destiny of his or her community.

Writing Systems: The Bases for Literacy

About 5,000 years ago an astute businessman in Mesopotamia discovered that he needed a system of keeping track of sales and inventories, rather than trying to remember the myriad details of his burgeoning enterprise (the growth of which he attributed to his ad agency—Hasan, Aziz, and O'Roarke—whose stroke of genius had been to saturate the whole area with criers who day and night extolled the virtues and values of the businessman's products). Although the details of my story might be inaccurate, in essence I'm telling the truth: writing developed as a method of record-keeping for business. Romantics, of course, wish that writing had started because the Sumerians were poets at heart and wanted to record their songs; a philosopher might lament the commercial origins of literacy and rewrite history to portray writing as the result and instrument of abstract pondering. But as it turns out, the evidence shows that literacy began in the very practical marketplace.

The Sumerian *pictographic* writing, however, had no offspring and thus stands alone in a chart showing the family tree of scripts. A pictograph is a symbol that stands for a word and is iconically related to its referent. Thus, the Chinese pictograph for "tiger" is recognizably a tiger, as are those for "deer," "elephant," and "horse." An *ideogram* is also a symbol that stands for a word, but it is unrelated to the referent iconically; it doesn't look anything like what it means. Both pictograms and ideograms are illustrated in Figure 1.

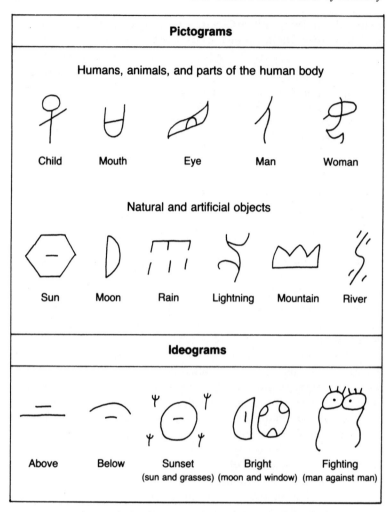

Figure 1. Chinese Pictograms and Ideograms.

As the Chinese language attests, picto-ideographic writing systems work well and even have certain advantages. For one, they can represent language groups and subgroups that when spoken are mutually incomprehensible. A speaker of Mandarin Chinese who cannot understand spoken Cantonese can nonetheless read what the Cantonese write, for they both use the same characters; in fact, there is only one character system. Two different languages—in principle, two as different as English and Russian—can be written logo-ideographically, for the script does not represent sound.

But these writing systems also have great disadvantages. To be able to read *The People's Daily,* one needs to know between four and five thousand characters! Chinese typewriters are massive, complex mechanisms, and computer displays are diffiuclt to construct. (In China I saw youngsters working with Apple IIe's in English, not Chinese. The bonus is obvious: the student learns both programming and a second language.)

Around 1100 B.C. the Phoenicians, a seafaring, mercantile tribe, achieved a major breakthrough: they invented a syllabary, that is, a system of notation that represented the spoken syllables of their language. Now writing was tied to sound, and the writing system was enormously simplified. Although the Phoenician syllabary didn't represent vowel sounds, it was economical and efficient and, compared with logograms, extremely simple to learn.

Suppose that the English syllables *tele* and *tel* (as in telephone and motel) were represented by T; the English syllable *phone* were represented by F; and the English syllable *mo* were represented by M. Then TF would spell "telephone," MT would spell "motel," and we could invent the new words MF "mophone" (obviously a phone in a motel), TT "teletel" (an ultralong-distance telegraph), FT "phonetel" (you decide the meaning), and so on. In other words, the syllabary enables one to write existing words and to coin new words that are decipherable on the basis of their sound.

This is a long step forward.

The Greeks took the ultimate step. They perceived the utility of the Phoenician syllabary and refined it into a twenty-four-character alphabet, from alpha to omega. And the Greek alphabet forms the basis of the Roman alphabet, which is essentially the ABCs of modern English. The basis of our literacy, then, is the twenty-four-character Greek alphabet (Figure 2).

The great Hellenic breakthrough lay in the realization that language consists of a small number of meaningful sounds (which linguists call *phonemes*) that can be endlessly recombined. Learn the signs for the sounds, and an infinite number of words becomes

GREEK		LATIN
Old	*Late*	
Ᵽ, А	A	A
Ⅎ, ⍭	B	B
⅂, ∧	Γ	C
△	Δ	D
⅂, ⍾	E	E
⅂, Y, V	Y (at end)	F (+U,V,Y at end)
I	Z	Z (at end)
日	H	H
⊗, ⊕	Θ	
⟨, ⟩	I	I
⅄, ⅄	K	K
⅃, ⅃	Λ	L
ꟽ	M	M
ꟼ	N	N
Ɨ	Ξ	X (at end)
O	O	O
⅂, ⅂	Π	P
ꟽ, M	(M)	
Ϙ, Ϙ	(φ)	Q
ꟼ, P	P	R
Ƨ, Ƨ, Ƨ	Σ	S
T	T	T
	Y,φ,x,ψ,Ω	U,V,X,Y,Z

Figure 2. The Greek Alphabet.

accessible. Comparing this simplicity with, for instance, Chinese makes the utility of the alphabet dramatic. An American child is en route to reading and writing when he or she is able to make the sound–letter correlation; a Chinese child must learn something on the order of 4,000 characters really to be headed toward literacy. The alphabet is a miracle of technology—which, as the chapter on reading will demonstrate, has its own problems. Figure 3 is a schematic history of writing systems.

The Social Basis for Literacy

Literacy is always grounded in a social context—as Burke likes to say, in a scene. The Brazilian tribes that Claude Lévi-Strauss speaks so eloquently of in *Tristes Tropiques*—a good "read" by any standards—had no reason for literacy, no social need to read and write. It would have been fatuous to bring them the daily newspaper, let alone the complete works of Milton or even the Bible. Yet they, like all other peoples, could learn to read the daily newspaper and Milton and the Bible if they felt the social need to do so. The Bible is an instrument of the felt need for a religion, not the beginning of that need.

In his brief and excellent discussion of literacy, John Oxenham outlines the historical-social forces that brought about literacy in the Western world.[6] First, as we have seen, was the entrepreneurial spirit, *commerce*. As the Phoenicians expanded their conglomerates from the site of the Garden of Eden outward toward Greece and the rest of the Middle East, they needed means of keeping track of transactions. Legend has it that the first letter of our alphabet, the *aleph* of the Semitic languages, derives from a picture of the head of an ox (Figure 4). Although one leading scholar on the development of writing, I. J. Gelb, questions that assumption,[7] nonetheless no one doubts that writing systems were invented to record the doings of commerce. As other parts of this book will indicate—and as everyone's experience attests—literacy is still a primary instrument of commerce.

Technology also demands literacy. Anyone who watches *National Geographic* specials on public television knows that preliterate societies have technologies of a certain kind, those which can be passed on orally and through direct observation: pottery mak-

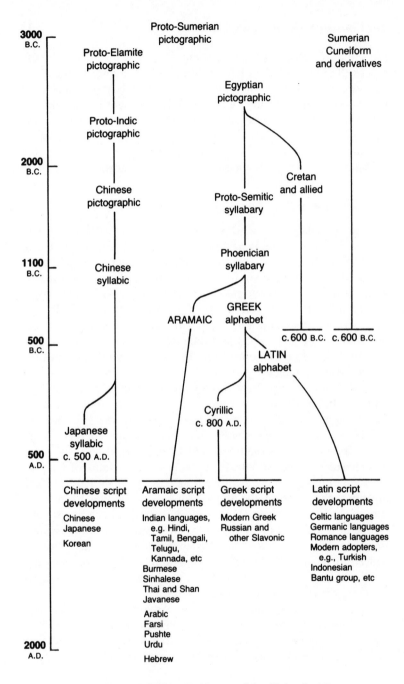

Figure 3. Schematic History of the Major Scripts.

Figure 4. From Aleph to A (Hypothetical Derivation).

ing and basket weaving; fashioning weapons such as the bow and arrow and the blowgun; making cloth from vegetable fiber or wool; and cooking. With more complex technologies, such as those which became common with the advent of the steam engine and the Industrial Revolution, literacy is essential, for these technologies are the result of plans and instructions, not simply direct observation. It was during the Industrial Revolution that the idea of mass education took hold—education not for culture or personal enrichment but to qualify workers for the industrial society.

Without printing, however, mass literacy would have been impossible.

The story of movable type and the printing press has been told often, yet it is a fascinating parable concerning the ways in which a simple technology can bring about revolutionary changes in society. By the time Gutenberg printed his famous Bible in 1455, the Chinese had been using movable type for centuries, but it was Gutenberg, with his serendipitous notion of movable type, who sowed the seeds that would blossom exponentially from the mid-fifteenth century to the present. Hand-copied books such as the Ellesmere Chaucer in the Huntington Library were often magnificent works of art, but they took enormous labor to complete (one thinks of the monk at his desk, tediously inscribing a text on vellum) and were extravagantly expensive. In other words, they were accessible only to the very few. Although we see the results of Gutenberg's invention all about us (since we are inundated by print), the statistics set forth in Table 1 are at least surprising, if not awesome.

As the 1455 Gutenberg Bible indicates, religion has been a major force for literacy in the Christian world. In 1521 Luther began his translation of the Bible into German to make the Book available to the laity, for Latin was a learned language inaccessible to those not in the priestly and scholarly classes.

TABLE 1. Book Production in the World

	Titles Published			Percent (of 1955 total)		
	1955	*1965*	*1976*	*1955*	*1965*	*1976*
World	269,000	426,000	591,000	100	158	219
Africa	3,000	7,000	11,000	100	233	366
North America	14,000	58,000	91,000	100	414	650
Latin America	11,000	19,000	31,000	100	172	281
Asia	54,000	61,000	100,000	100	113	185
Europe	131,000	200,000	269,000	100	152	205
Oceania	1,000	5,000	5,000	100	500	500
USSR	55,000	76,000	84,000	100	138	152

Source: Adapted from John Oxenham, *Literacy: Writing, Reading and Social Organisation* (London: Routledge & Kegan Paul, 1980), p. 12.

Literature has also been a major force for literacy—and in the category "literature" I will include all texts that are read primarily for pleasure, not just the texts approved by members of the "high culture" and academics. Romance novels, for example, "account for some 30% of the sales of mass-market books, tens of millions of books a year. In 1980, there were an estimated 12 million readers of romance novels; by 1983, 20 million."[8] Janet Dailey, one writer of popular fiction, published sixty-nine romances between 1976 and 1985—nearly seven per year! These books have sold more than 100 million copies, or about eight times more than the total number of copies of *Huckleberry Finn,* one of America's best loved and most admired classics, since Mark Twain published his book in 1884.[9] We may deplore the taste of people who read romance fiction rather than the works of Mark Twain, Nathaniel Hawthorne, William Faulkner, and other "classic" authors, but we cannot argue that people no longer read literature.

Of course, there are other factors that make for literacy (for instance, a person's curiosity), but we can see that literacy depends on its social context and conversely helps create that context. It is helpful to think of the individual within the literacy scene as being motivated by a need to do something with reading and writing, as well as by a need to become solidly a member of a society; stated another way, the motives for literacy are instrumental and integrative. On the one hand, when the preliterate Jack-or-Jill-of-all-trades (or, to use a term favored by Lévi-Strauss, *bricoleur* or *bricoleuse*) learns to read and write, he or she is enabled to become an engineer; on the other hand, by learning to read and write, he or she moves toward integration with educated society and its cultural ideals.

Literacy and Mind

In *The Psychology of Literacy,* a book to which I will refer often, the authors, Sylvia Scribner and Michael Cole, quote the following story told by a Wesleyan missionary in the Fiji Islands:

> As I had come to work one morning without my carpenter's square, I took up a chip and with a piece of charcoal wrote upon it a request that my wife should send me that article. [The chip was given to a Fijian chief to deliver] but the Chief was scornful of the errand and asked, "What must I say?" . . . "You have nothing to say," I replied. "The chip will say all I wish." With a look of astonishment and contempt, he held up the piece of wood and said, "How can this speak? Has this a mouth?" [When the errand had been successfully performed] the Chief tied a string to the chip, hung it around his neck and wore it for some time. During several following days, we frequently saw him surrounded by a crowd who were listening with intense interest while he narrated the wonders which the chip had performed.[10]

Here is the stark line between the primeval forest of illiteracy and the village or city of literacy. What will be the consequences when the chief leaves his forest and comes to reside in the village or city as a fully entitled member of the literate society? That question has intrigued anthropologists, psychologists, historians, and others at least since Plato wrote his *Phaedrus.*

In one fascinating book, the classicist Eric Havelock argued that alphabetic literacy was the basis for Platonic philosophy—in effect, for Western thought. Oral language, said Havelock, is concrete, unsuited to abstract speculation and logic. Literacy, in contrast, not only enables abstract thought but demands it.[11] Extending Havelock's thesis, Jack Goody and Ian Watt pointed out that written language is static—as I like to say, an array in space—allowing one to scan backward and forward, to compare one utterance with another. Without this characteristic of written language, the sequentiality of logic and comparisons of one text with another to check veracity would be impossible. The logic of Aristotle, which is the basis for Western systematic thought, was the result of literacy.[12]

We can easily grant that St. Thomas Aquinas could never have accomplished his monumental project—justifying the ways of God to man—without writing, and it is equally obvious that what we know as science and technology are literacy based. Yet we are left with a troubling question: does literacy change the fundamental nature of the human mind? It is inconceivable that literacy would not have an effect on cognition, the nature of one's thought and one's ability to think; but the dimensions of that effect—or, more properly, those effects—is a matter of speculation and debate. Literacy enables one to do more elaborate kinds of thinking than would be possible without reading and writing—to create elaborate technologies and philosophical systems—but through such activity, does the fundamental nature of the thought process change? This is the question we shall now explore.

All such inquiries begin with the work of A. R. Luria, one of the great pioneers in the study of cognition and brain function. In the 1930s Luria investigated a rapidly changing area of Central Asia to find out how schooling and literacy affected cognition. He discovered that unschooled, illiterate people tended to respond to thought problems in concrete, context-bound ways. For example, the syllogism was a mystery to these people; their responses were puzzlement. What Luria encountered was something like the following exchange that I have concocted for illustrative purposes:

Psychologist: All polar bears are white. Sascha is a polar bear. What color is Sascha?
Peasant: How should I know? I've never seen Sascha. Your question doesn't make sense.

Does the response show an inability to think logically? In answering that question, we should take two factors into account: *genre* and *context.*

In a somewhat roundabout way, I will make the point about genre. I am very good at working American word puzzles: the New York *Times* crossword, the anacrostic in *Harper's* magazine. Yet I once spent several hours attempting to work the London *Times* crossword and failed miserably, finally discarding the newspaper in defeat. The reason I am skilled at doing the New York *Times*'s crossword puzzle and not that in the London *Times* is my acquired familiarity with the unstated "rules" and general patterns that occur in the New York paper's puzzle. I have simply internalized the various features that make the *Times*'s puzzle a weekly variation on a theme, just as romance novels are variations on themes. Or take another tack. Suppose someone shows you a mechanism, obviously complicated. You don't know what its function is or whether it's part of some larger, even more complicated thingamabob. Suppose, further, that you are asked to name the function of the mechanism. That is something like the dilemma that faced the preliterates whom Luria tested.

Jack Goody, an anthropologist, studied the LoDagaa of northern Ghana. He found that they were skilled counters but had very little concept of multiplication—because, Goody argues, they lacked the multiplication table, which is a written aid to arithmetic. Yet they had developed extremely efficient methods of counting the 20,000 cowries that were normally given as "bridewealth." First, the counter made a pile of five by putting two and three together; the piles of five were assembled into heaps of twenty; and five twenties were put together for a hundred. When Goody naively began to count cowries in the usual one-two-three manner, the LoDagaa laughed at his "primitive" ineptness.

We assume that preliterates, then, have the mental faculties necessary for higher mathematical reasoning. As Goody says, "The difference is not so much one of thought or mind as of the mechanics of communicative acts. . . ."[13]

Interestingly, a LoDagaa tribesman would be baffled by a request that he count. His response would be, "Count what?" In Goody's words, "The LoDagaa have an 'abstract' numerical system that applies as well to cowries as to cows. But the ways in which they use these concepts are embedded in daily living."[14] If preliterates have the basic mental abilities to do abstract thinking, what will elicit it? Obviously, either a change in the society or a change in the individual's place in the society.

In a massive and highly influential study of the Vais, a people who live on the border between Sierra Leone and Liberia, Sylvia Scribner and Michael Cole were able to compare the effects of literacy on people who had attended school and those who had gained their primary literacy from friends or family members. The Vais have three very different literacies: one in their own script, one in English, and one in Arabic. They are proud of their own writing system. Visitors are told, "There are three books in this world—the European book, the Arabic book, and the Vai book; God gave us, the Vai people, the Vai book because we have sense."[15]

In their late teens and early twenties, young Vai men learn the script from some individual, not in a formal class. People who acquire the ability to read the Vai script also gain the ability to write, and both of these abilities develop in an amazingly short time, two or three months on the average, though some learn the script sufficiently well to communicate in it within a couple of weeks.

A second kind of education takes place in schools modeled after those in the United States, but attended by only a small minority of Vai children. In these schools, instruction is in English—with the result, according to Scribner and Cole, that the average child, after attending the school, will be able to decipher a brief letter, but will not have sufficient literacy to enter more complex tasks.

The third kind of education is Qur'anic. At age five or six, most of the Vai boys and some girls begin to memorize the Qur'an, reciting it aloud under the promptings of an imam. The children are not learning to read in any real sense, but to pronounce; the imam gives them the general meaning of what they are pronouncing in chorus.

In sum, Vai literacy is local, familial, used for village-to-village correspondence; English is the official national language of Liberia, and communication with the central government in Monrovia is in English; and Arabic is the ritual, religious language.

Scribner and Cole were able to study the effects of three influences on cognition: literacy (in three different scripts), schooling, and urbanization. The English schooling had an effect on the ability (1) to explain reasons for sorting (categorizing), (2) to give logical explanations, (3) to explain grammatical rules, (4) to give instructions for games, and (5) to answer hypothetical questions about name switching.[16] In other words, schooling—as opposed to literacy in the script without schooling—gave the Vais important (and to some extent predictable) skills and knowledge. That is, knowledge of grammar presupposes the explaining of grammatical rules. Most of us would say that the gains discovered by Scribner and Cole amount to development toward mental sophistication,

TABLE 2. Effects of Literacy: English Schooling and Vai Script

Broad Category of Effect		English Schooling	Vai Script
Categorizing	Form/number sorting	XXXXXX	XXXXXX
Memory	Incremental recall		
	Free recall	XXXXXX	
Logical	Syllogisms	XXXXXX	
reasoning			
Encoding and	Rebus reading	XXXXXX	XXXXXX
decoding	Rebus writing	XXXXXX	XXXXXX
Semantic	Words	XXXXXX	XXXXXX
Integration	Syllables		XXXXXX
Verbal	Communication game	XXXXXX	XXXXXX
explanation	Grammatical rules	XXXXXX	XXXXXX
	Sorting geometric figures	XXXXXX	
	Logical syllogisms	XXXXXX	
	Sun-moon name switching	XXXXXX	

Source: Adapted from Sylvia Scribner and Michael Cole, *The Psychology of Literacy* (Cambridge, Mass.: Harvard University Press, 1981), p. 253.

but that judgment is, of course, only from the standpoint of our culture. Urbanization gave Vais the ability to categorize—that is, to sort numbers of objects into meaningful groups.

In broad summary, Scribner and Cole found that Vais who attended English school made gains in their ability to categorize, to remember, to undertake logical reasoning (syllogisms), to encode and decode, to achieve semantic integration, and to give explanations. Vais who were literate in their own script, but had not attended English school, made gains in the ability to categorize, to remember, to encode and decode, to achieve semantic integration, and to give verbal explanations of certain kinds. Table 2 makes the comparison graphically.

Neither English schooling nor Vai literacy improved incremental memory, but Qur'anic literacy did. Vai children memorized the Qur'an by rote and recited it without necessarily being able to explain or translate; they didn't actually read, but apparently the exercise improved their ability to remember long texts and series (their ability to memorize). We would also expect Vai literacy to improve the ability to integrate syllables, as the script is a syllabary. Finally, we see that in "logical" operations, English schooling did have a positive effect, whereas Vai literacy did not. The strong implication is that the effect on such operations comes about not through literacy per se, but through the uses to which it is put in a social situation.

We are left with our original question. Does literacy affect higher-order cognitive processes? The answer seems to be "It all depends—on purposes and scenes."

A bit of sermonizing is perhaps now in order.

It makes little sense to consider literacy in the abstract. People gain literacy for reasons, and those reasons come about because of scenes—situations, social conditions, cultural values and norms, the ethos of the family. Changing the status of literacy means changing the nature of society, hence the aspirations of those who make up the society. The puzzlement of the Fijian chief can be translated into classrooms across America, with millions of children puzzling about the uses and meaning of reading and writing. Certainly a standard essay from our tradition—a piece by Charles Lamb or John McPhee—is as enigmatic to some children as the wood chip was to the chief. What can it say to me and mine? How does it "talk" meaningfully to me? Does it have a mouth? A soul?

To acquire literacy is to change one's value system if not one's cognitive equipment. Perhaps a personal example will illustrate the difficulties of changing one's values. My wife and I are at least relatively intelligent and as prosperous as most academics. We read the Los Angeles *Times* and live in a perfectly respectable suburb, drive relatively acceptable cars (a Dodge and a Buick), and can talk about the news of the day. We subscribe to the right magazines and actually read most of them. We have, then, all of the appurtenances of respectability. Yet we're intensely uncomfortable in fancy restaurants—not that we don't have the smarts to know which fork is for the salad and which spoon is for the soup, but almost any restaurant with a French name is not our turf, is antithetical to the value system that we have inherited from our families and all that we have held dear. For us to be at ease in these fancy eateries, we would have to be different people, with different values, with different heritages—yet we cherish our values and our heritages, and we don't want to be different people. (Sophisticates in one sense, we have applied good Western logic to our situation, thus: our values are clearly the best available; if they weren't, we'd change them. After all, who wants to live a life of second-rate values?)

When you ask the chief to acquire the literacy to survive and thrive in a modern technological society, you are asking him to move from his forest tribe—with its infinite variety, its rich culture of oral tradition and myth, its complex *bricolage* technology, its plenty for the gathering, its nature as an extended family—you are asking him not only to gain a new technology (the rifle in place of the blowgun), but a whole new set of values, a radically different world view, an abnegation of all that he has been. And to deny one's self is the ultimate denial.

Nor will I admit to the charge of dewy-eyed romanticism, a belief in the noble savage inhabiting a Garden of Eden. Every home turf is a postlapsarian Eden for those in it. I think of the squalid little Nevada mining camp that is my real past and of the narrow, isolated Mormon community in which my wife grew up, and I can say that necessarily they were for us Edens. Who, after all, wants to leave the Garden?

Of course, we do leave, must leave, but the migration is not without its traumas, and only the less-than-human deserts the Garden with no regrets; only the Neanderthal with no past looks inexorably forward, with no backward nostalgic glances.

Here is the dilemma. In conferring literacy, you are destroying a past, and except for the mentally deranged, the past must be worthwhile and elicits strong allegiance.

Spoken Word and Written Word

In *The Presence of the Word,* Father Walter Ong's thesis is simple and troubling (his argument is not simple, but is nonetheless troubling): that literacy brings about alienation.[17] At the most rudimentary level, we can understand that a note can never be as personal as a face-to-face message, me-to-you. If we extend the metaphor, we can say that a village operates on a face-to-face basis, one person talking to another or others, with the living word. When that word is written, a technology intervenes, and we are no longer dealing with an actual human who has spoken, but rather with a text that presumably speaks for the human. Ong writes:

> Primary orality, the orality of a culture which has never known writing, is in some ways conspicuously integrative. The psyche in a culture innocent of writing knows by a kind of empathetic identification of knower and known, in which the object of knowledge and the total being of the knower enter into a kind of fusion, in a way which literate cultures would typically find unsatisfyingly vague and garbled and somehow too intense and participatory. To personalities shaped by literacy, oral folk often appear curiously unprogrammed, not set off against their physical environment, given simply to soaking up existence, unresponsive to abstract demands such as a "job" that entails commitment to routines organized in accordance with abstract clock time (as against human, or lived, "felt," duration).[18]

Father Ong is saying that without literacy there is concord, agreement, understanding—at least potentially so. And that could well be the case, for without literacy there is no chance to compare one statement with another, one text with another.

Oral cultures have formulaic knowledge, communal and shared. With print, however, the knower is potentially separated from the known, with the result that he or she can step back and look "objectively" at his or her noetic universe in ways that are impossible with orality. "This separation," says Father Ong, "makes possible both 'art' (*techne*) in the ancient Greek sense of detached abstract analysis of human procedures, and science, or detached abstract analysis of the cosmos, but it does so at the price of splitting up the original unity of consciousness and in this sense alienating man from himself and his original lifeworld."[19]

One might say, then, that literacy is the basis for skepticism. As a case in point, we can take the Bagre myth of the LoDagaa, discussed at length by Goody in *The Domestication of the Savage Mind*. The myth deals with the human relationship with God and wild creatures and also with life's problems. Its ending is poignant:

' . . . we still perform,
so that one day
we may help each other.
These things we do,
though they can't banish death?'

'But this our matter [ritual],
I had thought that
it was able
to overcome
death?'
'It can't do that.'[20]

The invocation to the myth is something like "The Lord's Prayer," known verbatim by everyone. We know, of course, that there are several versions of "The Lord's Prayer," depending on the version of the Bible that one uses, but we also know the exact parameters of variation because we have the text and can compare one version with another or our own current recital with the authority of the text. Such is not the case with the twelve-line invocation of the Bagre myth. The current version of the invocation (and of the 10,000 or so lines of the entire myth), as spoken by the reciter, is the "correct" version, for there is no external model to serve as a standard.

What we have in the Bagre myth and its reciters is a model of the Garden before the fall into literacy. It would never occur to the LoDagaa Adam to question the meaning "behind" the myth, its truth. The meaning is simply there (somewhere) to be uttered on ritual occasions in the form of a 10,000-line recitation.

As Father Ong has argued, the first move out of innocence and toward skepticism is the printed text rather than the work recited in the living human voice. The final step—one that has been taken only in the latter half of the twentieth century—is the denial that either the spoken or written word contains determinate knowledge or truth.

Jacques Derrida is the secular skeptic *par excellence,* the Lo-Dagaa tribesman after the fall into the history of Western literacy from Plato through Locke to our own day.[21] His work is largely a reaction against the doctrine of presence.

In the West we have taken it for granted that upon occasion we have truth "up here" in our minds—that is, have definite knowledge—and that books have a definite meaning that finally, even in difficult cases, can be worked out. That is, we have uncritically believed in *presence:* that knowledge or truth is present and available. As one scholar says, the metaphysics of presence "locates truth in what is immediately present to the consciousness with as little mediation as possible."[22] A useful oversimplification explains that truth is consciousness; we must get behind the words to get at truth.

But Derrida argues that there is no "truth" behind the words. And suppose there were. How could you get at it except through language? The problem is that meanings are built with words, and words take their meaning primarily from other words; thus, in the quest for meaning, we are imprisoned within language, and there is no way out. You might say that we can define a word by pointing to its referent, "out there" in the real world; yet in the second chapter of this book we will find that such a method of definition is totally inadequate to account for meaning. You can define "cat" by pointing to a number of cats, but you can't define "ailurophobia" that way.

In fact, Derrida tells us that writing does not reveal meaning; it creates it, and reading recreates it.

> It is because writing is *inaugural,* in the fresh sense of the word, that it is dangerous and anguishing. It does not know where it is going, no knowledge can keep it from the essential precipitation toward meaning that it constitutes and that is, primarily, its future. . . . Meaning is neither before nor after the act.[23]

Meaning is in the act of writing and the act of reading, not in anyone's mind, including the mind of God.

Derrida speaks of the end of the book, for the idea of "book" is that of a totality, a definitive statement.[24] Derrida does not mean that there will be no more paperbacks or hardbounds, but rather that their value will change; they will no longer be repositories of truths or definitive statements. The book, in this postlapsarian's world, is nothing more than an invitation for more books, commentary on commentary without end, hence without the hope that finally one of the texts will reveal *the* truth.

Coda

We began with Jorge Luis Borges. We will let Kenneth Burke have the final word.

> Where does the drama [of human relations] get its materials? From the "unending conversation" that is going on at the point in history when

we are born. Imagine that you enter a parlor. You come late. When you arrive, others have long preceded you, and they are engaged in a heated discussion, a discussion too heated for them to pause and tell you exactly what it is about. In fact, the discussion had already begun long before any of them got there, so that no one present is qualified to retrace for you all the steps that had gone before. You listen for a while, until you decide that you have caught the tenor of the argument; then you put in your oar. Someone answers; you answer him; another comes to your defense; another aligns himself against you, to either the embarrassment or gratification of your opponent, depending upon the quality of your ally's assistance. However, the discussion is interminable. The hour grows late, and you must depart. And you do depart, with the discussion still vigorously in progress.[25]

2

How Language Works: Some Basic Concepts

> If men were wholly and truly of one substance, absolute communication would be of man's very essence. It would not be an ideal, as it now is, partly embodied in material conditions and partly frustrated by these same conditions; rather, it would be as natural, spontaneous, and total as with those prototypes of communication, the theologian's angels, or "messengers."
>
> KENNETH BURKE
> *A Rhetoric of Motives*

The first chapter outlined some of the more general socio- and psycholinguistic concepts necessary to an understanding of the nature of literacy. The present chapter will explore how language works and, in the process, attempt to hack through some of the thornier issues that arise in discussions of reading and writing.

The Trouble with Grammar

Do the following sound familiar?

A noun is the name of a person, place, or thing.
   Person: George Washington
   Place: Washington, D.C.
   Thing: Washington Monument
Infinitives should not be split.
   Incorrect: I want to quickly leave.
   Correct: I want to leave quickly.

A pronoun must agree with its antecedent in person and number.
Incorrect: Everyone put their books on the desks.
Correct: Everyone put his or her books on the desks.

These are examples of "school grammar," the variety of grammar that most of us are familiar with: a combination of statements concerning the nature of language (e.g., the definition of "noun") and rules concerning language use. Children often study grammar throughout virtually the whole of their twelve years of grade and high school.

Among the educated—one might say "the solid middle class"—the belief in grammar amounts virtually to a faith: children should be taught to use "good" grammar and, conversely, the teaching of grammar is at the heart of "language arts," those subjects which involve speaking, reading, and writing. Yet no term is more commonly misunderstood than "grammar," and because an understanding of it is essential to discussions of reading and writing, a bit of sorting out is in order. Just what is grammar?

At least three senses of the word grammar are important to us: the school grammar that most of us are familiar with, the grammar in our heads, and scientific grammar.[1] The distinctions among these three grammars are crucial to an understanding of the processes of and problems with reading and writing.

It is the case that native speakers have a virtually complete grammar of the language in their heads—obviously so, for language results from the rules that make up its grammar. Now this "internal" grammar can't have any resemblance to school grammar, for school grammar describes and regulates language, but does not produce it. The grammar in our heads enables us to produce sequences such as (1) *the pretty little six-year-old Swedish girl* and to recognize that the following is not "English": (2) *the Swedish six-year-old little pretty girl.* (An asterisk preceding a word, phrase, or sentence indicates that in the opinion of the author, the usage would be unlikely to occur in the language of a native speaker.)

As we will see hereafter, it is important to realize that we all possess and use this grammar without thinking about it or learning it through traditional instruction. Furthermore, we obviously follow rules, but are unable to state them explicitly. Somehow we have internalized the rules that enable us to use language, but we are unaware of having acquired them or of their nature. It would be difficult, if not impossible, for most of us to explain the rules whereby we know that *the pretty little six-year-old Swedish girl* is idiomatic English but that **the Swedish six-year-old little pretty girl* is not.

It is convenient to call this internal, tacit grammar "competence," and that is the term we will adopt for the remainder of this discussion when we refer to that grammar-in-our-heads which enables us to use language—which, in fact, constitutes language. (An analogy might help here. The game of football or chess *is* the rules that make it up, and that is also the case with language.)

We will call the third variety of grammar that concerns us "scientific," although into the barrel with that label we could throw a great diversity of systems and theories. In some ways scientific grammar and school grammar are alike, but in other ways they differ radically, and these differences have brought about enormous and destructive misunderstandings. It is important to recognize that scientific grammar attempts to account for what *is* in langauge, not for what might be there. On the one hand, scientific grammar is to language what anatomy is to the human body: an attempt to give an accurate account of features and structures. On the other hand, scientific grammar is an attempt to construct a competence model, that is, a system of rules that will allow machines to use natural language in the same way that humans do. (In this sense, grammar and artificial intelligence are identical, but scholars in the field are not even approaching the era envisioned by the computer HAL in the movie *2001*. Later on, we will discuss competence models and artificial intelligence more fully.)

One example of problems brought on by a failure to understand the nature of what we are calling "scientific grammar" occurs in the introduction to *Paradigms Lost*, by John Simon, who always has something to say about language. He bemoans the advent of "descriptive (or structural) linguistics . . . that statistical, populist, sociological approach, whose adherents claimed to be merely recording and describing language as it was used by everyone and anyone, without imposing elitist judgments on it."[2] The point is, of course, that one might attack the descriptive linguists because their work is faulty or inadequate, but hardly because they are not judgmental.

For example, the linguist William Labov did a well-known study of Hawaiian Creole, of which the following is an example, although in the written version we only approximate the pronunciations and accents of the speakers, two teen-age boys:

B: I tell you dis. Had one pheasan' in deah.
H: Oh, up by duh ranch in Molokai me and Buli and my cousin go, eh. Every time we wen go for catch the chicken somebody hadda start the car. Ah, you go to grab her, then the pheasan' fly 'way.[3]

In his role as a scientist, a descriptive linguist, Labov's obligation was to characterize and analyze the language, not to judge its beauty or adequacy, just as an anatomist is obliged to account for the features and structures of the human body, but not to evaluate their esthetic appeal. Of course, the description of language, though useful and even necessary, is only one aspect of the whole range of fields of language study, and certainly evaluation of the effectiveness and esthetics of various usages is both legitimate and necessary; but we should not confuse description (the "anatomy" and "ecology") of language with evaluation. The linguist, as linguist, must tell us where and when "ain't" is used and cannot deny that "ain't" is a well-established word in English; the critic must evaluate the use of "ain't" in situations, both contemporary and historical—which is not to say that one can't be both linguist and critic, provided the two functions are not confused.

The problems of constructing a competence model, a HAL, seem to be overwhelming. (HAL, by the way, is a simple code for IBM: H-I, A-B, L-M.) If a true competence model were developed, we would be unable to determine whether we were talking to a computer program or to a human being through the computer. Our conversations with the machine would have all characteristics of the professional talk that we carry on with colleagues or the chatter that accompanies our white wine and canapés. But consider a few of the difficulties that the programmer of a competence model encounters.

Two well-known sentences in the artificial intelligence (AI) lore are **(3)** *The cat fell off the roof because it was sick* and **(4)** *The cat fell off the roof because it was slanted*—perfectly simple for you and me to understand. However, to interpret these sentences, the computer must know a great deal about how the world works: that roofs are often slanted, but are not sick (except in the metaphorical sense, and that introduces complexity on complexity); that cats can be sick, but not slanted (except in figurative ways that it would take some doing to explain); that it is quite a usual occurrence to find cats on roofs. It would, as a matter of fact, be extremely difficult to program an adequate definition of "cat" into a computer, and a slanted roof is meaningful only in relation to buildings and other kinds of roofs. In other words, the competence model involves not only structures, but also world knowledge.

Let's do a little experiment. Suppose that we're programming a computer to use the verb "drink" in an idiomatic way. We can tell the machine to choose a subject, the verb, and an object to generate sentences such as **(5)** *People drink sherry.* But how do we program so that the computer won't choose an inappropriate noun as subject?—**(6)** **Chairs drink sherry.* And what about the noun object?—**(7)** **People drink ice.* We take it for granted that chairs can't drink anything, even though like people they belong to the noun category, and that ice is undrinkable; but the computer must be "told" all this and a very great deal more before it can begin to use the verb *drink* in sentences that we would take to be idiomatic English.

The point is simply that the grammar in a human head is complex beyond the ability of present technology to duplicate it. Yet somehow we all learn this grammar and use it automatically. The processes whereby we learn and use grammar-in-the-head will be the subject of much of the discussion that follows throughout this book.

The Meaning of "Meaning"

Language means. Always. Therefore, we must consider the nature of meaning. We listen and read to gain meaning; we speak and write to convey meaning. But an obvious objection arises. Don't we at times use language in nonsense ways, just for the sake of making sounds or marks on paper? Yes, of course—yet is such activity meaningless? Well, that depends on our interpretation of "meaning," and it is to meaning in language that we now turn.

We can start with the word, the smallest independent meaningful unit in language. (There are meaningful units other than the word, but they are not independent. For instance, prefixes such as *pre-* are meaningful, but they don't stand alone: *pre*supposition, *pre*monition, *pre*test.)

At first glance, the problem of word meaning seems relatively simple. For example, how does a child learn the meaning of the word "cat"? Mama points to a cat and says the word and to another cat and says the word. Ultimately, the child points to a dog and says "cat," but Mama says, "Not 'cat.' That's a doggy." Through the process of trial and error, the child eventually learns that certain features differentiate cats, dogs, horses, and pigs, and is able to apply the appropriate name, triumphantly labeling all the denizens of the local zoo.

This view of meaning has been appealing, especially in the first half of the twentieth century with its now passé behaviorist (stimulus–response) bias, but it is unable to account for any but the most rudimentary "meanings" that we would naturally assign to words. The German philosopher Gotthold Frege, with a brilliantly simple example, demolished this *referential* view of meaning. He told us that "evening star," "morning star," and "north star" all refer to something that we at other times call "Venus."

It would be difficult to define "house" by pointing at a number of houses: bungalows, French provincial two-stories, a house near me that is a converted water tank. But consider the insuperable difficulty of defining "condominium" merely by pointing. At one moment the large structure on the corner is an apartment house, and the next day it is a condominium, with no change in its structure, features, or tenants—only a change in the covenant by which people agree to define it. In other words, a condominium is not a physical structure, but a construct of language. And such is the case with "democracy," "free trade," and even, if you will, "religion"—which is not to say that there are not such things as democracies, free trade, or religions.

This example is of great moment for us. In terms of language, it displaces us from the "real" world of things into the unstable and chimeral world of words, where a "condominium" is not an entity, but a verbal construct. We define "condominium" not by pointing, but by retreating, symbolically at least, to the dictionary. We define words with other words. Even "cat"—for there is no way to understand the concept "cat" without the semantic structure of which it is a part: *The cat fell off the roof because it was slanted; the cat fell off the roof because it was sick.*

But our understanding and generation of language do not stop or even begin (as we shall see) with words: the words must occur in language structures. It is easy to see that the same words in different structures convey different meanings: **(8)** *Man bites dog.* **(9)** *Dog bites man.* It is perhaps not so easy to understand that different structures can convey essentially the same meaning:

(10) The truck collided with the bus.
(11) The truck and the bus collided.[4]

To understand the nature and problems of reading and writing, we must comprehend the *propositional* nature of language, for the proposition is the basic structural unit of meaning in language. Normally we read texts not word-by-word, but proposition-by-proposition. A proposition is a *predicate* (main word, pivot, not a predicate in the school grammar sense) and the other nouns, adjectives, adverbs, and verbs that relate to it. Thus, the following is a one-proposition sentence:

(12) The pilot banked the plane.

The verb "banked" is the predicate, and "the pilot" and "the plane" are noun phrases relating to the predicate. We can change the syntax (word order) of the sentence without changing the relationship of the predicate and the noun phrases:

(13) The plane was banked by the pilot.

In both **(12)** and **(13)**, "banked" is the action, and "the pilot" is performing the action on "the plane."

In reading **(14)** *The pilot who was in command banked the plane,* we derive the meaning of two propositions, something like this: *the pilot banked the plane* and *[the pilot] was in command.* The following examples of multipropositional sentences are pretty much self-explanatory:

(15) Noticing the helicopter, the pilot who was in command banked the plane.

the pilot banked the plane
[the pilot] noticed the helicopter
[the pilot] was in command

(16) The pilot thought that he was lucky to have avoided a collision.

the pilot thought SOMETHING
he was lucky
[the pilot] had avoided a collision

In other words, when we comprehend language, either spoken or written, we derive clusters of meaning relationships called "propositions," not simply discrete meanings of words.

To complicate matters further, the situation in which language is used determines meaning to a great extent. For example, is the following a threat, a promise, or merely a statement?

(17) I'll give you five minutes to complete your work.

Obviously, we don't know what sort of *speech act* it is until we establish a context for it. If a mother says it to a child who has been dawdling, it is probably a threat, but it would be a promise if it were bedtime and the child had asked for just a few minutes more to complete something that interested him or her. Virtually all of the time,

(18) Could you raise the window?

is a request, not a question, although it has the interrogative form.

Words in propositions gain part of their meaning from use, from what the speaker or writer intends them to count as. Take the one-word utterance "Beautiful!" We cannot determine whether it is praise or blame until we put it in context and thus determine what the speaker intended.

(19) Beautiful! You managed to miss the whole point of my instructions.

(20) Beautiful! That's the most perfect swan dive I've ever seen.

Language in Action

The discussion from here to page 39 will be an outline of *speech act theory,* a branch of *ordinary language philosophy.*[5]

When I speak or write, I use words in conventional structures, as we have seen. However, I also have an intention: to promise, to state, to ask, to apologize, to threaten, to explain, and so on. Thus,

(21) I promise I'll wash the dishes tonight

and

(22) I promise I'll disinherit you if you don't mow the lawn.

are—or at least could be—quite different kinds of speech acts: **(21)** we would normally take as a promise, and **(22)** is undoubtedly a threat. And we can determine these values because we have a sense of the way the world works.

In the jargon of speech act theory, the *illocutionary* force of **(21)** is that of a promise; the illocutionary force of **(22)** is that of a threat. So part of the meaning of every speech act (whether oral or written) is its illocutionary force, the user's intention. However, this formulation leaves out an essential component: the hearer or reader. Because you cannot read my mind, you must interpret my illocution. Take the following exchange as an example:

(23) *Wife to husband (at a party):* It's getting late.
      Husband to wife: It's only eleven.

The wife, we can assume, was not merely making a statement, giving information, but was *intending,* "It's time to go." And the husband was not correcting misinformation, but was really saying, "Let's stay a bit longer." Yet at face value, according to the dictionary, the husband and wife were merely exchanging information. In fact, the husband interpreted his wife's illocution and responded with his own *perlocution:* a perlocutionary act is a response to an illocutionary act.

We can see, then, that the tapestry of language comes about through the warp of illocution and the woof of perlocution, an intricate weaving of intention and response. Since conflicts among nations and races often come about through misunderstanding of illocution and perlocution, the subject is worth pursuing through two classic examples:

(24) *Gracie:* On my way in, a man stopped me at the stage door and said, "Hiya, cutie, how about a bite tonight after the show?"
George: And you said?
Gracie: I said, "I'm busy after the show, but I'm not doing anything now," so I bit him.
George: Gracie, let me ask you something. Did the nurse ever drop you on your head when you were a baby?
Gracie: Oh no, we couldn't afford a nurse, my mother had to do it.[6]

In this comic drama, Gracie's first problem is her misunderstanding of "bite." She takes an intended metaphor literally. But when George asks her if she had been dropped on her head when she was a baby, his illocutionary intention was an insult, something like "You're nuts!" Gracie takes his utterance as a request for information and gives him a "straight" answer.

(25) A young man on a train to Lublin, Poland, asked a prosperous merchant, "Can you tell me the time?"
The merchant looked at him and replied: "Go to hell!"
"What? Why, what's the matter with you! I ask you a civil question in a properly civil way, and you give me such an outrageous answer! What's the idea?"
The merchant looked at him, sighed wearily, and said, "Very well. Sit down and I'll tell you. You ask me a question. I have to give an answer, no? You start a conversation with me—about the weather, politics, business. One thing leads to another. It turns out you're a Jew—I'm a Jew, I live in Lublin, you're a stranger. Out of hospitality, I ask you to my home for dinner. You meet my daughter. She's a beautiful girl—you're a handsome young man. So you go out together a few times—and you fall in love. Finally you come to ask for my daughter's hand in marriage. So why go to all that trouble? Let me tell you right now, young man, I won't let my daughter marry anyone who doesn't even own a watch.[7]

This classic Jewish anecdote gives an analysis of a speech exchange that didn't work because the perlocutionary response to the illocutionary intention was not understandable. The point of the humor is the merchant's explanation of his response.

But we can pile complication upon complication. Suppose a private says to a general, "Stand at ease, soldier." Granted, the private would probably be reprimanded or court-martialed, but our question is this: did the private give a real order? If the private somehow thought he had the authority to give an order to a general, then his speech act was a genuine order (as misconceived as it might have been). If the general believed that the private intended a real order and was not just wise-cracking, then the general would conclude that the private was not insubordinate, but somehow misinformed or unbalanced, and would perhaps recommend psychiatric therapy.

However, we can turn to a real-life situation involving modes of *mitigation* and *politeness*.[8] Suppose a teacher says to a middle-class child,

(26) Junior, this is very sloppy work. Now you take that composition and write it over again.

The child is likely to reply politely with some kind of mitigating term, such as

(27) Aw, do I have to?

or

(28) I'll do it tomorrow.

The illocutionary force of either **(27)** or **(28)** might well be complete denial, the intention being "I won't do it." In any case, we would not expect a middle-class student to give an out-and-out "No!" to the teacher. However, some children not in the middle-class speech community might well respond simply (and candidly) "No!" The usages they have inherited from their language group do not include certain modes of mitigation and politeness, although every language has its own ways of expressing these niceties. The result of such discrepancies between language communities is often confrontation, brought on by failures in understanding.

And this is how language progresses: my intention, your interpretation of that intention. For any of it to work, we must share the language system and world knowledge. You must be able to guess what my response will be, and I must be able to guess what your intention is. When cultures clash, this cooperative endeavor breaks down, and conflict ensues, for we project and understand intentions on the basis of our cultural heritage.

Language transactions progress within an unwritten, but clearly perceivable set of "laws" that we might call "the cooperative principle."[9] When we speak or write, in effect we give the hearer or reader a four-part guarantee concerning

> **(29)** *Quantity:* I will give you all the information you need to understand what I'm getting at, and no more than is necessary.
> *Quality:* I will be reliable and truthful.
> *Relation:* Everything in my discourse will relate to my point.
> *Manner:* I will be as clear as possible.

Now a language user can violate these principles for one of two reasons: purposely, to create a special effect, or inadvertently, through inattention or lack of skill in language use.

For example, in the following marvelous course description, Woody Allen primarily violates the principle of relation—and does so zanily:

> **(30)** *Fundamental Astronomy:* A detailed study of the universe and its care and cleaning. The sun, which is made of gas, can explode at any moment, sending our entire planetary system hurtling to destruction; students are advised what the average citizen can do in such a case. They are also taught to identify various constellations, such as the Big Dipper, Cygnus the Swan, Sagittarius the Archer, and the twelve stars that form Lumides the Pants Salesman.[10]

Virtually nothing in the passage relates to what we might conceive as a course in astronomy, but when Woody Allen tells us that the sun is made of gas, a fact that all his readers know, he also violates the principle of quantity by giving us more information than we need.

Or think about manner. "The Gettysburg Address," with its eloquent language, is considered one of the world's great masterpieces of public address: "Fourscore and seven years ago, our fathers brought forth upon this continent a new nation, conceived in liberty and dedicated to the proposition that all men are created equal." Certainly nothing could be more appropriate to the occasion. However, used on another occasion, such as a child's spilling of orange juice on the living-room rug, elevated language is comic:

(31) On Sabbath last, the first son of my first son inadvertently and without malicious intent did overturn the vessel containing his orange juice, thereby staining the carpet in the parlor of our dwelling.

Sometimes, of course, language that should be perfectly clear in manner is opaque, for reasons that we cannot determine. The following—quoted in the August 25, 1986, *New Yorker*—is from the Iowa City *Press-Citizen:*

(32) A woman wearing a bold gold bracelet, a well-crafted lapel pin and tasteful earrings shows attention to detail and quality. The rings that catch one's eye as she points to her chart or pensively balances her gold pen on her chin make her ring as good as gold.

The last sentence of this example does make sense if you think about it in the right way.

It might be said that the problem with grammatical and spelling errors in writing is one of manner; in most writing situations they are simply inappropriate. But more about this later.

The principle of quality is easily illustrated. We tend to place more credence in information from the New York *Times* than from the *National Inquirer*. Most people place great confidence in the statements of professionals—lawyers, engineers, physicians, architects—about their fields. When we consider the quality of a statement or piece of writing, we are really asking about its credibility.

James Boyd White, a professor of law at the University of Chicago, discusses the difficulty of legal language for laypersons. The law is difficult to understand, he says, not because we don't know the definitions of the words, but because of what he calls the "invisible discourse" of the law. "Behind the words, that is, are expectations about the ways in which they will be used, expectations that do not find explicit expression anywhere but are part of the legal culture that the surface language assumes."[11] It might be said, in other words, that nonlawyers do not know how the cooperative principle works in legal language.

Readers as Writers

We can begin to see the complexities of writing and reading. If the writer's audience ("general public," "college students in the United States," "people who subscribe to the *New Yorker*") is unknown, the writer must draw on a great deal of cultural knowledge to provide readers with the right quantity of information; must somehow establish her or his credibility and possibly that of her or his sources (quality); must avoid irrelevancies, realizing that what might be irrelevant for one group of readers is to the point for another group (relation); and must write in a style that is appropriate to her or his purpose, readers, and subject (manner). If the writer misses in any of these respects, the reader will be forced to decide whether the miss was intentional (and thus figurative, for some special effect) or unintentional (and thus evidence of incompetence).

In fact, you might say that all writers must construct the proper conditions for their readers, inviting them to participate in the language transaction offered by the text. It is simply a fact that every reader is incapable of inhabiting some texts, chooses not to inhabit others, and feels perfectly at home in yet others. The writer must construct a text in which the intended readers will feel "at home."

Interestingly enough, much of the meaning that we get from a text, a piece of writing, is what the author does not supply, but which we must "fill in." The reader must, in a real sense, construct the text.[12]

Here is an interesting experiment that you can perform to demonstrate how the gaps in texts are filled. Tell the following story to a group; then, after ten minutes, ask the group to repeat the story to you.

(33) The company picnic was held on the shores of Lake Crystal. George arrived at the noisy, lively gathering somewhat late, but soon got into the swing of things and was crooning an old song with his comrades, a beer in one hand and a hot-dog in the other. After three hours, George was more than ready to leave. He was soaking wet and extremely angry.

Almost certainly your hearers will tell you that George either fell or was thrown into the lake, even though the story does not say as much. Furthermore, your hearers will remember the story as if it did directly state these *implications*. In other words, much of what readers get from a text is what they supply, not what is "there."

Some years ago, I was teaching as a visitor at the University of Iowa. I had been talking about meaning with a group of graduate students and in the course of the session cooked up this passage, which I wrote on the board:

(34) My wife and I love abalone. Whenever we go to Salt Lake City, we eat out. Bratten's serves wonderful seafood.

The students, of course, could supply the necessary "bridging as-sumptions" to make sense of the text: Bratten's is in Salt Lake City, and the Winterowds eat abalone at Bratten's. Nonetheless, my stu-dents felt that the text was strange and that it would be unlikely to occur in real-world discourse. At this point I bet them a pound of Amana cheese that in context, with the proper audience, it could be taken as a real-world instance of language use. Shortly thereafter, the class and my wife and I went out to dinner. While waiting in the lobby for our table, I casually said, "My wife and I love abalone. Whenever we go to Salt Lake City we eat out. Bratten's serves wonderful seafood." My wife forthwith responded, "Yes, and it's strange that, living practically on the seashore, we go to Salt Lake for good seafood." Because of her world knowledge—which she shared with me—the utterance was perfectly coherent, with no obvi-ous gaps. For her there was no strangeness whatsoever.

Proper Words in Proper Places: Usage and Dialect

Finally, we need to understand what is meant by *usage*. It is simply a fact that "nutty" is a well-established word in English, used from coast to coast by virtually all langauge groups, as in *Herb's* nutty *as a fruitcake*. We can prove this universality by listening for the word in the speech of various groups. However, we also know that many groups would not use "nutty" in relatively formal language. Suppose a middle-class, college-educated man is discussing his aged and beloved uncle, who has become senile. He would hardly say, "Uncle Bert is getting nuttier by the day," but he might say something like "Every day Uncle Bert's mind slips more and more."

The study of usage determines (1) what groups use given words, expressions, and pronunciations and (2) the situations in which these groups would be likely to use those locutions. Thus, we could say that "nutty" is a slang word used by speakers in informal situations.

A *dialect* is a variety of language, marked by distinctive features, that is spoken by a social, geographical, or even professional group. Now, everyone speaks a dialect—that is, belongs to a speech community—and a language is nothing more than the collection of dialects that make it up. All of us recognize the Southern, Northeastern, and urban black dialects, and in the United States there are many more, including the prestigious upper-class ("Oxbridge") British dialect, which is now a great asset for secretaries to some business executives.

Because usage and dialect are intimately connected, we should think briefly about the nature of dialect. We realize that dialects vary in their social, political, and economic power, depending on the situation of use. Urban black English *counts* for almost everything at Central Avenue and 102nd Street in Los Angeles, but has negative value in the hierarchy of, say, United Airlines, to choose an American industrial enterprise at random. To think that the president of the airline might speak urban black English is so outrageous as to be mere fantasy, but much farther down on the organizational chart, we would be astonished if the captain of a 747 made announcements in this dialect and would even be surprised if a flight attendant used this variety of English in dealings with passengers.

The way we talk counts for a great deal; that is simply an ineluc-
table fact of life. Yet no language or dialect is somehow better or
worse than any other in the total scheme of things. If I want my
language—hence my entire cultural stance—to count, I must use
the dialect appropriate to the group that I want to join. (And, of
course, several dialects might count equally with a given group.)

If you grow up in central Los Angeles, you almost certainly
speak the urban black English dialect; it is the coin of that language community. And if you grow up in central Utah, you acquire
the Sanpete dialect, which is what people use in that peaceful,
"backward," and Edenic region. In discussing dialect, I like to use
Sanpete as an example, for in doing so, I am not subject to charges
of racism or elitism. Like all other dialects, Sanpete differs from
what might be called network standard English in pronunciation,
vocabulary, and structure.

pronunciation: the /ar/ combination is pronounced as /or/ would be
   in network standard: Norma /Narma/, corn /carn/, fork /fark/
      "Pass the /carn/." "Don't you have a /fark/?"
vocabulary: "man" for "husband"; "drink" exclusively for "water," not soft drinks or alcoholic beverages
      "Ross is /Narma's/ man." "Do you want a drink [of water]?"
structure: "and them" for "and the others"
      "Let's drive over and see Ken and them [Ken and his family]."

The families that speak this dialect are respected members of the
community. Some of them at least are unaware that they speak a
minority dialect, but their language is no problem to them. Of
course, that is the paradox: within the speech community, the
dialect itself is an asset, yet some speech communities lack social,
economic, and political power. It is axiomatic that if the king of
Spain lisps, those who want to be in *his* speech community will lisp
also (and that, my colleagues who teach Spanish tell me, is a historical fact about Castilian). Thus, perfectly acceptable usage in one
dialect group can be unacceptable in another.

The occurrence of the "r" sound among speakers in New York
City is a case in point.[13] Speakers in the lower socioeconomic class
almost never pronounce the "r" sound, saying, roughly, /gahd/
(guard), /cah/ (car), /beh/ (beer), /behd/ (beard). Among the upper

middle class, however, the "r" is pronounced about 20 percent of the time in casual speech, about 25 percent in careful speech, and about the same number of times when the speaker reads aloud. When members of the upper middle class are given word lists to read aloud—that is, when their attention is called to pronunciation—they pronounce the "r" about 55 percent of the time.

With the lower middle class, however, something dramatic happens. In casual speech, careful speech, and reading aloud, speakers pronounce the "r" slightly less frequently than do members of the upper middle class, but in word lists, when their attention is focused on pronunciation, they pronounce the "r" 80 percent of the time.

The lesson from these data, gathered by the linguist William Labov, is dramatic and can be interpreted as follows. Apparently the president of the bank, a member of the upper middle class, is secure in his social position and thus secure with his language; but the teller, aspiring upward, is aware of language features that carry with them prestige and entrée to higher social circles (for dialect is often one appurtenance of upward mobility).

People shift their styles of speaking depending on

1. their relationships with their hearers. Notice how your own manner of speaking changes according to the person (or people) you are addressing. Probably your tone of voice, your vocabulary, and even your posture respond.
2. the context in which the language is used (e.g., church, street corner, office, family room). Notice how your own manner of speaking changes according to the "scene."
3. the topic. Discussions of, for instance, the immortality of the human soul evoke different manners of speech than discussions of people's favorite desserts.

Thus, speakers change their style and level of usage according to the situation. It is when the speaker is unable to make these stylistic shifts that trouble arises. For example, a person who is unable to master the jargon of CBers—"Breaker, breaker, this is Roarin' Roxy"—will remain an outsider in that speech community and would need a great deal of practice in order to make her language count in the give-and-take of highway talk.

In school grammar, we may find a rule that says, "Do not end a sentence with preposition," but to learn how and if that rule counts, we would look at usage studies—and would find that in modern English all language groups end sentences with prepositions. Of course, we could argue, though I would not do so, that ending sentences with prepositions debases the language or is illogical, but that question is one beyond usage. When we study usage, we merely want to find out what is, not what we think should be.

How many levels of usage are there in a language or dialect? Of course, that depends on how you make the distinctions. Are the following slang: **boondocks, broad, clip joint,** and **prof?** *Webster's Third International,* the prestigious unabridged dictionary, labels all of them slang. How about **flick, slut,** and **passel?** The *Third* does not label them as slang.

In fact, we will avoid the whole controversy over levels by saying that we must judge language in use. Either it works or it doesn't. Either it is acceptable for its occasion or it isn't. To make the judgment, we need to know the situation.

Yet we do sense that some language use is informal or jazzy and that other use is formal. The sense that we have is adequate for our purposes, and we will not enter a debate about niceties. The point is that appropriateness depends on the speech community and the situation in which the language occurs.

We will, however, cling to the distinction between language that a native speaker of any dialect would be likely to use (we can call it *grammatical*) and one that would mark the speaker as non-native (we will call it *ungrammatical* and mark it with an asterisk [*]). Thus, the following are grammatical in that native speakers would be likely to generate them:

(35) Those children are noisy.
Them kids are noisy.
My father is at home every night.
My daddy be home every night.
That's the program with which I worked.
That's the program I worked with.
Barry don't have no money.
Barry has no money.
the pretty little six-year-old Swedish girl.

And the following are ungrammatical in that native speakers would be unlikely to generate them.

(36) *Those childs noisy.
   *My father is every night at home.
   *That are program I worked with.
   *Barry, he no money have.
   the Swedish six-year-old little pretty girl.

The important point is this: not all of the above utterances are equally "good" or effective from the standpoint of their ability to communicate in a given situation, even though the sentences in example **(35)** are all grammatical from the standpoint of language used by native speakers of English.

By Way of Summary: Focus on Written Language

Our purpose has been to explore the ways in which language works, how it conveys its meaning. Now we will briefly relate all this to reading and writing.

Grammar

When we speak of grammar and advocate that students learn it as an aid to reading and writing, we must understand the differences among the grammars of the language. School grammar can be very useful, giving students information about the educated use of language, but it does not supply the grammar-in-the-head or competence that is the very foundation of language. (In the next chapter of this book we will discuss ways in which children gain competence.) Furthermore, we must recognize that scientific grammars are very useful, giving us information about how language works and how it is used in various situations and places by diverse groups.

Structure

We have seen that the basic structural unit of language meaning is the proposition, and in later discussions we will explore the implications of this principle for reading and writing.

Meaning

The point of the entire discussion of meaning is that meaning comes about through a transaction between the speaker or writer and the hearer or reader. The writer must give the reader the necessary cues for him or her to put the text together meaningfully. And one thing we didn't say, but strongly implied: meaning is not "down there," on the page, but "up here," in the mind of the reader (or hearer). Thus, when we discuss reading, we must consider what is necessary for the reader to use the information—the cues and clues—supplied by the writer to construct a meaning.

Usage and Dialect

No word, phrase, or other stretch of language is either good or bad in some abstract way, but only in context. Usage studies tell us what kinds of language various groups of speakers find acceptable and unacceptable. Dialect and usage overlap in discussions of language, for acceptable usage in one dialect may be unacceptable in another.

In Chapter 5 we will discuss the fact that there is really only one prestige "dialect" in writing, although there are many in the spoken language. Because of this, dialect at times seems to interfere with the ability to learn to write.

And we can sum up the gist of this chapter as follows: the tapestry of language is woven through the warp of the writer or speaker's intention and the woof of the reader or hearer's response.

3

Learning: First Language, Second Language

Once upon a time and a very good time it was there was a moocow coming down along the road and this moocow that was down along the road met a nicens little boy named baby tuckoo. . . .

His father told him that story: his father looked at him through a glass: he had a hairy face.

JAMES JOYCE
A Portrait of the Artist as a Young Man

What happens when people learn to read and write? How do children and adults gain these abilities? Chapter 5 will deal specifically with learning to read, and Chapter 7 with learning to write, but some discussion of language learning in general is necessary if one is to understand the more specific details of learning to read and write. The present chapter will outline children's early language development and then will discuss the social basis of language acquisition and the important distinction between two kinds of learning. The last section of this chapter, "Two Kinds of Language Learning," is especially important for what is to follow; it is based on the work of my colleague Stephen Krashen of the University of Southern California's Department of Linguistics.

Early Language Development

At one year and three months, a child utters single words:

(1) More. [reaching for a cookie]
No. [resisting being put to bed]
Ball. [pointing to doorknob]

Very soon, the child is producing utterances of two or more words, as in examples **(2)** through **(4)**.

(2) (1 year, 8 months): Allgone lettuce. [looking at empty plate]
More read. [holding up a book]
Mommy sleep. [of mother lying down]
(3) (2 years, 1 month): Andrew that off. [wanting to turn off light]
Where go car? [holding toy car]
Pants change. [wanting to change his pants]
(4) (2 years, 8 months): What he can ride in?
He not taking the walls down.
I want to open it.[1]

Equally intelligent children develop their language competence at different rates, but in general we can say that some time after the first year, the child begins to utter one-word "sentences," and before the end of the second year he or she is able to manage quite complex sentences (e.g., the statement "I want to open it"), but has not yet mastered the forms of the interrogative ("What he can ride in?") or of the "to be" verb ("He [*is*] not taking the walls down"). Nonetheless, the child has learned an enormous amount—has acquired enough competence to function well in complex language situations.

How does the child gain a first language—English, Hindi, Russian, Chinese, French, Tagalog, or any other? In the first place, no language is any more or less difficult than any other for a child to learn: regardless of the native language, children develop their competence at about the same rate, the German child of about a year and a half producing the same kinds of one-word "sentences" as her or his American counterpart: "*Mehr*" ("more"), "*Nein*" ("No"), "*Ball*" ("ball").

These one-word utterances are more complex than at first glance they might seem, for they express complete intentions—or, in the jargon, have illocutionary force. "More" is clearly an attempt to bring about an action on the part of the hearer (i.e., it is a "directive"); "no" expresses the child's feelings (i.e., it is an "expressive"); and "ball" gives information about the state of things (i.e., it is a "representative"). We can "translate" these one-word utterances into conventional sentences:

(5) More = "I want another cookie."
No = "I don't want to go to bed."
Ball = "That's a ball."

And, of course, this is exactly the same thing that the native does when the tourist makes a one-word statement:

(6) *Tourist: "Bahnhof?"* ["How do I get to the railroad station?"]
Native: [Responds with gestures and one or two words of broken English.]

In real-world situations, then, hearers do everything possible to interpret the full intention of the speakers, be they young children or foreigners. The mother hearing her child utter "more" or other one-word "sentences" uses *rich interpretation*[2] in the attempt to discover a complete meaning. Her response is always to what she thinks the child intends by the utterance, not to its form.

And such is also the case when the child, now approaching three years, uses more complex, though ungrammatical, expressions such as "What he can ride in?" Typically, the mother would answer the question and would not correct the grammar. In fact, correction would be of no use to the child—would, as a matter of fact, stop the language transaction.

(7) *Child:* What he can ride in?
Mother: *No, Sammy, not "What he can ride in?" The correct form is "What can he ride in?"

The child must discover the rules of the grammar-in-the-head, of competence, through hearing language and attempting to use it to convey meanings that have real-life validity. The child is performing real speech acts:[3]

Making statements about the way the world is (representatives):
Seeing clouds across a moonlit sky, a child of two says, "Moon walk," meaning "the moon is moving."

Attempting to get the listener to do something (directives): A
   mother told her three-year-old son not to eat any more candy;
   the boy responded, "Candy is for to eat," meaning something
   like "please let me do what comes naturally. What else is candy
   for?"
Making promises, vows, pledges (commissives): "I be good,
   Mommy."
Expressing emotions (expressives): At two and a half, a child says,
   "I sorry, Aunt Boo."
Making declarations, such as "I'm through with this!" meaning,
   "By these words I tell you that I won't do this any more."

For language learning to take place, the response to these speech
acts must be to their intention, not to their grammar.

The Social Basis of Language Acquisition

In the process of trying to communicate—listening to meaningful
speech and making utterances that count as real speech acts,
including representatives, directives, commissives, expressives,
and declarations—the child is automatically, unconsciously acquiring the grammar-in-the-head that constitutes language. This process cannot be hurried by direct instruction in either school or
scientific grammar. The child is genetically programmed to learn
language at a given rate and according to natural sequences.
   Simple observation reveals that a process more complex than
imitation is going on. In the first place, the child's utterances are
not like those she or he hears, except when adults attempt to
communicate in "baby talk." The child is unconsciously sorting out
and internalizing the rules of language according to a biological-
psychological pattern over which adults have no control. In the
second place, almost from the start the child makes utterances that
are unique, that he or she has never encountered from others. This
creative, generative quality of language comes about because the
rules allow for an infinite number of "games," just as the rules of
football do not predetermine every move in the game, but make
the game possible nonetheless.
   The "errors" that children make reveal aspects of the learning
process. Children learn a rule—for instance, that the -s suffix cre-

ates a plural—and they apply it universally: book*s* and foot*s,* dog*s* and sheep*s*. In fact, they must learn the plural forms of "foot" and "sheep" separately, as discrete items. Some children learn common irregular forms, such as *went* and *saw,* as discrete items before they learn the general rule for creating past tense. These young learners may at first use the correct forms and then, having learned that the -ed suffix creates past tense, overgeneralize and use the incorrect forms *goed* and *seed.* For example, Sarah used *went* from her twenty-seventh to her forty-seventh month, at which point she changed to *goed,* using that form for a couple of months, after which she changed back to *went.* Clearly she was working out the rules of grammar for herself—without realizing that she was doing so.[4]

What is the nature of adult conversation with young children? First, the talk is largely about the here-and-now: commentaries on what the child is doing ("That's right, build a tower with your blocks"), remarks concerning the immediate environment, naming ("That's a kitty"), describing ("She's warm and fluffy"), or stating relationships among objects ("The kitty's in her basket"). Second, the adult takes turns with the child, giving him or her an important lesson in the nature of conversation. The adult gives the child opportunities to respond and even invites him or her to do so, as in the following:

(8) *Child:* Dere rabbit.
  Adult: The rabbit likes eating lettuce. Do you want to give him some?

Finally, adults make corrections, but only concerning the veracity and accuracy of children's statements. Thus, if the child calls a dog "horsy," the adult is likely to correct him. As we said before (and this is an important point!) children virtually never receive correction of the forms of what they say—until they enter school, of course.[5] This point is so vital to our discussion that I will restate it: in natural language learning, the child attempts to convey meanings and receives responses to those meanings, not to the surface form of the utterance.

By the time the child enters school and is ready to begin learning to read and to write, this grammar-in-the-head is well on its way to complete development. Once competence is gained, school grammar can be useful to inform the child of the norms of usage. For example, if from the speech community the child has learned to say *Them is the tickets to the game,* school grammar can inform her that the acceptable usage in so-called prestige dialects of English is *Those are the tickets to the game.* Since we will be dealing with this matter at some length hereafter, we will let the matter drop for now.

The Two Kinds of Language Learning

We have implied that there are two kinds of language learning. On the one hand, children (and adults) learn their language in trying to use it. They don't think about rules or grammar; they do no drills; they simply try to convey meanings and intentions, believing that these will accomplish something, will count as real communications. In the process, the child builds up the competence, the grammar-in-the-head, that makes language work. On the other hand, children (and adults) can consciously memorize and apply rules to "correct" or regularize their language use. For example, if a young girl has learned from her speech community to say *They was going to the park,* rules and exercises in how to apply them can teach her to say *They were going to the park.*

The first type of language learning is unconscious and automatic. We will call it *acquisition.* Children and adults acquire language.[6] The second type is conscious and governed by overt rules. We will call this sort of learning *drill.* Children and adults can learn some features of language through drill.

A true story, slightly embellished for dramatic effect, demonstrates this distinction and its importance. A bride and her husband honeymoon in Vienna, where the wife has a Fulbright scholarship to study at the university for a year. The wife has a minor in German, can read it fluently, and can manage fairly well in speaking, but the husband has no previous knowledge of the language. Yet he must function in a German-speaking society: must do the shopping, find the men's room, get from one place to another in the city, exchange pleasantries—in other words, must at least have the language at the survival level. And very soon, within a couple of weeks, he is getting along very well. He can't, to be sure, discuss the philosophy of Kant or the subtleties of Mozart, but he can successfully carry out his day-to-day obligations. He learns to do this without any drill, without ever consciously studying the language. In fact, he is very much like the child acquiring a first language: he attempts to make himself understood and receives meaningful responses. In the process, his ability develops rapidly.

Like the child, he has made important discoveries about the language—for instance, that *der* is the German equivalent of *the*. Now he can talk about *der Mann* (man), *der Frau* (woman), and *der Mädchen* (girl). But as we all know, pride goeth before a fall, and to his dismay he learns (undoubtedly from a Viennese intellectual who corrects his grammar) that the matter is not so simple. In German, he discovers, nouns have gender: masculine, feminine, and neuter. And articles must correspond with the gender of the noun. Furthermore, the German language marks its cases: nominative, genitive, dative, and accusative. Thus, it is *der Mann,* but *die Frau* and *das Mädchen.* Not only that, but in German one says,

(9) Der *Mann ist alt.* (nominative case: The man is old.)
Sie ist die Frau des *Mannes.* (genitive case: She is the wife of the man.)
Ich gab dem *Mann meine Uhr.* (dative case: I gave the man my watch.)
Ich sah den *Mann.* (accusative case: I saw the man.)

What to do to master these complications!
The wife, having anticipated the difficulties her husband would face, has brought to Vienna her copy of Hauch's *Essential German,* which she used in her first language course in college. She flips the book open and shows him the following paradigm or set of rules:

	Masculine	*Feminine*	*Neuter*	*Plural*
Nominative	der	die	das	die
Genitive	des	der	des	der
Dative	dem	der	dem	den
Accusative	den	die	das	die

Pouring him a cup of tea, the wise wife says, "Now memorize these rules, and you'll be able to use the German definite article correctly."

The husband is a quick study. After two cups of tea, a wedge of Sacher Torte, and a good deal of mumbling, he says triumphantly, "I've got it!" Then he spiels it out: "Masculine nominative *der,* masculine genitive *des,* masculine dative *dem,* masculine accusative *den,* feminine nominative *die.* . . ." He has learned the paradigm through drill; he knows it by heart.

Young Adelheid Kaltenbrunner, a maid in an acquaintance's household, has not learned the paradigm through drill. In fact, when asked to give the rules for use of the definite article, she is at a loss; she stumbles and mumbles and finally gives up. Yet when she is speaking, she doesn't ever make a mistake in using definite articles. Adi knows the system of definite articles, but in quite a different sense from the young husband's knowing: Adi has acquired the rules in the developmental process.

Now, we might ask what difference the process of learning makes as long as the learning has taken place. In fact, the difference in learning through acquisition and through drill is enormous. Just consider this: Adi can use the acquired rules without ever stopping to think of them; she simply does what comes naturally. The young husband, however, can use the rules only by consciously thinking about them: "Let's see, *Haus* [house] is neuter, and I'm using it in the dative case, so the correct form of the article is *dem.*" Now he can utter his sentence: "Ich wohne in dem Haus" (I live in the house).

Of course, if the husband were to attempt to apply these "drill" rules during actual conversation, he would be stymied, for he would be forced to pay so much attention to form that he wouldn't be able to carry on the intricate process of generating and expressing meaning. Indeed, the more attention we must pay to form, the less attention we have in reserve for meaning. Acquisition gives us much greater power than does drill.

The point that we are driving at, and that will concern us often hereafter, is that language ability (including the ability to read and write) must be largely acquired, not learned through drill. This fact is one of the most difficult ones facing teachers when they attempt to give learners of any age the ability to read and write.

The sequel to the story of the young husband is, fortunately, a happy one. In his day-to-day use of German—with friends, merchants, government officials—he simply forgets about the rules he has learned through drill and concentrates on getting his meanings and intentions across. When we are speaking, we simply don't have time or the psychological reserve of attention to think about consciously learned rules and paradigms. Fortunately, in most writing situations, we do have time. As we shall see, it is wise to encourage students to take multiple passes at the texts they are writing, concentrating first on what they want to say and, then, after they have expressed themselves to their satisfaction, going back over the text to regularize punctuation, grammar, and spelling, using the knowledge that they have learned through drill—but that is the subject of another chapter.

To summarize the lessons embodied in the story of the young husband who gained the ability to speak, read, and write German: he acquired competence just through attempting to use the language. In his day-to-day encounters with the language, he was not conscious of rules or grammar; his attention was focused exclusively on what he wanted either to communicate or to understand. On the basis of the unconsciously acquired competence, the language learner is able to begin to use the second langauge, and in so doing he or she gains more input, which creates greater competence.

However, as we saw, the young man also learned rules and paradigms through drill. In doing this, he created what might be called a *monitor* that allowed him to "correct" or regularize his output whenever he had time to do so.

Figure 5 visually recapitulates the gist of this chapter. The lan-

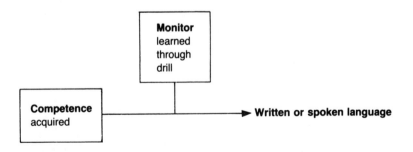

Figure 5. The Relationship of Monitor and Competence to Written and Spoken Language.

guage learner acquires competence (grammar-in-the-head and, obviously, a good deal more) through using language: getting meaningful input (in the form of listening or reading) and attempting to create meaningful output (in the form of speaking or writing). In any case, competence is the basis for language production and comprehension. Through conscious drill with rules and paradigms, children and adults can also learn certain features of language (such as the rules for capitalization or punctuation), and if the language user has time, he or she can monitor the speech or writing produced in order to "correct" or regularize it.

When we discuss writing later in this book, we will explore the specific application of this "monitor theory" to the composing process. Right now it is important for us to remember that there are two ways of learning any language, whether a first language, a second language, or a second dialect. We have called these ways of learning acquisition and drill. These two kinds of language learning apply with equal validity to the processes of learning to read and write, the subject of this book.

4

To Read

The reader of the Text could be compared to an idle subject. . . .
[T]his fairly empty subject strolls along the side of a valley at the
bottom of which runs a *wadi* (I use *wadi* here to stress a certain
feeling of unfamiliarity). What he sees is multiple and irreducible; it
emerges from substances and levels that are heterogeneous and
disconnected: lights, colors, vegetation, heat, air, bursts of noise,
high-pitched bird calls, children's cries from the other side of the
valley, paths, gestures, clothing of close and distant inhabitants. All
these *occurrences* are partially identifiable: they proceed from
known codes, but their combination is unique, founding the stroll in
difference that can be repeated only as difference.

ROLAND BARTHES
"From Work to Text"

Meaning is not "in" the text, but if the text is successful, it supplies
the reader with the wherewithal to derive meaning. The text is the
medium or agency whereby the writer conveys a semantic intention to a reader. In this chapter we will discuss the nature of texts
and how readers use texts to derive meanings.

The "Thing" We Read: A Text

Starting with the very basics, we need a word to denote the class
of "things" that we read, including books, letters, newspaper
reports—everything from the child's first primer to the novels of
Charles Dickens, from a set of instructions for assembling a kite
to the laws of the land. It is convenient to call all of these *texts,*
the term used in this book. Roughly speaking, texts have one

feature in common: each batch of writing that we take to be a text somehow hangs together and is not just a series of unrelated parts.

The following is a good example of textuality:

> Charles Fillmore once opened a class on text analysis with the following demonstration of textness. Imagine a sign posted at a swimming pool that says, POOL FOR MEMBERS' USE ONLY. Now imagine a sign posted at a swimming pool that says, PLEASE USE REST ROOMS, NOT THE POOL. And now imagine these two warnings placed together: PLEASE USE REST ROOM, NOT THE POOL. POOL FOR MEMBERS' USE ONLY.[1]

Meaning Again: Down There or Up Here?

The second chapter of this book laid out some basic concepts regarding meaning. We must now return to the subject of meaning to ask the strange question "Where is it?" You're reading a book right now. Is the meaning "in" the book, to be extracted like gold nuggets from a mine, or is it elsewhere? To continue the metaphor: as a reader, are you like a miner, digging out the meaning contained in the book? Or are you more like a cabinetmaker, using the materials afforded by the book to construct a meaning?

A bit of reflection will convince you, I think, that readers are cabinetmakers, not miners. To get right to the point, meaning is not "down there" on the page, but potentially "up here" in your mind. The text enables you to construct the meaning.

How the Text Generally Works

You might think of the text as set of instructions that you follow in order to achieve a given result. Some of these directions refer you "inward" to other instructions in the system, and some of them refer you "outward" to your knowledge of the world.

A simple example will clarify this idea. Take the following mundane text from the WordStar 2000 manual:

(1) Files are easier to handle when they're organized into directories and subdirectories.

The first word, "files," directs you outward, to search your knowledge of the world for its significance. Since you know the word is in a computer manual, you understand that it does not refer to a bunch of papers in a cabinet, and if you know something about computers, you understand that in this context "file" means a data set stored in the computer's memory or on a disk. The word "they," however, does not refer you to your knowledge of the world "out there"; it points inward, back to the word files, from which "they" gains its meaning.

In the linguistic jargon, the "pointing" function of language is known as "reference," and reference that directs one outside the system of the text itself is called *exophoric* (as the word "file" directs readers toward their knowledge of the world). Reference that directs one toward another part of the text is called *endophoric* (as with the word "they," which derived its meaning from another word in the text).

To act on the "cues" that make up the text, readers must have (a) the proper world knowledge and (b) competence with the language system. I cannot read a scholarly paper, written in English, concerning advanced mathematics (unless by "reading" one means not understanding, but merely pronouncing the words of the text), and I cannot read a scholarly paper on literacy written in Arabic. The easiest explanation is that a text is a set of exophoric and endophoric *cues* that enable readers to construct meanings—which implies what we will again state directly: meaning is ultimately "up here" in the reader's mind.

Now let's demonstrate these principles somewhat more extensively, with the first paragraph of "Clever Animals," by that admirable thinker and prose stylist, Lewis Thomas:

1 Scientists who work on animal behavior are
2 occupationally obliged to live chancier lives than
3 most of their colleagues, always at risk of being
4 fooled by the animals they are studying or, worse,
5 fooling themselves. Whether their experiments involve
6 domesticated laboratory animals or wild creatures in
7 the field, there is no end to the surprises that an
8 animal can think up in the presence of an investigator.
9 Sometimes it seems as if animals are genetically

    10 programmed to puzzle human beings, especially
    11 psychologists.[2]

First, a reader must know the *system,* the language and its written representation, in order to use the "cues" that it affords. For example, a reader must be able to relate *who* (1) back to *scientists* (1), for by itself *who* has no meaning, even though it is the subject of the propositiion *who work on animal behavior,* which would be meaningfully incomplete without the knowledge that *who* "stands for" *scientists.* Again, the reader must relate *they* (4) back to *scientists* (1), even though three plural nouns intervene: *lives* (2), *colleagues* (3), and *animals* (4). In fact, the reader makes the text "hang together" by knowing how to relate one part to another.

The Cue System

We will now explore the cue system in more detail.[3] The reader employs three cue systems in deriving meaning from a text: *graphophonic* (having to do with the correspondence between the printed or written symbols and the way words are pronounced), *syntactic* (having to do with the arrangement of words in propositions and sentences), and *semantic* (having to do with meanings).

There is a correspondence between the graphic system of the text as written and the sound system (*phonic* system) of the reader's spoken dialect. So much goes without saying. It is obvious, however, that there is not a letter-by-letter correspondence, for a word such as *phthisic* (meaning "tubercular") contains only five *phonemes:* roughly /tizik/. Not so obvious, but hardly astounding, is the fact that proficient readers derive meanings from print (the *graphemes*), not from sounds (the phonemes). That is, meaning is derived from the configuration on the page without the mediation of sound. Even though there is a rough graphophonic correspondence between the written and spoken versions of the text, proficient readers use this correspondence rarely, to "sound out" a word in the attempt to gain its meaning.

When we see readers "sounding out" their words, we know that they are having difficulty. Of course, children just beginning to read do a great deal of sounding out, but as they progress in their ability, they do less and less vocalization and subvocalization.

The function of the syntactic cue system is obvious. There is all the difference between *My grandson loves girls* and *Girls love my grandson*. The syntactic system determines the parts of speech that can fit into the various "slots" in the sentence. In the sequence *Girls love* _____, the empty slot can be filled only by a nominal (such as boys, candy, music, sports) or an adverbial (such as in the spring, all the time, passionately, with caution). Hence, the following are acceptable:

(2) Girls love *boys.*
Girls love *candy.*
Girls love *music.*
Girls love *sports.*
Girls love *in the spring.*
Girls love *all the time.*
Girls love *passionately.*
Girls love *with caution.*

But these, which fill the empty "slot" with words and phrases other than nominals and adverbials, are ungrammatical:

(3) *Girls love *beautiful.*
*Girls love *although.*
*Girls love *into.*

Meaning in a sentence is not, of course, a mere 1 plus 1 plus 1 sum of its parts, a principle that is easily illustrated by the fact that no one is really uncertain about the meaning of the following: *The yacht dropped its* _____ *in the harbor at Avalon.* In other words, we use our world knowledge—here called the semantic cue system—to fill in the blank.

In learning language we acquire the graphophonic, syntactic, and semantic information that we need in order to derive meaning from the text.

Other Kinds of Knowledge Readers Need

Readers must also have what we might call *genre* knowledge—that is, a familiarity with the conventions of various categories of texts.

For example, the more poetry we read, the easier it is for us to read poetry, but a person who has never read a poem will probably be stymied by even a simple lyric, such as the following delightful bit of verse I came across recently:[4]

Creature

At night,
When I write,
There's a long dark
Creature
Spawned by light
Who clings to me
Like a parasite,
But she won't bite—
In fact, she's rather shy
And only likes to versify.

Like other poems, this one uses sound effects (rhyme and alliteration), figurative language (personifying a shadow as a shy female creature), and irregular typography—features that for many of us present no difficulty (since we have genre knowledge), but which are significant hurdles for people who are inexperienced with poetry. In like fashion we encounter scientific reports, interoffice memoranda, legal briefs, dunning letters, institutional advertisements, sets of instructions—all of which are genres with their own conventions that we must learn.

Reading the text by Lewis Thomas also demands a great deal of world knowledge—for instance, a general understanding of what science is and does. Besides having a definition of *scientists* (1), we need to know that scientists perform *experiments* (5) and in general what experiments are, that these experiments sometimes involve *domesticated laboratory animals* (6) and at other times *wild creatures* (6); and we must, of course, have some knowledge about laboratory animals and wild creatures. We must be aware that *psychologists* (11) are generally classed as scientists, and we must know what *genetically* (9) means and be able to relate it to *programmed* (10), with all of that word's cybernetic connotations. And this is only a small part of what we must know beforehand in order to read (that is, understand) such a text.

Obviously, we must bring a great deal of knowledge to the text, else we will be able to get nothing out of it, for we read with our minds. In fact, we always bring more to the text than we take away. In the case of example (1), we learn that scientists working on animal behavior are likely to be fooled. In my case at least, that is new information, and it makes me want to continue the essay to find out how animals fool scientists or scientists fool themselves.

Why Read?

Perhaps we now agree on a general idea of what a text is, but we need still, I think, to be more specific about reading. One obvious reason for reading is, of course, to gain *information,* which is data that reduce uncertainty, that make choices easier. For example, if I tell you that I have a playing card in my pocket and ask you to guess what suit it is, you need only two bits of information to be certain. First you ask, "Is it a red suit?" If I answer "no," you are now certain that the card is either a spade or a club. You ask, "Is it a spade?" and whether I answer "yes" or "no," you are sure about the suit of the card.

The reduction of uncertainty is almost never as simple as the process illustrated in the foregoing example, but the principle concerning information holds—both *visual* information relayed to the brain by the eyes and *nonvisual* information derived by the brain from the reading process.

If I pick up an article from a mathematics journal and read it aloud to you, pronouncing every word accurately, but not understanding any of the concepts, have I actually read that text? No— for reading obviously involves at least partial comprehension. This leads us to a truism that will not, hereafter, seem quite so obvious: we read to gain meanings, not sounds.

Reading is often called "a psychological process," which it certainly is. (A person interested in becoming a reading "specialist" would study psychology, among other subjects, and not ophthalmology. As Braille demonstrates, we can read without using our eyes.) Kenneth Goodman, whom we will discuss shortly, calls it "a psychological guessing game." But there are good reasons for viewing reading as an *act.*[5] If we do take this view, then we will consider reading from a number of important angles.

Motive and Motivation

Reading is not purposeless activity; it always has some motive or whole web of motives, from the need to kill time while one waits for a bus to the necessity of deciphering the instructions on an income tax form; from the lure of the lurid to a love of poetry; from idle curiosity to the thirst for knowledge. No one will read or learn to read without a strong motive. When we consider the problems of literacy that are so much a part of the news nowadays, we must start by asking what motivates people to gain the ability to derive meanings from texts.

Scene: The Social Setting

Reading and learning to read always take place in a scene, a time and a place, and scene is closely related to motive. For example, it is a well-established principle that, in general, children who grow up in homes where reading takes place and is a valued activity learn to read and do read.[6] A good offhand way to predict how successful children will be on reading tests is to look about their homes; if one sees books, magazines, and newspapers here, there, and everywhere, chances are the children from that home will be good readers—not in every case, to be sure, but often enough to prove the validity of the test.

We can, of course, broaden the concept of scene to include not just one home, but a social group or an entire society. The social nature of literacy is vividly illustrated by a study of reading in three cultures: a school-oriented Philadelphia community, a nonliterate society in New Guinea, and Sino-Vietnamese families in West Philadelphia.[7] Among the school-oriented Philadelphians, reading was taken for granted; as one parent asked, "If you don't read, how do you know?" In this community, adults took on the role of helpers-facilitators, answering questions and encouraging the children. Story-reading was an accepted and beloved part of the day.

Among the Kaluli of New Guinea, "Looking at books is seen as neither instructional nor entertaining." Those adults who have gained literacy have done so in order to read the Bible. But the entire attitude toward reading in Kaluli is in direct contrast to that among the families studied in Philadelphia. As researchers Bambi Schieffelin and Marilyn Cochran-Smith state:

> In general, adults do not want children handling the literacy booklets or even looking at them because the booklets were valued and could be damaged easily. Osowola was the only adult in the village who looked at books with her child. The few men who were learning to read and who practiced their reading at home did not share the booklets with their children.

Kaluli society had some books, to be sure, but it was not a "bookish" society.

Among the Sino-Vietnamese of West Philadelphia, an interesting reversal has taken place. The children, who attend school, transmit literacy information to their parents, helping them learn English, translating documents for them, and so on.

The point, of course, is that scene determines to a large extent the sort of literacy that will develop and even the ways in which it will develop.

Agency: The "Channels" of Literacy

Thinking about agency, the means whereby text is conveyed to readers, takes us into questions about books versus magazines and newspapers—and also versus television and the computer. This is a question that we will return to periodically, but for the moment we must dispel some misconceptions. A "book" in the form of electronic data on a computer is nonetheless a book, though unprinted and unbound. Reading text from a computer is essentially the same process as reading text from a printed medium. Print is an array in space, whether on the screen or on the page, and we use the same visual and psychological processes to gain meaning from the screen as from the page. (We "flip" the pages on the computer screen by pressing a function key.) Yet the technology of the book and of the computer are radically different, and the technology of the computer in itself may give children motives for learning to read.[8]

We are perhaps not aware that for the young child, becoming familiar with the technology of the book is a major accomplishment: learning to turn the pages and discovering that they are not only filled with pictures, but connected with meanings. In early life, the child "socializes" himself or herself to books, making them a part of his or her existence. As the child matures, story time—hearing stories that come from books read by Mommy or Daddy—becomes an essential part of life. Learning to read involves attitudes toward books as well as "skills."

Here is just one example of how what we call agency affects meaning.[9] In a phone booth, I read

(4) Lift receiver.
Deposit coin.
Listen for dial tone.
Dial number.

Here is a text with no "voice," no "color." It is clear and efficient but uninteresting, without depth.

But give the same text a title, and put it in a book called *Now Poetry:*

(5) AT&T
Lift receiver.
Deposit coin.
Listen for dial tone.
Dial number.

Now it has a wry, ironic voice, satirizing the colorless impersonality of big business; the poem has color, "off-color," one might say, with its definite overtones of sexuality: coins in slots, fingers in dials. . . . Yes, it's a remarkably rich instance of language use—as long as it's in a book called *Now Poetry,* not on the wall of a phone booth. (And, by the way, this anecdote could well be interpreted "scenically," the phone booth being one scene and the book another.)

The Reader

Of course, not all children from "ideal" scenes develop into avid, efficient readers. Without speculating on the mysteries of genetically programmed personality differences, we know that there is an ill-defined condition termed "dyslexia" that creates sometimes insuperable hurdles for learners, and we will talk about it and other conditions later. For the moment we can say that in thinking about reading, we must take account of motives, scenes, agencies, and individual differences among readers.

What the Eye Tells the Brain

In 1906, a French oculist, Emile Javal, made a discovery that surprised him: readers do not steadily sweep their eyes across a line of print, but instead make jumps and pauses called *saccades.* You can verify this discovery easily: just watch a reader's eyes. The *fovea* is the area of the eye where the receptor cells are most densely packed, and readers bring target words into the range of the fovea by saccading, fixating on the target for about a quarter of a second. The "information" that is transmitted to the brain, however, is not only what the fovea picks up, for the *parafovea,* surrounding the fovea, also gains data, though less sharply defined. The rate of movement is influenced by the difficulty, for the reader, of the material being read and by the length of words.[10] However, the point that we should tuck away in our memories right now is this: the visual system transmits to the the brain only a small fraction of the information available from the text, and skilled readers do not progress word by word, let alone letter by letter.

Somehow, with a relatively small amount of visual information, the reader is able to construct a meaning. In fact, the more familiar the material in the text, the less "information" from the text is needed in order for the reader to gain meaning. With "easy" texts, the length of the saccades increases, and pause time decreases—which is really only to say that difficult texts take more time and effort to read than easy texts.

A number of factors make texts difficult for readers, the most obvious of which is blurred or dim print. But a discussion of reading will be much easier for a psychologist who brings a great deal of information to the text than for a layperson who has relatively little information about the subject in her or his store of world knowledge.

The Basic Unit of Reading: The Proposition Once More

The meaning of one word in a text "hangs fire" until the reader can relate it to the other words in its proposition. Thus, in general, "normally" (if there is such a thing as normal reading), we progress from proposition to proposition. Schematically, reading a sentence takes place something like this:

(6) Knowing that dinner was ready, Kim washed her hands.

The reader gains the incomplete proposition (*someone*) *knowing that dinner was ready* and holds it in suspension until he or she finds who did the knowing, namely, Kim, at which point the meaning of the first proposition is closed, and then the reader is ready to go on to the second proposition: *Kim washed her hands.*

Readers remember the content of propositions, but not their surface forms.[11] For example, when we read the sentence

(7) Wanting to be accurate, the scientist who did the calculations was careful.

the information that we gain and store in memory is something like this:

(8) careful: scientist
want: (scientist)
accurate: (scientist)
do: scientist, calculation

More prosaically, we gain the information that (1) the scientist was careful, (2) it was the scientist who wanted, (3) the scientist was accurate, and (4) the scientist did the calculation—four complete propositions. If readers cannot gain this information, they are not readers of the sentence in question.

From

(9) To kill time, Alvin did a crossword puzzle.

we remember something like

(10) kill: (Alvin), time
do: Alvin, crossword puzzle

and after a very short time we cannot determine reliably which of the following was the source of meaning:

(11) Alvin killed time by doing a crossword puzzle.
(12) Doing a crossword puzzle, Alvin killed time.
(13) Alvin killed time. He did a crossword puzzle.
(14) To kill time, Alvin did a crossword puzzle.

This is only a rough-and-ready example and explanation, but it does make the point that in attempting to derive meaning from texts (or using texts to construct meaning), readers sort out the propositions. It is impossible to read word by word. Newscasters, for instance, typically read about fourteen words ahead of the one they are pronouncing at the moment. How would you pronounce the "read" in the following if you were moving from word to word without having gained the whole proposition?

(15) *I read a newspaper this morning.*

The phrase "this morning" determines whether the word is to be pronounced /red/ or /reed/.

(16) I read /reed/ a newspaper every morning.

The phrase "every morning" determines the pronunciation of "read" as /reed/, not /red/.

A Psycholinguistic Guessing Game

Kenneth Goodman, whose work in reading has been very important, calls the act of reading a psycholinguistic guessing game.[12] What does he mean by this?

The term "psycholinguistic" shouldn't put us off, for it simply implies that reading involves mental (psycho-) activity with a language (-linguistic) system. Psycholinguists study the psychology of language. What Goodman says—and you can verify his claims by thinking about your own reading—is that readers *sample* texts (as we have seen when we talked about saccades focusing on target words); *predict* meanings on the basis of the world knowledge they bring to the text; and *confirm* or *disconfirm* these predictions. And we can see how this process works by thinking about an example sentence (although people read whole texts, not individual sentences). In the following example, the x's represent type so blurred that it is seemingly indecipherable.

(17) We flew to New York in xxxxxxxxxxxxx.

On the basis of what we know about the world, we would simply "read" this as something like

(18) We flew to New York in [a jet, plane, 747].

In fact, it may turn out to be irrelevant whether the actual phrase was *jet, plane,* or *747* if the passage goes on in this way:

(19) We arrived at five in the morning.

Any of the guesses for the missing text works equally well. Suppose, however, that subsequent text reads

(20) But we flew to Dallas in two hours.

The reader will now suspect that the missing phrase in **(17)** had to do with time and go back to confirm or disconfirm. Perhaps the new information gained from **(20)** will allow him or her to decipher the blurred type and conclude that the sentence actually said

(17a) We flew to New York in five hours.

The information brought to the text will make even blurred type more readable!

In thinking about reading, we are, of course, interested in texts more extensive than sentences. Except in unusual circumstances, people don't read isolated sentences, but rather texts, groups of sentences arranged to convey complex meanings. In regard to these whole texts—newspaper articles, books, reports, memos,

whatever—Goodman's sample-predict-confirm (or disconfirm) formulation holds up well, at least in the case of efficient readers. In
fact, at a later time we will apply the principle as advice for readers
to increase their efficiency.

Comprehension: Is There a Meaning?

Early in this chapter we asked, "Where is meaning?" Because
readers construct meanings on the basis of the cues provided by
texts, we must now ask whether there is such a thing as *a* meaning,
stable and definitive.

The goal of reading—whatever its motives—is comprehension:
understanding in a complex and deep sense. Comprehending *Anna
Karenina* entails empathizing with the characters, for part of the
meaning of the book is its emotional charge. Comprehending a
poem entails appreciation of the technical skill of the poet. In
other words, comprehension includes information but goes beyond
it. We can say that we try to comprehend the author's *meaning* if in
this term we include emotion, style, values, and so on.

We have seen that there is nothing "in" the text to comprehend;
the text, as a conventional system, enables us to construct or derive
a meaning that we assume is what the writer intended. The text
mediates between the writer and the reader, but does not somehow
encapsulate meaning as a vial of perfume encapsulates fragrance.
We have been so used to the idea of meaning-in-the-text that it is
difficult to realign our thinking to meaning-in-the-head. Using our
knowledge of the language system and our world knowledge (and
the two are finally inseparable), we are able (in many cases, but not
all) to construct a meaning that we assume represents the author's
intention; that is, we believe that we comprehend.

This leads us to one of the most interesting debates currently
going on about the nature of meaning: does any text (the Bible, the
United States Constitution, a novel by Hemingway, a poem by
Robert Frost) have *a* meaning, determinate and stable? Or is meaning indeterminate, unstable, changing with time and scene? To
take a simple and obvious example: the meaning of "pornography"
is an important issue, for even in our liberal age, pornography is
illegal in many localities. Complicating the issue is the fact that for
one person a work is pornographic, whereas for another it is simply

in bad taste. My wife and I, relatively conservative in our values, experience this clash with our son, a Presbyterian minister. What we consider merely bad taste, hence protected by the First Amendment, he often considers pornographic, hence illegal. Of course, neither my wife and I nor my son have the ultimate truth about the actual meaning of the word in use, for our values differ. In fact, it is inconceivable to me that there could ever be one clear and indisputable meaning for "pornography," valid now and throughout history for all groups.

One might argue, of course, that there is a final and "true" meaning of "pornography," perhaps in the mind of God—as well there may be—but appeals to a deity never settle arguments over meanings. I do not mean here to seem impious; I am merely limning some of the difficulties in arguing that a word, let alone a complex text, has one unchanging and unchanged meaning.

A name much associated with the attack on the idea of determinate meaning is Jacques Derrida, whose writings, though dense sometimes almost to the point of impenetrability, argue against the Western faith that any book contains or can convey a definite, unchanging meaning.[13]

Derrida uses the term "writing" in a very special way, to include both spoken and written texts, but since we are concerned here with reading, not hearing, we will sidestep the intricacies of his reasoning and simply talk about "writing" in the ordinary sense. Meaning, he says, has no habitation before it is written. It gains its substance on the page, but the moment it is written that substance disappears. What remains is the system that we have been discussing: a structure of cues that we can use to reconstruct a meaning. Yet we have no assurance and can have no assurance that the meaning we reconstruct is the one that the writer encoded on the page or pages. We can assume that we share a knowledge of the system with the writer and that our world knowledge and his or hers are similar, yet we can never be sure that the writer and we as readers have identical world knowledge. We are, after all, genetically and socially different individuals, living, perhaps, in different eras. And, as we have seen, we must apply our own knowledge in order to derive meaning from a text; in fact, that is exactly what the text invites us to do, demands of us.

If there is one stable, unchanging meaning in the Bible, why has debate over it continued for millennia? If the Constitution means exactly what it says and nothing else, why do we have the Supreme Court? If any book is the "last word" on a subject, why does the author publish a second and third edition, and why do some books generate commentaries upon commentaries?

One genial scholar argues against this skepticism: E. D. Hirsch, Jr., says in effect that meaning comes from somewhere, from some human intention, hence is not unstable or indeterminate.[14] For example, we may find it difficult to discover just what the drafters of the Constitution intended, but we know that the meaning of the Constitution is *theirs,* not whatever we might want it to be. Thus, our obligation is to find out what they intended. After all, the nation agreed to this covenant, and the Founders gave us a method of changing the terms of the pact when they included the possibility of amendment.

In our discussion it is not necessary to solve the problem of determinate versus indeterminate meaning. However, we need to be aware of the problems of claiming that a text means just this or that and only this or that—for all readers at all times. *Communities of readers* do often agree on the meanings of texts.[15] When such agreement is reached, meaning is in fact stable and determinate for those communities. In other words, we might say that through discussion (dialectic), groups of readers come to agree upon a meaning, in which case the meaning is once again not in the text, but part of group consensus. Furthermore, it is important to point out that we agree about meanings more often than we disagree.

Gist: The Heart of the Matter

When we set out to read a text, we have one overriding interest: to understand its *gist,* its main point, what it is getting at in the larger sense. For example, *Anna Karenina* is clearly about a group of Russians, but that is not its gist. Suppose we were administering a comprehension test to a group of students—*What is* Anna Karenina *about?*—and received the following two answers from different students:

(21) It's about Russians.
(22) It's about the search for meaning in life.

We would feel that the student who responded with **(21)** had not comprehended or attempted to comprehend the book. In contrast, we would feel that the other student had attempted really to "read," even though this student's answer is somewhat oversimplified.

In the process of reading, we continually seek the highest-level idea or theme that will allow us to organize or make sense of the subordinate details. This is the case in fiction and scientific literature, in poems and sets of instructions.[16] (In reading instructions for operating a camera, we know that the highest-level idea is something like "to operate this camera, do the following." If we did not realize this, the individual details would be meaningless.) If we cannot find this highest-level generality, this gist, we will be puzzled by the text and will not comprehend it even though we can recite the details. Thus, when we read, we hold information and ideas in suspension in our memories until we can relate them to other, more important aspects of the text.

Writers often begin with a direct statement of their gist or main idea. For instance, in the first chapter of *Class,* Paul Fussell says,

(23) In this book I am going to deal with some of the visible and audible signs of social class, but I will be sticking largely with those that reflect choice. That means that I will not be considering matters of race, or, except now and then, religion or politics.[17]

Such a statement has great value for readers, giving them the controlling idea to which they can relate the subordinate ideas, concepts, and information in the text.

Coherence: How Texts "Add Up"

A *coherent* text is one in which we can see how the details relate to the gist or main theme. The less we can perceive this unity, the more incoherent we feel the text is.

This point about coherence is important for the consideration of teaching reading and writing. Obviously, those learning to read must gain the ability to find gists and relate subordinate parts to those gists, and just as obviously those learning to write must have ways to guide their readers toward gists. These are ideas that we will pursue further in the discussions of learning to read and to write.

As we think about coherence, we might decide that readers progress from concept to concept, putting them together in some kind of hierarchical structure so that when this organizational chart is complete, comprehension has been achieved. Yet we have seen that readers do not progress simply from concept to concept. After all, in a short essay, one concept—such as comprehension—might sprawl across many sentences, paragraphs, and pages. In fact, one second-level concept might be made up of several at the third level, and a third-level concept might contain some from the fourth level, and so on, down to the individual propositions that we have discussed earlier.

Cohesion: The "Glue" That Holds Texts Together

Texts are not only coherent; they are also *cohesive.* That is, we are able to get from one segment to another without puzzling over relationships.

The "glue" that holds the bits of texts together is fairly simple—like the flour-and-water paste we made in grade school, not the exotic modern adhesives that suspend an automobile at the end of a cable over the Grand Canyon, one drop cementing the Ford to the wire rope. In fact, the adhesive consists of

1. our ability to know what is *referring* to what,
2. what has been *substituted* for what,
3. what has been *deleted,*
4. what *means the same* as something else, and
5. how *conjunctions* (and, but, for, or, etc.) function.

In other words, the glue consists of (a) *reference,* (b) *substitution,* (c) *ellipsis,* (d) *synonymy,* and (e) *conjunction.*[18] Of course, we all have this knowledge, having gained it as part of our competence in language; yet it is worth thinking about, particularly as it does cause problems for those learning to write.

We are able to get from one segment of the text to another because we know that some words or phrases refer to other words or phrases:

(24) *Christopher* played with his *ball.* HE tossed IT.

(25) Norma dislikes *parties* THAT are boisterous.

(26) *Beulah's cholesterol was high.* THAT is why she stopped putting cream in her coffee.

We often substitute words and phrases to avoid the monotony of repetition:

(27) *Scholars* love *knowledge* above all else. LEARNED PEOPLE are willing to give up creature comforts for *WISDOM*.

The rules of language dictate that we delete words and phrases, the meanings of which are supplied elsewhere. We continually employ ellipsis. In fact, the following, without ellipsis, would be ungrammatical in most usages:

(28) *The choir sang "Abide With Me," and the choir sang "Rock of Ages."
(29) *Kenneth studied psychology, Kenneth studied history, and Kenneth studied economics.

The normal form of these sentences would be

(30) The choir sang "Abide With Me" and "Rock of Ages."
(31) Kenneth studied psychology, history, and economics.

When we read a text, we track behind groups of words and phrases that we take to have the same or similar meanings. To illustrate this principle, we can look at the *semantic chains* in an example that we considered earlier, the passage by Lewis Thomas. The "links" in the *scientist* chain are emphasized to illustrate how these semantically related words and phrases serve to bring cohesion to the text:

(32) 1 SCIENTISTS who work on animal behavior are
      2 occupationally obliged to live chancier lives than
      3 most of THEIR COLLEAGUES, always at risk of being
      4 fooled by the animals THEY are studying or, worse,
      5 fooling THEMSELVES. Whether THEIR experiments involve
      6 domesticated laboratory animals or wild creatures in
      7 the field, there is no end to the surprises that an

8 animal can think up in the presence of an INVESTIGATOR.
9 Sometimes it seems as if animals are genetically
10 programmed to puzzle HUMAN BEINGS, especially
11 PSYCHOLOGISTS.

Making Texts More Readable

The following pairs of sentences have the same propositional structure and thus mean at least approximately the same thing, but in each case the first one is easier to read than the second.

(33) It is odd that Martha said that Mary claimed that George is bonkers.
That Martha said that Mary claimed that George is bonkers is odd.
(34) The child pulled down the poster that his mother had just put up in his room.
The child pulled the poster that his mother had just put up in his room down.
(35) The horse that was galloped around the track died.
The horse galloped around the track died.

Clearly, sentences that mean nearly the same thing can be more or less difficult to read, and such is also the case with longer texts: essays, articles, books, or letters. *Readability* is obviously a big issue in the textbook business, as educators demand that the level of reading difficulty be adjusted to the students who will use the books. Thus, we hear about readability tests and scales designed to determine if materials are at the appropriate level. In a short article, Robert M. Gordon has made what I think is a definitive statement on these reading scales, and I will quote almost his entire essay:

> Educational publishers are intensely aware of the need to control the reading levels of their materials. Both the demands of the educational marketplace and the real needs of students for informative, interesting, and comprehensible materials contribute to this awareness. But many educators question whether the demand for materials that test out "at or below grade level" is the most helpful way to meet these needs.
>
> So, for fun, I decided to perform an experiment that might shed some light on the question of readability from a little different angle.

Ever since the first time I read Plato's *Parmenides,* I marvelled at how simple, straightforward language could be used so that the result was comprehensible only with the greatest difficulty. . . .

What, I wondered, would be the readability of this dialogue?

To answer this question I randomly chose a passage from the text. I applied two common readability tests: the Dale-Chall (1948) as revised by Powers et al. (1958). . . . [In the passage, the italicized words are those listed by Dale-Chall as "unfamiliar."]

> "Well then," said Parmenides, "If there is a one, of course the one will not be many. *Consequently,* it cannot have any parts or be a whole. For a part is a part of a whole, and a whole means that from which no part is missing; so, *whether* you speak of it as 'a whole' or as 'having parts,' in either case the one would consist of parts and in that way be many and not one. But it is to be one and not many. *Therefore,* if the one is to be one, it will not be a whole nor have parts." (137c–d)

The results of this experiment are astounding. The passage tested at a fourth-grade level on the Dale-Chall, and at grade six on the Fry graph. . . .

I readily admit that this experiment is nonscientific and somewhat fatuous. And I certainly am not advocating a regular program of Plato in junior high schools. But I do hope that these results will lead many of us to pause and remind ourselves of the limitations of readability tests and reconsider some of the roles we ask these tests to play.[19]

The problem with readability tests such as the Dale-Chall and Fry[20] is that they do not take account of meaning. Dale-Chall uses two criteria: average sentence length and number of words not on the test's list of familiar words. Fry also uses two criteria: number of sentences per 100 words and number of syllables per 100 words—in effect, sentence and word length. These figures are normed with target populations, and school systems and publishers have a quantitative measure of readability, which seems to be valid in general and over the long haul.

Yet Gordon's brief essay provides a telling critique of these "contentless," "quantitative" measures of readability. The passage from *Parmenides* would be difficult not only for a child, but also for an adult who was completely unfamiliar with Platonic thought and the dialogue genre that Plato used.

Certain textual and syntactic features make texts easier to

read—again, in general, but not always. Because these are readily applied and easy to understand, it is worthwhile to run through them briefly.

Using Typographical Resources

Underlining, italics, and subheads can help the reader get through a text. These graphic cues are, however, "noisy"; that is, they are intended to attract attention to themselves. If they are overused, they lose their saliency and become merely an unconscious annoyance, like the background noise in a factory or on the freeway.

Making Lists

A good way to enable the reader to remember a series of points is to list them, as in the following example from this chapter:

(36) The "glue" that holds the bits of text together is fairly simple—like the flour-and-water paste we made in grade school, not the exotic modern adhesives that suspend an automobile at the end of a cable over the Grand Canyon, one drop cementing the Ford to the wire rope. In fact, the adhesive consists of
   a. our ability to know what is *referring* to what,
   b. what has been *substituted* for what,
   c. what has been *deleted,*
   d. what *means the same* as something else, and
   e. how *conjunctions* (and, but, for, or, etc.) function.
   In other words, the glue consists of (a) *reference,* (b) *substitution,* (c) *ellipsis,* (d) *synonymy,* and (e) *conjunction.*

The typographic segmentation in the first list is extremely useful for readers, as it visually isolates items.

Using Examples

Examples help explain concepts, as in the following from this chapter:

(37) One obvious reason for reading is, of course, to gain *information,* and information is data that reduce uncertainty, that make choices

easier. For example, if I tell you that I have a playing card in my pocket and ask you to guess what suit it is, you need only two bits of information to be certain. First you ask, "Is it a red suit?" If I answer "no," you are now certain that the card is either a spade or a club. You ask, "Is it a spade?" and whether I answer "yes" or "no," you are sure about the suit of the card.

Using Verbs Instead of Nouns

In general, ideas are easier to understand when they are expressed with verbs rather than nouns. For example, the first sentence is easier to read than the second, although they both mean approximately the same thing:

(38) The light *illuminated* the room brightly. The *illumination* of the room by the light was bright.

And here is an even more dramatic example, the first version of the passage in a verbal style, the second heavy with nouns:

(39) To write readable prose, you must follow certain principles. For example, express your ideas with verbs rather than nouns whenever possible and avoid uncommon words. At times, however, the less readable version of a sentence will fulfill your purpose better than the more readable one. You must use judgment.

To write readable prose, *the following* of certain principles is necessary, for example, *the expression* of ideas with verbs rather than nouns and *the avoidance* of uncommon words. At times, however, *the fulfilment* of your purpose is better achieved with the less readable version of a sentence than the more readable one. *The use* of judgment is necessary.[21]

Getting to the Point[22]

As we have seen, a sentence is either a single proposition or a combination of two or more propositions. If we look at the following awkward sentence, we can begin to understand the operations necessary for a reader to gain closure of meaning from it:

(40) That Vitamin C prevents colds, the scourge of mankind, is known by everyone.

In order to gain closure, the reader must find the main pivot word (*predicate*), which in this case is *is known,* and organize the rest of the sentence around it. The crucial pivot comes near the end of the sentence; hence, the reader must hold a great deal in mind before she or he can begin to sort out the meaning relationships. Schematically, it works something like this:

> is known by
> everyone.
>
> (colds are) the
> scourge of humankind

That Vitamin C prevents colds

But another version of the sentence puts the predicate-pivot at the beginning of the sentence and lets the reader begin to organize immediately, without strain on memory:

Everyone knows
> that Vitamin C
> prevents colds
>
> (colds are) the scourge
> of humankind

And here are some further examples of delayed closure:

(41) Whatever the family couldn't buy at the country store located at the crossroads five miles from town they did without.
(The family did without whatever they couldn't buy at the country store located at the crossroads five miles from town.)
(42) The program was a concert of relatively pleasant newly discovered Appalachian dulcimer music.
(The program was a concert of relatively pleasant dulcimer music that had been newly discovered in Appalachia.)
(43) To bake potatoes on an open bonfire, as we did when we were kids, was always a great adventure. (It was always a great adventure to bake potatoes on an open bonfire, as we did when we were

kids.) The point is that the original is less readable (harder to process) than its revised version, not that it would be more or less effective in a given context.

Relative Readability

As we have seen, through various maneuvers sentences can be made more or less readable, and rearrangement of passages can also increase or decrease their readability. The variable that can never be completely controlled, however, is the knowledge that a reader brings to the text.

All reading is a tradeoff between what the reader brings to the text by way of background knowledge and the information that the reader gains from the text. The completely informative text would be unreadable, for everything in it would be "news." For example, if I were having trouble reading a text in advanced mathematics, I would not take a course in reading, but rather one in math. Regardless of sentence structure and other factors, a text presenting complex ideas will be difficult to read—though less so for the expert in the field handled by the text.

In Summary

A text is a structure of cues and clues through which the reader can construct a meaning—presumably the one that the writer intended. These clues, however, direct the reader in two directions; inward to the textual structure itself, and outward to the reader's knowledge of the world.

Thus, reading problems are almost never strictly "technical," having to do with eye movements or lack of experience with the cue system; they also involve knowledge that the reader brings to the text. Hence, "remedial" reading programs must give students not only the "skills" of "processing" text, but also the knowledge requisite to make sense of cues that point outward. Reading instruction is not only a physiological and psychological problem, but also a problem of culture.

Reading is not an isolated activity, but a human action that, like all actions, has motives and takes place in a given scene, through diverse agencies such as books, magazines, TV monitors, pamphlets, billboards, and graffiti, to name a few. When we begin to diagnose reading problems and propose solutions, we must take account of reading as a human action.

Our logic leads us to the conclusion that texts are not stable and eternal, conveying a single undisputed meaning to all readers through all time; instead, they can and do mean differently to various groups in diverse scenes. The process of arriving at one "true" meaning involves negotiation among communities of readers, who debate, discuss, study, and at last (sometimes) agree on meaning.

A coherent text, one that hangs together with no loose ends, is one from which the reader has been able to gain a main idea or gist and one in which all the parts relate hierarchically and systematically to this gist. As we will see, the problem of coherence is a large one for teachers and their students who are learning to write.

Readability is a quicksilver term, for it involves not only the structure of the text, but what the reader brings to the text. This leads us to the conclusion that in teaching children (and adults) to read, we are involved in a much larger enterprise than merely teaching technical skills.

In the next chapter, we will explore the problems of learning to read—including such topics as cultural literacy, phonics, dyslexia, and speed reading.

5

To Learn to Read

One of my most persistent memories is about reading. I can remember being told by my mother to turn off the lights and go to sleep. She always seemed to tell me this at the precise moment when I was completely engrossed in a book and did not want to put it down. However, not wanting to anger my mom, I would lay the book down on the floor beside my bed, kiss my parents good nght and turn off the light. As soon as I heard their bedroom door close I would quietly open my bureau drawer and take out the flashlight I had hidden in there. With only an occasional pause to reassure myself that my parents were still in their room, I would read until the wee hours . . . until I had finished the book or had fallen asleep trying.

Of course, this meant I didn't sleep much, and as a consequence, I detested getting up early, but even at the age of eight, I made a conscious decision that reading was much more fun than sleeping.

My mother was a teacher, so even when I was very small she would read to me. We had a very "scientific" method of determining what we would read: she would spread some picture books out on the floor, and I would point to the one that I liked. Since I couldn't read yet, I picked the ones with the pretty colors or the nice picture on the cover. . . .

I remember many people being surprised by my love of reading. Some of my babysitters, expecting me to spend the entire evening in front of the television, were amazed to see me pick up a book, grab a handful of candy from the candy dish and disappear into my room, quiet as a mouse the entire night.

One of my favorite books is *Gone With the Wind*. I have read that book at least six times and I could probably read it six more. The first time that I read it was on a family vacation to Europe. We had flown to London and were staying at a friend's home. When we arrived at the house it was very late, and everyone got settled in their rooms and went to sleep. I was in the daughter's room and as she was fifteen, six years older than I was, I was fascinated by all the things that she had in her room. I was drawn like a magnet to the bookshelf where I saw the biggest book I had ever seen. I pulled it off the shelf and carried it over to the bed. I started reading it at about 3:00 a.m. and was still reading when my father came in to wake me at 8:00 a.m. I was only nine years old, and I hadn't slept in nearly twenty-four hours, but the book was so interesting it didn't seem to matter. . . .

My love of reading is something that I treasure. It has certainly made school reading assignments less of a chore, but there is more to it than that. As long as I have a book to read I can sit for hours and not get bored. I have learned the pleasure of being able to entertain myself. I enjoy every kind of book I can find; I read love stories, mysteries, plays, autobiographies, biographies, science fiction and satires. I have favorite books that I reread when I have no new books, and even though I know the plot and even most of the dialogue by heart, I still would rather read a book than do most anything else.

CAROLINE M. BLEIFER
University of Southern California

When we think of how easy it seems for some children to learn to read, we are justifiably puzzled at the difficulty that other children have. My older son was reading well before he entered school—taught, apparently, by his cousin, four years older than he, as they played "school," she the teacher and Geoff the pupil. Both of our sons grew up in "readerly" environments: their parents, grandparents, and aunts and uncles are all addicted readers, and various relatives spent countless hours reading stories to them. Like many similar children, they "grew into" reading naturally.

Importantly, the context in which they and other children learn to read is very different today from what it was before World War II. Ralph W. Tyler, emeritus director of the Center for Advanced Study in the Behavioral Sciences, reminds us that

in 1800, the unskilled in all categories constituted more than eighty
percent of the labor force; in 1900 they made up sixty percent; and in
1980, about six percent. It was only after World War II that rapid
changes in the occupational and social structure created sharp new
demands for education and many more opportunities for employment
in such fields as education, health, recreation, social services, administration, accounting, and engineering. Consequently, schools are now
expected to educate all (or nearly all) children rather than sort out high
performers and proficient test takers and to encourage members of that
group alone to go on with their education.[1]

In the last decades of the twentieth century, universal education
has become not only a democratic ideal, but also a social and
economic necessity, particularly when we realize that "by 1990
about fifty percent of the work force will be manufacturing objects
and producing food. The rest will occupy most of the time just
communicating."[2] But even though reading seems so easy and inevitable to most of us, estimates of the number of functionally
illiterate adults in the United States range from 25 to 57 million—a
vast quantity in a society that increasingly trades in information,
not products. In Chapter 8 of this book, we will explore the social
and individual consequences of literacy. For now, it is enough to
remind ourselves that the ability to read and write is intrinsic to all
aspects of education.

The Development of Reading Ability

Many children, like my son, learn to read without systematic instruction and before they start school, in rare cases beginning as
early as a year and a half. In a marvelous book titled *GNYS AT
WRK* (a five-year-old's spelling for "genius at work"), Glenda
Bissex tells how her son Paul taught himself to read and write
before he entered school. Interestingly, Paul began to write before
he could read, and when he was just over five years old, he was
using invented spelling. In one instance, after attempting to attract
his mother's attention while she was engrossed in a book, he
printed her a note with rubber stamps: RUDF. No, his mother
replied, she was not deaf, and she put down her book and attended
to Paul. Writing stirred Paul's interest in reading, but he wrote

apparently for the sheer pleasure of achieving mastery, not for any extrinsic reward.[3]

Whether in school or prior to school, the learning of reading progresses through some fairly clearcut stages.[4] These will be discussed briefly in the next four sections.

Letter and Word Recognition

When a parent says /bee/, the child is able to point to a B and has thus made the letter-sound connection, which in the previous chapter we call *graphophonic* (from *grapheme,* the letter or letter combination, and *phoneme,* the meaningful sound). (We should remind ourselves that groups of letters—graphemes—often represent one phoneme: *ph*ysics /fiziks/, *taught* /tot/. Of course, this more complicated recognition develops later than that of the one-for-one correspondence of B /bee/.)

The child, of course, in developing competence, has learned that the sound /bee/ is meaningful: *b*ig and *p*ig do not mean the same. Thus, the child is bringing world knowledge and growing competence in language to bear on recognizing the grapheme and associating it with the meaningful sound. To associate the letter B and the sound /bee/ is not merely to respond to a stimulus automatically, but to engage in a complicated mental process. At this stage children also begin to recognize words. "Cheerios" is on the box that contains the delectable little donuts that Daddy so deftly flips up and catches in his mouth. Children are learning to match a visual pattern with a sound pattern that has meaning for them.

Should parents then systematically "drill" their children in graphophonic recognition? My answer is an emphatic No. You will recall that we made a sharp distinction between learning language through drill and acquiring language through experience in meaningful situations. Games, the give-and-take of proto-conversations, playfulness, the seriousness of really trying to communicate—these should and do provide the occasions for learning. One can gain a monstrous image in thinking about drilling a child in letter recognition: the parent as Gradgrind, the schoolmaster in Dickens' *Hard Times,* setting aside an hour a day to go through systematic exercises, rewarding the child for accurate responses and punishing him or her for inaccuracies or refusal to cooperate. Such a parent-child relationship is pathological.

Reading Sentences

The next step is a large one, for it involves not only relating the word with its sound and its sound with a meaning, but also untangling the relationships of words with other words. Think of the following two sentences:

> **(1a)** Bozo [the clown] tells Donald [Duck] to hop up and down.
> **(1b)** Bozo promises Donald to hop up and down.

In **(1a)**, Donald will do the hopping, but in **(1b)** Bozo will. Carol Chomsky found, however, that younger children make Donald hop in both instances.[5] The children have not yet acquired the competence to establish the relationships that will give them an accurate reading of the sentences. It also takes children some time to acquire the competence necessary to understand that the following pair mean essentially the same thing:

> **(2a)** Christopher sees Mommy.
> **(2b)** Mommy is seen by Christopher.

For young learners, the subjects of the sentences (Christopher and Mommy) both do the seeing.

Reading Stories

Very young children can learn to "read" stories. In one instance, a child of two and a half was able to arrange six pictures in a sequence that represented a plot.[6] If you think about it, this is quite an intellectual accomplishment for the child; it represents burgeoning world and genre knowledge. A story is a series of events, one after another, and everyone who has been around children knows their insatiable appetite for endless stories: "Then what?" and "What happened next?" are among their most frequent questions. Yet when the concept of plot enters, the situation complicates itself immeasurably, for plot implies cause-and-effect and motives.

The novelist E. M. Forster gave an example of a mere story: "First the king died, and then the queen died." The story gains a plot when the element of *why* enters: "First the king died, and then the queen died of grief." Now the question becomes not "What happened next?" but "Why did the queen die of grief?"—and we are into the morass of human relations.

Stories, then, are the child's first introduction to reasoning *literately,* which is not to say that one must be literate in order to reason. But a story would be inexplicable to a child if that child did not have the world knowledge to supply and interpret motives. Once again, we see that reading is not merely a technical process of working out the relationship between printed symbols and the sounds that they represent and sorting out the relationships among words in sentences.

Pleasure Reading

This last step is perhaps the most important. In it, reading becomes its own reward, a pleasure and a way of life. If the child does not take this step, he or she will forever be a handicapped reader or a nonreader.

The literature on reading is full of reports about stimulus-response, behaviorist models of reading instruction. Years ago I was on a doctoral committee of a student who attempted to motivate students to read by giving them money for attaining steps of proficiency as measured by tests. His effort was a dismal failure. Children and adults don't read for immediate rewards, but simply because they are readers.

I worked some years ago with a well-meaning but misguided father whose son was profoundly deaf and had difficulties with both reading and writing. The father was an engineer and had convinced himself that systematic drills, based on modern linguistic science (about which, surprisingly, he knew a great deal), would be the answer to his son's problems. He approached me to concoct a set of drills keyed to inadequacies that I would find in his son's reading and writing skills. Of course, the situation was complicated; because of his deafness, the son was unable to go through the natural developmental process that we have been outlining. Yet I knew what everyone who thinks about the situation knows:

that language develops in the give-and-take of an environment in which learners immerse themselves in language (in other words, in the world of talk and print that most of us inhabit), then attempt to convey meanings, and finally get responses to those attempts. Therefore, I suggested as a first step that the father supply his son with copious reading material, which the father proceeded to do. He bought stacks of "good" books, classic novels, essays by the best thinkers, and technical discussions of scientific fields. These expensive stacks lay untouched about the house. Then I suggested that the father simply provide books on subjects that the boy was interested in. The father was resistant; after all, he told me, his son's primary interest was model building, hardly an uplifting intellectual enterprise. Nonetheless, at my suggestion the father provided his son with books and magazines about models.

I wish that I could report success. Unfortunately, the father and son disappeared from my scene, and I have no idea how the boy progressed. Nonetheless, I'm sure that I was on the right track, even though I am equally sure that some children, for more reasons than we could enumerate, will never become readers. For such children we must provide alternate means of learning and communicating. That, however, is a subject we will deal with when we turn to dyslexia.

Phonics and Whole-Word Approaches

For many people, learning to read and phonics mean virtually the same thing, and the debates over phonics versus the whole-word method of instruction are often heated. With phonics, learners are drilled in letter or letter-group and sound correspondence. For instance /p/ and /b/ are contrasting pairs, and children can be given materials designed to emphasize the contrast: The *poor puppy put* his *paw* in the door, The *big boxer barked before* he *bit*. Or, of course, word lists can be presented: bad, bed, bid, bud. Among other problems with these methods is their artificiality, but they are no more unnatural than having learners identify individual whole words on flash cards.

The following discussion will sort out some of the problems with phonics and make some recommendations concerning the use of that method in instruction.

We know that language learning does not take place from the bottom up; that is, learners do not begin with the smallest parts of language (phonemes, syllables) and after mastering these go on to words and then to sentences. We also know that direct instruction in the total sound system of the language would be such a massive enterprise that we would reserve it for graduate school. In other words, if we want to do a "thorough" job with phonics, we must either teach a few rules with thousands of exceptions or thousands of rules with few exceptions.

Here are some of the words that children in my neighborhood in California hear from the time they are born: bologna, buoy, playa, sushi, tamale, yacht. Again, children learn to pronounce *ashes* /a-sh-ez/ and *mishap* /mis-hap/, not to mention *through, though, tough,* and *trough.* What kind of systematic phonics instruction would be necessary to teach children to pronouce these "anomalous" words, which are not, after all, so exceptional? Clearly, thoroughgoing instruction in phonics is unfeasible—even, if you will, crazy to consider.

In a letter to relatives, nine-year-old Denise wrote:

I had my ears pierced. I bought myself a pair of *earings,* lipstick, and *ruge.* I had a big *suprize.* I'm *staring* in a *mellow drama.*

Denise used phonetic spellings: earings, ruge, suprize (representing her pronunciation of the word), staring, and mellow drama. To learn the correct spelling of these words, she would need to see them. Let's pursue this matter a bit further. Suppose that Denise encountered the word "rouge" out of context, in a list. She might well pronounce it /rowj/ and be unable to derive its meaning. If, however, she encountered it in context, she would probably know how to pronounce it because she would know its menaing:

(3) The makeup artist applied lipstick, eye shadow, and *rouge* to the star.

Learning to read thus involves knowledge of both the phonemic (sound) and graphemic (print) systems.

Contrasted with phonics as a method of instruction is the *whole-word* or *look-say* approach. Children or adults are taught to recognize whole words (for instance, from flash cards) without the mediation of sound or phonics.

If you are looking for a definitive, scientifically established answer to the question of phonics versus look-say methods, you will be be disappointed. As Insup and M. Martin Taylor say in their excellent book *The Psychology of Reading,* "The relative advantages of look-say and phonics in laboratory experiments depend on the kind of material and task, and hence the findings have little practical value."[7] Doing what comes naturally, parents and aunts and uncles have used phonics sensibly all along. As children are learning to read, adults often pronounce words that the children stumble over. We have all have heard adults say "Now you can sound that word out" and then coach children in the pronunciation of the target word.

Children acquire most of their phonic knowledge in the same way that they acquire grammar-in-the-head or competence: through language experience aided and abetted by some direct instruction. Taylor and Taylor summarize thus:

> Phonics teaches how to sound out letters and letter sequences, and is suitable for teaching regular words. Armed with phonics skills, children can decode new words on their own. The contrasting method, look-say, associates a whole word with its meaning and sound, and is the quickest and easiest way to introduce young children to reading. It is particularly suitable for teaching irregular words. In look-say, letter-sound relations are left to children to induce from known words. English has both regular and irregular words, requiring a combination of the two methods for teaching children (and adults) to read.[8]

Dyslexia

In his excellent book *Understanding Reading,* Frank Smith has only the following to say about our topic: "failure [to read] need not be attributed to *dyslexia,* a disease that only strikes children who cannot read, and which is invariably cured when they can read."[9] However, Taylor and Taylor have no doubt about the existence of a condition that is normally termed dyslexia. They say, "Developmental dyslexia is a severe and persistent difficulty suffered by intellectually normal children in learning to read,"[10] a condition with the following characteristics: "(a) persistence to adulthood; (b) peculiar and specific nature of the errors in reading and spelling; (c) familial incidence of the defect; (d) greater incidence in males than in females; and (e) normal if not high intelligence."[11]

In one study, students who were identified as dyslexic were compared with a group that were, according to the investigators, not dyslexic, but generally backward in reading. The dyslexics were from homes of "adequate" socioeconomic status. Over a five-year period, the "backward" group, those with lower IQs than the dyslexics, made more progress in reading and spelling than did the latter group, but the dyslexics advanced more rapidly in arithmetic than did the other group,[12] indicating both mental ability and ability to learn.

It would seem, then, that there is a condition, however, ill-defined, that we might name dyslexia. Yet we also know that low socioeconomic status is associated with reading problems, whatever we call them. Should we say, then, that dyslexia is confind to economically secure children and that children of poverty who have trouble with reading are victims of the social system? Children of poverty have more tooth decay than middle-class children, and it is caused, in a sense, by social conditions; changing the social conditions would undoubtedly decrease the amount of tooth decay in these groups, but some individuals would still be more prone to caries than others, for genetic heritage differs from individual to individual. There is no doubt in my mind that most children are simply born with the neurological equipment to become good readers, but some are not (and I don't mean those with brain lesions or other obvious problems). It is an accepted fact that some people are better coordinated than others, have faster reflexes, are better equipped to be athletes or ballet dancers. Why should we deny that such differences exist in the "equipment" necessary for reading?

Taylor and Taylor (upon whose work I am relying for much of the technical background in this discussion) take it for granted that dyslexia exists and classify dyslexics according to the difficulties they have. The first type (in the jargon, phonetic-linguistic dyslexics), find it difficult to convert letters into sounds; in other words, they can't pronounce unfamiliar words or make the graphophonic connection, but they can "sight read" words that are familiar to them. Presumably, they have learned exclusively—or at least primarily—by the whole-word method. The second type is just the opposite. These dyslexics can, with some difficulty, sound out words, but they cannot "sight read." (In the jargon, these are visual-perceptual dyslexics.)

We have already contrasted the phonic and whole-word methods of early reading instruction. Phonetic-linguistic dyslexics appear to learn only by the whole-word method and visual-perceptual dyslexics only by phonics. Perhpas—just perhaps—the dyslexic is unable to integrate two different sorts of mental processes that are necessary for reading.

Speed Reading

Woody Allen told of taking a speed-reading course. After finishing it, he read *War and Peace* in fifteen minutes. "It was about Russians," he said.

I would like to advance four propositions and then follow them up. First, almost everyone can increase his or her reading speed with *all* materials. Second, the more detail the reader wants, the slower will be the reading speed. Third, unfamiliar (hence difficult) material takes longer to read than familiar material. Fourth, reading speed depends on the purpose for reading.

Most readers are less efficient than they might be. If your purpose is to cover a given text as rapidly as possible, you are ill-advised to read carefully and sequentially. Think of what Kenneth Goodman said about the nature of the reading process as a psycholinguistic guessing-game: sampling, predicting, and confirming or disconfirming. And think also about the necessity of finding the gist so that the details can be related to this highest-level generality or point of the text.

Readers who want to "process" a text with maximum efficiency will scan several times, attempting to get a general idea of what the main point is. They will look for summaries and will notice subheadings. They might even read the first sentences of the paragraphs. This will be a rapid process, taking them through a chapter in this book, for instance, in a very few minutes. In other words, they will sample liberally and quickly so that they have a basis for predicting. Then they will circle back and test their predictions, confirming or disconfirming them. Once the reader has gained a sense of the overall point of the text, he or she will make another pass, this time "reading" more closely to gain detail that relates to the whole picture. Depending on the purpose for reading, the reader will attempt to integrate more and more detail into the totality, a process that finally may demand very close reading. *However—and this is axiomatic—close reading should never precede scanning.* The image is that of a bird after prey, circling high and broadly, scanning the territory for movement, then zeroing in with increasingly tighter circles, before the final plunge.

All this can be stated in a set of "rules of thumb" for efficient reading:

> *Scan* the territory, perhaps more than once. Try to find main points, to get the lay of the land. Look at first sentences of paragraphs, subheads, and summaries if there are any. (Summaries often appear at the ends of chapters.) Next, *predict* what the point of the text is. Then *confirm* your prediction by reading more closely. If close scrutiny *disconfirms* your expectations, start the process again.

If your purpose is to get the gist of a novel—the plot—you can read a detective story very quickly, as John F. Kennedy was reputed to have done. But you cannot speed-read Jacques Derrida's *Of Grammatology* unless you want only the vaguest notion of what it is about, although you can certainly read it more efficiently than most people do. If you are an expert on ichthyology, you may be able to read a treatise on that subject very quickly; the less you know about the subject, the more time you will invest in reading if you want not only to comprehend the general idea, but also to understand local details.

Purpose has much to do with how we read. If we want merely to know the plot of *Great Expectations,* we can read it very rapidly, skimming, skipping, and circling back to pick up essential details that we missed. Few, however, would want only that much from the book, for it offers the chance to experience and live through Pip's great expectations. Such a purpose slows reading down, sometimes even to almost a snail's pace.

Suppose, however, that you are a scholar—say, a biochemist—and you need to keep up with the myriad publications in your field. All you want from these pages and pages in journals and books is basic information. You don't want to savor the language or admire the deftness of metaphor. Then it will be the case that much of what you read you can comprehend almost at a glance, although other texts will contain new and unfamiliar material that will demand more time and a more detailed reading.

Your method of reading, which almost everyone can improve, is only one factor in speed reading. The more detail you want to grasp and integrate, the longer it will take you to complete the text. The more familiar the material is, the faster you will be able to read. And if your purpose is to enjoy the text as a text, not to use it merely as a source of information, you will read more slowly—in the case of a novel, for instance, contemplating the characters as they grow in your mind, enjoying the language of the author, and thinking about the relevance of the ideas and events to your own life.

Cultural Literacy

During the summer of 1987, *Cultural Literacy* by E. D. Hirsch, Jr., remained high on the national list of best sellers for several weeks, a fact that gives evidence of widespread concern about both literacy and culture. (A book much akin to *Cultural Literacy, The Closing of the American Mind* by Allan Bloom, was higher and remained longer on the lists.)

Now, the crux of the issue regarding cultural literacy—which Hirsch defines as "that knowledge that enables a writer or reader to know what other writers and readers know within the literate culture"[13]—is not "whether" but "what." For how could literacy be other than cultural? Might one conceive of a disembodied literacy, an abstraction, independent of scene and a tradition of texts? How could reading specialists teach students the "skill" of understanding "the patience of Job" or "sour grapes"?

Hirsch is one of many who present evidence that literacy is critically declining in the United States and that the need for literacy is ever more compelling. For example, regarding the scholastic aptitude tests, Hirsch states that "out of a constant pool of about a million test takers each year, 56 percent more students scored above 600 in 1972 than did so in 1984. More startling yet, the percentage drop was even greater for those scoring above 650—73 percent."[14] This brings us to the subtitle of Hirsch's book, *What Every American Needs to Know*, to which we might add the sub-subtitle *in Order to Be Literate.* The answer is crucial. One needs some specialized knowledge and a great deal of general knowledge: *intensive* and *extensive* learning.[15]

It seems to me that this reasoning is impeccable. To understand this morning's newspaper, I need an enormous reservoir of general knowledge concerning Kurt Weil, HMOs, the American Kennel Club, the Persian Gulf, the Supreme Court, and on and on. But to function in my profession, I need to know about and understand in depth such matters as "illocution" and "perlocution" (from speech act theory). (And to understand the letters I receive from friends, I need equally specialized knowledge.) This reasoning leads to the inevitable question: of what does cultural knowledge—hence cultural literacy—consist?

Hirsch and his colleagues Joseph Kett, a historian, and James Trefil, a physicist, all of the University of Virginia, answer the question with a list of some 4,500 or 5,000 items, developed primarily by the three principals. The list includes the American Legion, bas relief, capital expenditure, deus ex machina, El Salvador, familiarity breeds contempt, Gresham's law, Heisenberg's uncertainty principle, Iwo Jima, Scott Joplin, the Kentucky Derby, Simon Legree, magnetic tape, neocolonialism, one man's meat is another man's poison, paleontology, quixotic, Ronald Reagan, serf, Talmud, unsaturated fatty acid, value judgment, Mae West, X-chromosome, Yosemite National Park, and Zapata.

I must now forestall objections to what Hirsch and his colleagues have done. First, they do not set themselves up as cultural dictators. Second, they view their list as provisional and invite the dialectic of response and critique: "The authors see the list as a changing entity, partly because core knowledge changes, partly because inappropriate omissions and inclusions are bound to occur in a first attempt."[16] I find it impossible to understand how anyone could object to the project of cultural literacy so far. Of course, one might argue for a radical individualism, with each person inhabiting his or her own cultural universe; however, I prefer a chummier sort of utopia, in which my neighbor and I can discuss not only the funny papers, but also Shakespeare. Hirsch is merely saying, "If we want to communicate, we must have a body of shared knowledge."

Hirsch repudiates formalism (drills, dry-run exercises) in theories of literacy, in educational practice, and in his own earlier work, yet clearly his cultural literacy project implies a kind of formalism. By this I mean that one does not become culturally literate merely by absorbing a body of information. The point can be made another way: one will not absorb a body of cultural information until one is attitudinally prepared to do so. As I have held throughout this book, the fundamental cause of the literacy crisis is the unwillingness or the inability of illiterate or marginally literate people to change cultures. The whole point of *Cultural Literacy* is that reading depends on cultural knowledge, and one gains that knowledge through understanding—and hence, in effect, joining the literate culture.

As mentioned earlier in this book, case studies of the development of reading and writing ability in individual homes (e.g., Taylor and Bissex) or among social groups (e.g., Scribner and Cole, Heath, Schieffelin and Cochran-Smith, and Scollon and Scollon) convey what is almost a truism: children in homes where reading and writing are highly valued unconsciously acquire cultural literacy almost inevitably, and those homes are part of societies or social groups in which literacy has value. And the "uses" of literacy within a society—the advantages that it bestows—determine not only the "level" but the consequences of literacy.

No one, I think, would argue with the premise that a higher level of national literacy will come only through a higher level of nationally shared information. The question is how to bring about that sharing—and, I suppose, in a discussion of cultural literacy and *Cultural Literacy,* the usefulness of a list in meeting this goal.

The distinction betwen acquiring language subconsciously and learning it consciously is important here. It will be recalled that acquisition takes place as a natural consequence of using language to communicate. For example, in the process of trying to get meaning from language and to make meaning with it, a child discovers the rules of grammar and uses them with more and more accuracy, which is to say that the child acquires the language system without consciously attempting to master rules. In fact, the number of rules that can be consciously mastered is extremely small, considering the complexity of language. In spite of the long school tradition, people do not learn language through studying "grammar."

The question I am leading up to, of course, is whether people can gain cultural literacy by studying lists or, indeed, by studying canons. Suppose the four or five thousand items in the *Cultural Literacy* list do, indeed, roughly map out the territory of our culture. How are students meaningfully to learn those items? I would argue that the key is acquisition, not conscious learning, and that acquisition takes place only when the focus is on semantic intention—on purpose, not on items. In fact, I think that the *deconstructionist* educational theories of Paulo Freire hold the answer to the question of cultural literacy. Freire would argue that we can achieve cultural literacy only through what he calls "problem-posing education." In effect, he proposes a productive redefinition of "acquisition" that holds that "learning" involves gaining information through attempting to deal with existential problems.[17]

Hirsch advances telling arguments against the content-neutral ideas of Rousseau and Dewey.[18] However, Freire would counter that culture has no hard-and-fast parameters, but is continually created by individuals who reinterpret what is and was and who contribute their own works to the immediate future. Thus, the problem of cultural literacy is not so much one of compiling lists as demonstrating through a dialogic and loving pedagogy that every human is part of the culture-making process:

> Thus the educator's role is fundamentally to enter into dialogue with the illiterate about concrete situations and simply offer him the instruments with which he can teach himself to read and write. This teaching cannot be done from the top down, but only from the inside out, by the illiterate himself, with the collaboration of the educator.[19]

Hence, Freire and his colleagues are skeptical of "primers."[20] From one point of view, cultural literacy, as developed up to this point by Hirsch, is primer-bound. In fact, the real problem in cultural literacy is not one of canons or lists but of creating and sustaining the dialogue whereby culture is made.

In Summary: Critical Reading

The final goal of reading is not merely to derive information from a text efficiently but to be able to evaluate that information—in other words, to read critically. Writings speak for their authors, and like other humans, authors can be prejudiced, ignorant of important facts and concepts, and mendacious—or wise, honest, knowledgeable, and reliable. A critical reader thinks carefully about what he or she reads, evaluates it, tests its logic and its facts, seeks its strengths and weaknesses. Critical readers learn more and certainly enjoy their reading more than do passive readers.

Novels, histories, essays, sets of instructions, newspaper reports, poems, personal letters, memos—these are all texts, for we have defined text as any piece of writing that conveys a coherent meaning. Thus, a dictionary and an almanac, useful though they may be, are not texts, for they don't add up to a single, unified meaning. The entries in an encyclopedia are texts, but the individual volumes are not texts themselves. However, one text may extend through several volumes.

A rule of thumb for texts is this: in a text the careful reader can get the gist of the writing and can, in general, see how the parts fit this whole. Of course, some texts are more coherent than others, and some contain unsolvable problems of interpretation; but if a piece of writing simply does not make sense at all, we do not call it a text.

Next, we have asked how texts convey meanings. It is useful to think of a text as a set of cues or instructions, inscribed by the writer, which enable the reader to construct a meaning—presumably the one intended by the writer. To use these instructions the reader must have adequate world knowledge as well as knowledge of the language system. A critical reader will always realize that he or she is (re)constructing the meaning and thus will beware of personal prejudices that distort what might be taken as the author's intention.

It is not to belittle philosophy, theology, law, and other disciplines to say that in essence they are words about words. (Although we don't want to become mired in philosophical speculation, it is perfectly reasonable to say that language constitutes all disciplines; the texts of a discipline are that discipline, though not its practice. For example, medicine is not what your family physician does when you visit her or his office, but rather the sum total of the texts concerning what she or he and other physicians do.)

According to H. P. Grice's cooperative principle, the author agrees that he or she will abide by a "contract" to

1. tell us all we need to know to understand the subject, but no more than we need to know;
2. tell the truth and have knowledge of the subject;
3. not introduce irrelevant material; and
4. be as clear as possible.

In other words, these maxims concern *quantity, quality, relation,* and *manner.* Writers violate the "terms" of this contract either intentionally or inadvertently, through error. Intentional violations create special effects such as irony and humor; unintentional violations most frequently puzzle readers. In attempting to understand and evaluate texts, readers can use the maxims as probes:

Quantity: Does the text supply all that I need to know about the subject? Does it contain more than I need to know? What is lacking? What is excessive?

Quality: Can I trust the information in the text? Is the writer being honest? Does the writer know what he or she is talking about? How do *I* know that the writer knows?

Relation: Is everything in the text relevant to the writer's point or gist? Does anything unnecessarily sidetrack the reader from the point?

Manner: In relation to the author's purpose, is the text as clear and easy to read as possible?

Intention is the vital stuff of discourse, written or spoken. Sometimes, in fact, the meaning of an utterance is almost nothing but intention—as when I say "Mmmmm!" after tasting my wife's pound cake, my intention being to express my satisfaction, gratitude, and approval. At other times the surface form of an utterance and its intention seem not to coincide, in which case the intention will always prevail. For example, suppose that in a stuffy room, George is sitting by a closed window. Greta says to him, "Could you open the window?" If George merely answers "yes" but takes no action, he will have misinterpreted Greta, for though her utterance looks like a question, it is actually a request ("Please open the window").

Your answers to analytic questions will depend on what you take to be the writer's intention, and there is no way that you can avoid assuming authorial intention behind any text. Here are a few of the questions for which critical readers seek satisfactory answers:

1. What is the gist of the text?
2. Is the quantity of information adequate?
3. Is the quality of information unquestionable?
4. Does everything in the text relate to the gist?
5. In manner, is the text as readable as possible, considering the author's intention?
6. What does the writer's intention seem to be?
7. What do I know and what do I need to know about the writer?
8. What sort of readers does the text seem intended for?
9. Is the organization effective?
10. Is the style effective?
11. What influence does scene (of composition and of reading) have on the text?

And now we turn to writing, the counterpart of reading.

6

To Write

That is why I started to write. To save myself.

I realized that no one could save me but myself. The prison authorities were both uninterested and unable to help me. I had to seek out the truth and unravel the snarled web of my motivations. I had to find out who I am and what I want to be, what type of man I should be, and what I could do to become the best of which I was capable.

ELDRIDGE CLEAVER
Soul on Ice

In this chapter I would like to explore the purposes for writing and to discuss what is often called "the composing process." Writing is an instrument of thought. Without writing, science, technology, philosophy, theology—all the monuments of human intellect—are inconceivable. But, as Eldridge Cleaver's statement indicates, writing is also a means of self-discovery and self-expression.

Writing and Inscribing

In this book "writing" means the mental activity that produces texts, not "handwriting" (penmanship). It is important to note that writing need not involve *inscription,* that is, making marks with pencil, pen, typewriter, or electronic impulse. Many writers dictate their texts into a recorder, and the taped words are then inscribed by a typist or word processor. The blind Milton wrote *Paradise Lost,* but his daughters *inscribed* it (wrote it down) for him.

However, one should not underestimate the advantage that inscribing gives the writer. If you mark your ideas down in some way as they develop, you can look back through them as you plan the forward movement—you can see exactly where you've been before you proceed. Any experienced writer knows that she or he spends a good deal of time looking backward in the text, and it seems that unskilled writers (we will call them "basic writers") don't scan backward as they attempt to move forward.[1] We might say that inscription is a technology of mind.

The Range of Writing: Writers' Purposes

Different purposes for writing create different writer-reader relationships, and one of the main skills a writer must develop is the ability to adjust the text to meet the reader's expectations.

Examples of this principle are always at hand. John Kenneth Galbraith, writing for other economists, can assume that they understand the details of monetary policy, Keynesian theory, and so on. When specialists write for the general public, however, the situation changes. Laypeople need explanations that would be irrelevant for experts; specialized terms need definition; reasons for the importance of the subject must be laid out.

Expert writers learn to produce "reader-based" texts, writings that are crafted with the intended audience in mind. Inexpert writers often produce "writer-based" texts that don't supply the background necessary for readers to construct the writer's intention.[2] For example, here are two explanations of the "GOTO" statement used in BASIC computer language. The first is from a book by David Simon for beginners who know nothing about computers or programming. The second is from an IBM manual.

(1) The GOTO statement is one way to tell the computer to repeat a sequence of statements. A GOTO statement consists of a statement number, the word "GOTO" (or "GO TO"), and a second statement number. When the computer encounters a GOTO statement, it does not continue to execute statements in numerical order. Instead, it executes next the statement whose number appears in the GOTO statement, and continues from there. Consider the following example (a rather stupid one):

```
10 LET A = 1
20 LET B = 2
```

```
30 PRINT A
40 PRINT B
50 GOTO 30
60 END
```

Statements 10 through 40 print the numbers 1 and 2. When the computer gets to statement 50, it goes back to statement 30, where it prints another 1. Then it continues on from statement 30 to statement 40 and prints a 2. When it comes to statement 50, the computer goes back to statement 30 again, where it again prints a 1. Then it prints a 2. When it comes to statement 50 again, it goes back to statement 30. . . .

In fact, this program succeeds a little too well: the computer will continue to print 1's and 2's . . . until the next power failure or the end of the world, whichever comes first.[3]

(2) Purpose: Branches unconditionally out of the normal program sequence to a specified line number.

Versions: Cassette   Disk   Advanced   Compiler

Format: GOTO *line*

Remarks: *line* is the line number of a line in the program.

If *line* is the line number of an executable statement, that statement and those following are executed. If *line* refers to a nonexecutable statements (such as REM or DATA), the program continues at the first executable statement encountered after *line*.

The GOTO statement can be used in direct mode to reenter a program at a desired point. This can be useful in debugging.

Use ON . . . GOTO to branch to different lines based on the result of an expression.[4]

The explanation from the IBM manual is clearly intended for people who know about computers, who need little background information. Simon's explanation is just as clearly for beginners, who need copious help at every step.

Table 3 is a schematic of one common way to sort out the manifold purposes for writing. Of course, as in all human acts, motives in writing are usually mixed. For instance, an anthropologist writ-

TABLE 3. Manifold Purposes for Writing

Purpose and Definition	Examples
Explanatory: to inform	Sets of instructions, reports, encyclopedia articles, most histories and biographies, *Beyond the Hundredth Meridian* by Wallace Stenger
Argument: to convince	Scientific papers, research papers, logical arguments, *The Panda's Thumb* by Stephen Jay Gould
Exploratory: to explore	Texts that outline problems without proposing solutions, texts that are "thinking in writing," *Pilgrim at Tinker Creek* by Annie Dillard
Poetic: to create imaginative structures	Poems, stories, novels, plays, *Far Tortuga* by Peter Matthiessen
Persuasive: to persuade	Advertisements, political speeches, appeals by charities, Lincoln's "First Inaugural Address"
Expressive: to express oneself	Private diaries, scribblings, laments, tirades, Pepys' *Diary*

Source: Adapted from Roman Jakobson, "Linquistics and Poetics," in *Style in Language,* ed. Thomas A. Sebeok (Cambridge, Mass.: MIT Press, 1960).

ing a scientific report on work with a remote, preliterate tribe may well take great satisfaction in his or her own skill as a writer and intend that the book be appreciated for its verbal artistry as well as for its informative value. And we can immediately begin to break down the seemingly clear-cut divisions between types of writing. For example, a text may be largely a dispassionate setting forth of facts to convince readers but may in fact persuade them to some action, such as voting for a candidate.

Purposes: Writer to Reader

Various categories of writing imply different writer-reader relationships. Several categories and relationships are discussed in the sections that follow.

Informative Writing

The writer of informative texts is an expert on a given subject—or at least the readers must accept him or her as such. If readers take a text to be informative, they do not ask of the writer, "How does he know?" In informative writing the writer is the expert, and the reader is the novice. As we will see, this principle creates problems in the schools, for teachers often ask students to write "informative" papers on subjects in which the teacher is an expert and the student is only a beginner. Thus, both student and teacher must assume poses, and here the writing act is to a great extent artificial.

What follows is a typical informative text from the *World Almanac*.[5]

Major Venomous Animals

Lizards
Gila Monster—up to 24 inches long with heavy body and tail, in high desert in southwest U.S. and N. Mexico; immediate severe pain followed by vomiting, thirst, difficulty swallowing, weakness approaching paralysis; no recent mortality.
Mexican beaded lizard—similar to Gila monster, Mexican west-coast; reaction and mortality rate similar to Gila Monster.

Argument

In argument the focus shifts away from the authority of the writer toward the nature of the contents. In scientific and research writing, the data convince. In texts based on reasoning (arguments for or against some proposition), success depends on the integrity of the argument, its "logic." Its chain of reasoning either convinces or fails to convince.

Samuel Johnson, the great eighteenth-century man of letters who compiled the first modern dictionary, wrote an argument for freeing a slave, Joseph Knight, who had been kidnapped as a child and sold to a Scottish gentleman. Knight's lawyer used Johnson's argument, and the court did, indeed, set Knight free.[6]

It must be agreed that in most ages many countries have had part of their inhabitants in a state of slavery; yet it may be doubted whether slavery can ever be supposed the natural condition of man. It is impossible not to conceive that men in their original state were equal; and very difficult to image how one would be subjected to another except by violent compulsion. An individual may, indeed, forfeit his liberty by a crime; but he cannot by that crime forfeit the liberty of his children. What is true of a criminal seems true likewise of a captive. A man may accept life from a conquering enemy on condition of perpetual servitude; but it is very doubtful whether he can entail that servitude on his descendants; for no man can stipulate without commission for another. The condition which he himself accepts, his son or grandson perhaps would have rejected. If we should admit, what perhaps with more reason may be denied, that there are certain relations between man and man which may make slavery necessary and just, yet it can never be proved that he who is now suing for his freedom ever stood in any of these relations. He is certainly subject by no law, but that of violence, to his present master; who pretends no claim to his obedience, but that he bought him from a merchant of slaves, whose right to sell him never was examined. It is said that, according to the constitutions of Jamaica, he was legally enslaved; these constitutions are merely positive; and apparently injurious to the rights of mankind, because whoever is exposed to sale is condemned to slavery without appeal; by whatever fraud or violence he might originally have been brought into the merchant's power. In our own time Princes have been sold, by wretches to whose care they were entrusted, that they might have an European education; but when once they were brought to a market in the plantations, little would avail either their dignity or their wrongs. The laws of Jamaica afford a Negro no redress. His colour is considered as sufficient testimony against him. It is to be lamented that moral right should ever give way to political convenience. But if temptations of interest are sometimes too strong for human virtue, let us at least retain a virtue where there is no temptation to quit it. In the present case there is apparent right on one side, and no convenience on the other. Inhabitants of this island can neither gain riches nor power by taking away the liberty of any part of the human species. The sum of the argument is this:—No man is by nature the property of another: The defendant is, therefore, by nature free: The rights of nature must be some way forfeited before they can be justly taken away: that the defendant has by any act forfeited the rights of nature we require to be proved; and if no proof of such forfeiture can be given, we doubt not but the justice of the court will declare him free.

Exploratory Writing

Writing is a means of expressing what you think about a subject, but it is also an instrument for discovering what you think, that is, for taking a mental look at the complications and enigmas of a subject. To a certain extent, of course, most writing is exploratory, for no one can predict with certainty what will develop from a complex semantic intention.

The writer of exploratory discourse is asking the reader to follow along, to investigate and understand points of view and attitudes, but the exploratory text does not seek the reader's agreement with some thesis; it does not set out to convince.

Imaginative Writing

The writer of imaginative texts asks the reader to enter a fictive realm and contemplate the artistic and moral structure of the work and the world it creates. All works of imaginative literature— poems, novels, plays—have informative and often persuasive value, but if a reader takes these works to be imaginative, his or her main purpose in reading is not to gain information. Usually the reader's attention focuses on the imaginative experience provided by the text and the pleasures afforded by the writing itself.

Persuasive Writing

Through persuasion the writer is attempting to bring about some action in the reader. With argument I may convince you that a given candidate is the best qualified and yet not persuade you to vote for that person. (Most smokers are convinced that cigarettes are unhealthful, but have not been persuaded to give them up.) To persuade, writers must convince the reader that they intend a benefit for the reader. (Holding a gun at someone's head is not persuasion, but coercion.)

Expressive Writing

Writers are their own readers in expressive discourse, writing not for someone else but solely for themselves. Examples of expressive writing are diaries and letters never intended to be mailed or read.

An Outline of Purposes

The following outline briefly breaks down the foregoing categories of writing according to the reader's and writer's purposes and roles.

Explanation
   Writer: the expert, reliably giving the reader all he or she needs
            for understanding
   Reader: the novice, accepting the authority of the writer

Argument
   Writer: the disinterested investigator setting forth the evidence,
            either data or reasoning
   Reader: the critical observer, weighing and evaluating the evi-
            dence

Exploration
   Writer: the open-minded but undecided investigator, outlining
            ideas, problems, doubts, and even tentative conclusions
   Reader: the open-minded observer, trying to comprehend the
            problem that the writer is exploring

Imagination
   Writer: the artist, creating a fictive realm and language struc-
            ture that are valuable in and of themselves
   Reader: the participant-observer, immersing herself or himself
            in the fictive realm and language structure created by
            the writer

Persuasion
   Writer: the honorable person attempting to bring about a
            change for the better in the behavior or thinking of the
            reader
   Reader: a person willing to change if the benefits seems real and
            feasible

Expression
   Writer: the writer
   Reader: the writer

Our outlines looks neat, tidy, and nicely packaged. But as Dick
Laine, the famous TV car salesman and announcer at wrestling
matches, used to say, "Whoa, Nellie!" What novel have you ever
read that was a "pure" structure of the imagination, that did not
have a persuasive motif, that was completely uninformative, that
didn't contain (in your opinion) evidence of the author's urge to
express herself or himself? What magazine article that you enjoyed
had no traces of verbal artistry for its own sake?

In other words, once we have made the clean cuts, the categories, we can begin to understand that they are (like most categories of human acts) mere stylizations, convenient perhaps, but finally, in the noisy, complex human crowd, basically false. No crime, I think, ever has a single motive; no act of charity is ever pure. Every act of writing results from a complex web or purposes, which makes our inquiry more difficult, but much more interesting. In "reading" the act of writing, we are immersed in a complex "text" that needs insight and patience to interpret.

One purpose for writing that we've overlooked is simply the joy of language play. Richard Lanham of the University of California at Los Angeles argues most strongly for the importance of the play motive. He says that "human nature is and always will be a battleground between play, game, and purpose."[7] Lanham says that we can't escape the play motive, for it is part of our biological heritage. Whether or not we are "hard-wired" for language play, we know that all groups, through all of recorded history, have enjoyed language play: rhymes, alliterations, puns, the "dozens," tongue-twisters, and more.

The Writing Process

Much current discussion of writing talks about a fourfold process: *prewriting,* in which phase the writer gathers ideas and plans; *writing,* when the writer forms the materials gathered during prewriting into a text; *rewriting,* the time when the writer reformulates, adding needed information, deleting unnecessary material, rearranging sentences and sections, and substituting one item for another; and finally *proofreading,* to regularize punctuation, spelling, and matters of syntax and grammar. Although this model captures something of the tasks a writer faces when she or he attempts to produce an adequate text, the process is recursive, not linear. That is, an expert writer gets ideas (generated by the developing text) as the writing progresses and incorporates them, rearranges sections as the text develops, and corrects spelling errors when they arise. For good writers there is an all-at-onceness about the process. In their composing process, good writers differ from basic or poor writers in their *planning, rescanning,* and *revising* efforts.[8]

Planning

Good writers plan more than inexpert writers—which does not mean that good writers prepare elaborate formal outlines, for in fact few writers use such outlines (unless forced to do so by a schoolteacher). Good writers do, however, make notes, and, as two researchers report, the least able writers "only sometimes think a long time before beginning to write, and rarely make any written plans or notes, preferring to begin by 'just beginning.' "[9]

Another important fact is this: good writers are more flexible than their less able peers. A good writer most often has a plan, but it is flexible, more like a strategy that can be adapted as the text develops. Less able writers tend to make inflexible plans and, unable or unwilling to change tactics when they hit a snag, are more readily stymied. The good writer is much like a quarterback whose game plan is flexible or even expendable, depending on developments.

Rescanning

In a study of college freshmen writers, Sharon Pianko found that the better writers paused frequently, to make plans for moving ahead, to rescan to determine if their plans were appropriate, and to reformulate.[10] Remedial writers tend not to rescan when they pause, as if they have no overall sense of where they want to go with their writing.

Revising

In regard to revising, the big difference between skilled and unskilled writers is this: skilled writers tend to make changes in content, adding some ideas and deleting others, reorganizing, and making substitutions. Unskilled writers are like "Tony," an unskilled college writer studied by Sondra Perl. Tony made 234 changes during the course of the several compositions that Perl observed, but only 24 of these had to do with content; the rest were changes in surface form (e.g., spelling, verb agreement, punctuation, and so on).[11]

Some Recurrent Motifs

For the past ten or twelve years, I have been asking my graduate students to do detailed reports on their own methods of writing, their composing processes. The following motifs arise repeatedly, illustrating something of the complexity that we ask writers to be involved with.

ATTITUDE

Attitude is, of course, one of the most important factors in writing. Enthusiasm for the process and the subject matter makes success a great deal more probable. In any case, here, from a student, is a typical statement about attitude:

> To begin with, I have a fear—sometimes ridiculous and crippling—of saying the obvious. This means worrying at length about what I will say. This worry is the first stage of the whole process.

THE EUREKA PHENOMENON

Discussed extensively by those who study creativity and experienced by all of us, this is the breakthrough moment when the solution to a problem appears, when an insight pops up. The student who wrote the following account of such a moment collaborated with a friend on TV scripts:

> Working on a boring, nonspontaneous scene physically and mentally exhausted us, so we decided it was time to take a break. We took off to Marie Callender's Restaurant—our favorite change of environment. Of course, we took our legal pad with us in case we came up with any ideas for scene two. Suddenly inspiration struck over the strawberry pie. Gags started pouring out of our mouths faster than we could shovel in the pie. Unlike the first scene, we didn't feel straightjacketed by the plot, and our imaginations were able to wander freely. We stayed at the restaurant until we had worked out the entire scene, and we were quite pleased to find it up to our usual standards of wit and ingenuity, albeit with a few coffee stains.

HEURISTICS

These are ways of getting the thought process started. Journalism's *who-what-when-where-why* is a heuristic, as is brainstorming. Many writers consciously use heuristics. Here are one student's thoughts on them:

> I've never made conscious use of a heuristic. . . . There was a time, though, that a series of questions for a Title III proposal did in fact act as a heuristic for a program I later put into practice. That effort was the germ for a basic skills program and the beginning of my finally successful effort to have a reading specialist hired.

JOURNALS

Many writers keep journals and use them as sources of ideas, as this student's statement attests:

> I think that using the journal for [this paper] might be seen as a logical development of my usual jotting process. Idea: could I continue to use the journal as a way of exploring issues, capturing ideas and speculations?

METHODS OF INSCRIPTION

Writers have strong feelings about their writing implements. Some need particular kinds of ballpoint or felt-tip pens, or certain typewriters or computers. Said one writer: "A pen was just too slow. I've found that I feel more fluid, further ideas and ramifications come faster with a typewriter."

PREWRITING

My students' methods of prewriting varied from making random notes on scratch paper to writing individual notes on three-by-five cards that could be arranged and rearranged. As one student said:

> I generally try to let my mind play with my subject for a time before I actually begin writing. Sometimes this involves a period of concentration with pencil and paper; other times it involves keeping a page or series of pages on which I make notes as ideas occur to me, often while I am working on something else.

PURPOSE

One of my students had this to say about purpose: "This dynamic [the reader-writer relationship] changes depending on my purpose and motives for writing. I write for three reasons—I have to, I want to, I need to. Although these are not mutually exclusive categories, they are motivations that produce different kinds of writing and writing processes."

REWRITING

Some of my students rewrote, like D. H. Lawrence, by starting afresh from the beginning. Others made changes almost sentence by sentence:

> I . . . write several drafts, the number depending on the considerations I discuss in the next section [of this paper]. I never throw away any drafts until the end (hence my cluttered desk). Usually, I write more beginnings than ends, because I find that when I return to the writing task, instead of picking up where I left off, I frequently start again at the beginning. Often, when I have numerous drafts, I cut, paste, and write. However, when I write the final draft, I try to write straight through from beginning to end without stopping. Although when the deadline arrives I am rarely satisfied with a paper, I type it or have it typed, and it disappears into a pile of similar offerings and finds its final form in the reader's hands.

RITUALS

Many writers go through elaborate rituals before they begin to write and during the writing process:

> My writing never starts as it should, with anything as simple as picking up my pen and writing. I have to go through several procrastinating routines—looking for pens, arranging my desk, getting up from my chair to take care of some detail in the house, shuffling through my papers, or staring earnestly out of the window.

SCENE

Many writers functions best in a particular setting or scene. Some can't function at all out of their familiar scene. Here are one writer's thoughts on scene:

> Every writer, playwright or prose essayist, serves his idiosyncracies. I have several. First, I demand a familiar, comfortable place. Only two places work: my desk at home or a long wooden table in a library reading room. Home can be almost anywhere; I once wrote the better part of a play in a series of bed-and-breakfast places along Scotland's east coast. I was only in each place a week, but I felt settled.

TALK-WRITE

Writers often want to hear what they've written and thus read their texts aloud to themselves, as this student explained:

> Any performance demands concern with an audience. As a writer, I feel like an actor readying myself for a performance. My composing process is a performance. Vocalization occurs as I write during each stage of the process; I try each line out loud, then repeat (and often change) it as I write. My sense of sound is my first critic and audience.

From Process to Transaction

When we focus on process, we have made a great advance in our understanding of writing. Suppose that we concern ourselves only with errors, with what went wrong after the text was produced. Then we can say to the writer, "You did this and this and this wrong." But if we are concerned with process, we can say, perhaps, "Here's how you might be able to write more successfully." It's axiomatic that a math teacher is not concerned only with the right and wrong answers, but with the process whereby the student went either aright or astray. Errors are clues that allow the instructor to teach correct mathematical processes. In the next chapter, we will explore the difference between correcting errors and providing help with writing, but for now we must refocus our concern, shifting from process to *transaction.* For, as the first chapter of this book demonstrated, *all language acts are transactional,* a speaker or writer transmitting a meaning through the spoken language or a written text to a hearer or readers. Because we are concerned with writing, we can ignore speaking and say that the text is the means whereby the writer communicates with the reader.

We can now refer back to Chapter 2 and quote one person who is working on the problem of artificial intelligence:

> The message from artificial intelligence appears to be that the utterance never provides all the information one needs for understanding. Neither the computer nor the human being, it seems, can be merely a language parser, sorting out information in the incoming signal. Both also need to be constructors of meaning. *Understanding is a constructive process which involves using the linguistic cues provided by other speakers [or writers] as a basis on which to build up a more elaborate and informative meaning representation.* This construction can only take

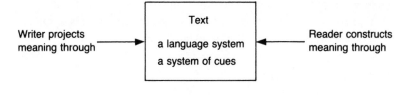

Figure 6.

place if the appropriate scenarios and linguistic patterns are already part of the comprehender's knowledge.[12]

This boils down to a fairly simple equation: the writer, using both his or her world knowledge and knowledge of the language system, creates a text from which the reader who has appropriate knowledge of both the language system and the world can (re)construct a meaning (Figure 6).

A Recapitulation

And now we can recapitulate, drawing concepts from the second and fourth chapters into the context of the act whereby text is produced. We know that writer and reader must share the language system and the system of cues that make up the text—and, of course, the language and cue systems are not identical. (When a text begins "Once upon a time," the informed reader is cued to expect a story.) And the world knowledge of the writer and the reader must overlap.

The writer has an intention and a meaning to project. We might say that the writer attempts to project a *semantic intention,* a term that covers "meaning" in the oridinary sense and includes such elements as connotation. The reader uses the text to reconstruct the writer's semantic intention. The text itself does not contain meaning, but enables the reader to reconstruct a meaning that, in most cases, he or she will believe is the semantic intention of the writer.

Both the reader and the writer are functioning according to the cooperative principle. That is, this principle establishes the norms by which intention may be judged. You will recall that the norms concern quantity; quality, relation, and manner. We have seen that purposeful tampering with these principles creates humor, irony, and other "special effects" in language.

The "Dialect" of Writing

We have also seen that the language—as spoken—is really a collection of dialects, some of which carry prestige and some of which do not. However, in writing there is really only one prestige "dialect," which we will call edited standard English, characterized by fairly rigid rules that determine such features as word choice, spelling, punctuation, verb agreement, pronoun reference, and other matters of syntax and grammar. In her landmark book *Errors and Expectations,* Mina Shaughnessy catalogues the ways in which basic writers violate the norms of the written dialect, edited standard English (ESE). Some of these are highlighted below.

Punctuation

In ESE, punctuation is fixed and almost totally predictable. Basic writers have not either learned or acquired the system and therefore produce texts erroneously punctuated or unpunctuated:

  (3) First of all the system, don't really care about the students, schools are always overcrowded and the students get the, impression that really there are some teachers, just like students just to Be there.[13]

Syntax

Shaughnessy says that her basic writers attempted to imitate the mature syntax (sentence structure) of ESE and in the process created tangles. The students had not acquired through reading the sentence-sense necessary to use syntax characteristic of ESE. The examples that follow are from *Errors and Expectations:*[14]

  (4) Most of the more demanding jobs have many people at which their financial status is very low or about average.
      (The jobs that are easy to get don't pay much.)
  (5) According to this statement which projects there are more jobs

available without college, was very obvious to me before enrolling.
(I knew before enrolling that there were more jobs for high-school
graduates than for college graduates.)

(6) On the point assumed that infants have quality for excepting beauty
more intellectual than grownups I fell are really true.
(I think it is true that children appreciate beauty more than adults
do.)

Spelling

People learn to spell by seeing words in texts, though probably
spelling lists can be helpful to those who have acquired some
competence as spellers. As Shaughnessy points out, the fact that
there is not a one-to-one correspondence between sound (phoneme) and written representation (grapheme) causes difficulties
for basic writers.

Vocabulary

On a television special concerning literacy, a worker in a textile
mill was asked, "If your boss handed you a document, could you
deal with it?" The worker replied, "I don't rightly know what a
document is. Is it a book or something?"

"Document" is a "bookish" word, one that people normally learn
from reading, not through conversation. Not only do basic writers
lack such vocabulary items as "document," they often use the wrong
forms of words. Shaughnessy cites the following examples:

(7) He is headed in a *destructional* way.
(8) People are judged by what they *product* on the job.
(9) He works without *supervise*.[15]

The Scribal Stutter

Basic writers fail to meet the expectations of readers of ESE in
many other ways. The task of spelling, punctuating, making verbs
and pronouns agree, choosing the right word, and trying to order
thoughts in syntactic structures is so overwhelming that frequently
the basic writer can't get beyond the first sentence in a composi-

tion. Trying to meet the expectations of readers of ESE, basic writers develop what might be called a "scribal stutter."

(10) *Start 1*
Seeing and hearing is something beautiful and strange to infant.

Start 2
To an infant seeing and hearing is something beautiful and stronge to infl

Start 3
I agree that seeing and hearing is something beautiful and stronge to a infants. A infants hears a strange sound such as work mother, he than acc

Start 4
I agree that child is more sensitive to beauty, because its all so new to him and he apprec

Start 5
The main point is that a child is more sensitive to beauty than there parents, because its the child a infant can only express it feeling with reactions,

Start 6
I agree a child is more sensitive to seeing and hearing than his parent, because its also new to him and more appreciate. His

Start 7
I agree that seeing and hearing have a different quality for infants than grownup, because when infants comes aware of a sound and can associate it with the object, he is indefeying and the parents acknowlege to to this

Start 8
I agree and disagree that seeing and hearing have a different quality for infants than for grownups, because to see and hear for infants its all so new and more appreciate, but I also feel that a child parent appreciate the sharing

Start 9
I disagree I feel that it has the same quality to

Start 10
I disagree I fell that seeig and hearing has much the same quality to

> both infants and parents. Hearing and seeing is such a great quality
> to infants and parents, and they both appreciate, just because
> there aren't that many panters or musicians around doesn't mean
> that infants are more sensitive to beautiful that there parents.[16]

The massive problems of producing edited standard English have
effectively stopped this person from writing. In the next chapter we
will explore ways to help disabled writers overcome their handicaps.

Writing and Thinking

In the first chapter we discussed the cognitive consequences of
literacy. (Is the preliterate tribesperson unable to think abstractly?
Does learning to read and write make one more logical?) Now we
should briefly consider what writing enables us to do that we could
not do without this "technology of the mind."

Whether or not writing and reading make a person more logical
or better able to think abstractly, one can say that without writing,
there would be no Century City and no *City of God*—that is, no
technological monuments, as represented by the Los Angeles en-
clave of Century City, and no monuments of thought, as represented by Augustine's *City of God.* This is not to say that preliterate societies have no technology or philosophy, which would be an
absurd claim; one merely has to look at, for instance, the bush
people of the Kalahari to realize that each member of a tribe is a
far better technician in a variety of fields than our neighbors in an
advanced society, and certainly these people have a religion entail-
ing a capacity for awe and mysticism as great as that of Christian-
ity, Judaism, or Islam.

If writing does not allow us to think any more "deeply," it does
allow us to think sequentially and to develop longer structures of
evidence or reasoning than we could hope to achieve if we had to
rely exclusively on memory. Even in relatively simple cognitive
tasks, we can experience the usefulness of being able to inscribe,
hence to look back in preparation for looking forward.

A simple example makes the cognitive uses of writing vividly
clear. In their classic text *An Introduction to Logic,* Morris R.
Cohen and Ernest Nagel outline the principles of the syllogism,
with which all of us are familiar:

(11) All musicians are proud.
   All Scotchmen are musicians.
   Therefore, all Scotchmen are proud.

Those of us who are familiar with the genre of the syllogism could solve this one without recourse to reading, hence writing. (People not familiar with syllogisms are puzzled by the simple logic involved in the solution—a subject we dealt with in the first chapter.) The syllogism just cited demands that we remember and consider only two premises: "all musicians are proud" and "all Scotchmen are musicians." We can easily keep this much in mind and arrive at the conclusion. However, when we come to the *sorites,* the situation complicates itself. A sorites is a logical chain in which there is more than one premise. We must be able to access more information. Thus, it would be difficult for most of us to arrive at the conclusion of the following sorites without being able to look backward at the premises, which are inscribed:

(12) All dictatorships are undemocratic.
   All undemocratic governments are unstable.
   All unstable governments are cruel.
   All cruel governments are objects of hate.

What, then, must we logically conclude about dictatorships? If we can scan the inscribed text, we will conclude that

(13) All dictatorships are objects of hate.

But many of us would be hard to put to follow this chain if the premises were not written down.

We should realize that most arguments, for or against the ideas that determine our futures, cannot be reduced to sorites, let alone syllogisms. Then we begin to appreciate the value of writing in our attempt to make sense of government, values, heaven and hell, the economy, human relationships, and the myriad concerns of this frustratingly interesting place that we call the world of our minds.

Writing allows writers to carry on a dialogue with themselves and enables readers to go back and evaluate statements, data, and premises. Writing is, indeed, a technology of mind.

A Unilateral View of the Real Value of Writing

I am reluctant to close this chapter on such a drab, pragmatic note. The metallic clank of the word "technology" is not the echo I want to resound.

In the third chapter, on reading, we saw that ultimately reading develops into an act for its own sake, the pleasure one derives from it. That should be the case with writing, yet one never hears the term "pleasure writing" as one does "pleasure reading." I think that this is a sad commentary on American education. As my colleague and friend Francis Christensen once said, we have sold our souls for a pot of message. We have, in other words, forgotten that the best reason for writing is the pleasure which the writer derives from the act.

I will conclude this chapter with an appendix that details the growth of a piece of writing from the germ of an idea to the final draft. However, before turning to that illustration of the composing process, I would like to summarize and polemicize.

A Polemical Summary

For some, "writing" means inscribing: making marks on paper or some other surface or causing characters to appear on a computer monitor. But writing can take place without inscription, for writing is the mental activity that may result in texts, not the physical activity of producing them. In short, writing is a way of thinking, and those who fail to realize this obvious fact reduce an important aspect of cognition to the level of a mechanical skill.

Equally disastrous is reducing writing to its most obvious utilitarian function: conveying information efficiently. No one who has thought about writing, the writer, and society would argue against the notion that conveying information efficiently is an important function of writing; however, other purposes are equally compelling: to convince and persuade; to amuse and move; to play. Writing not only conveys information; it creates knowledge. Through writing, writers get to know themselves.

The writing process is more complex than traditional lore makes it out to be. According to the old textbook tradition, a writer discovered a clear-cut thesis, made an outline of the development of that thesis, and then, using the outline as a blueprint, filled in the details. Studies of successful writers show, though, that the composing process is not a clear-cut series of steps, but is typically a recursive cycle of what might be called prewriting (or gaining ideas), writing, and rewriting. Good writers plan, but seldom do formal outlines; pause frequently to look back over what they have written; revise content, not just grammar and syntax.

The crucial idea regarding both oral and written language is this: all language acts are transactional whereby the speaker or writer attempts to convey a semantic intention to a hearer or reader. Thus, theories and discussions of writing that focus singlemindedly on the writer, to the exclusion of readers, are flawed. The cooperative principle—with its maxims of quality, quantity, manner, and relation—is in fact a demonstration of the transactional nature of language.

Finally, writing is both an instrument of mind, enabling the sequential, logical thought that is necessary for science, technology, and philosophy, and a means of self-expression and personal growth for the writer.

APPENDIX

For the third edition of a composition textbook of which I am the author, I traced a piece of writing from its inception through its final draft.[17] The following is my account of how that piece of writing came to be—in effect, a detailed case study of my own composing process.

The first bit of writing that I did is what you see in Figure 7. I knew that I wanted to set the scene: White Pine County, Nevada, an isolated mining district in the 1940s. Two people were extremely important to me during these years: Glen A. "Dunc" Duncan, a high-school teacher, and my father. And it seemed to me that certain events in my life at that time were so important that I could focus on them to give an account of how my interests developed.

I could, then, have started to write, telling first about White Pine County, then about Dunc and my father, and finally about certain important events. However, I needed to do some more thinking and planning, so I did a bit of *brainstorming*.

With this technique, the writer simply starts recording anything that comes to mind about his or her subject, letting one word, idea,

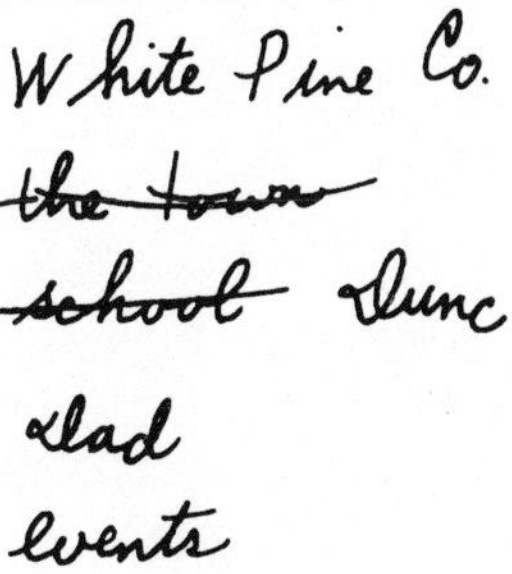

White Pine Co.

~~the town~~

~~school~~ Dunc

dad

events

Figure 7.

or image suggest another. The secret to brainstorming is to turn off the censor. The idea is to try not to judge whether an idea is good or bad; it is easy to discard useless items later, and furthermore, sometimes an idea that initially seems useless or even ridiculous turns out to be quite useful.

As usual at this stage of my writing process, I began to develop a cluster. A very useful technique for generating and organizing ideas, *clustering* is actually a variation on brainstorming, and I find it extremely helpful in much of my writing. Figure 8 is the first phase of my cluster. As this figure indicates, I had decided not to deal with the whole area in which I lived but only with my hometown, McGill, and my home within that town. (The high school that I attended was in Ely, thirteen miles from McGill.) I had also decided to write about both of my parents, and "Dunc" as a single topic had expanded to "school." At this point, I might have begun to write a six-part essay that could be outlined as follows:

   I. Introduction
  II. Scene
     A. Home
     B. The town
 III. Parents
     A. Mother
     B. Father
 IV. Events
  V. School
 VI. Conclusion

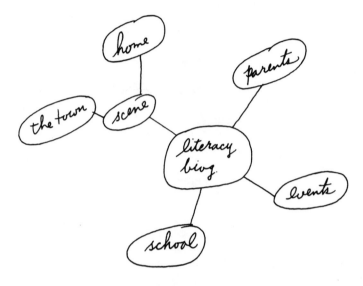

Figure 8.

However, my ideas had not "cooked" long enough; I needed to think some more about details and connections. You can see the results of that "cooking" and thinking in Figure 9. I added details about my home: the coldness of my bedroom during the winter, the electric blanket that saved me from frostbite, the cocker spaniel that shared the room with me, and the coal stove in the kitchen. These details were to play a part, I felt, in the text that I was getting ready to produce.

I also added details about the town: the mill and smelter that dominated it, the dust and smoke that shrouded it, and the drabness that characterized it. I decided to tell about "cultural" resources available to me: the radio programs that we could receive only at night, the small library, and the movie theater.

A section on my parents was no longer part of my planning, but I was sure that my mother and father would take their parts in the events that I intended to relate. Those events were three, and they would, I thought, give a sense of what my early reading experiences had been like. (The essay itself would explain some of the items that I included in the cluster as reminders to myself: "Trelawny," "mint patties," and "green olives.")

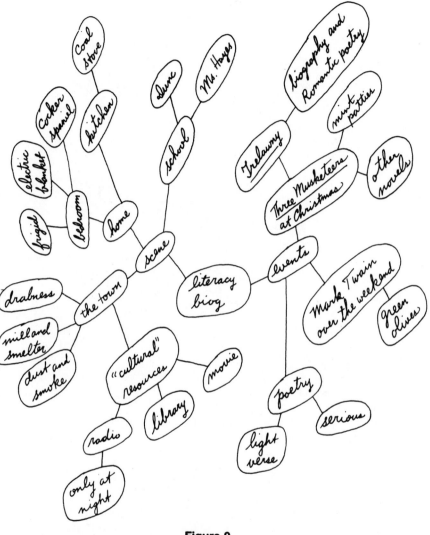

Figure 9.

But I had a final adjustment to make in my cluster. Initially I had thought of "events" as happenings in my home, but I realized that Dunc's sixth-period English class was also an event, so I added it to the "events" category. Because of Dunc I grew to love the poetry of

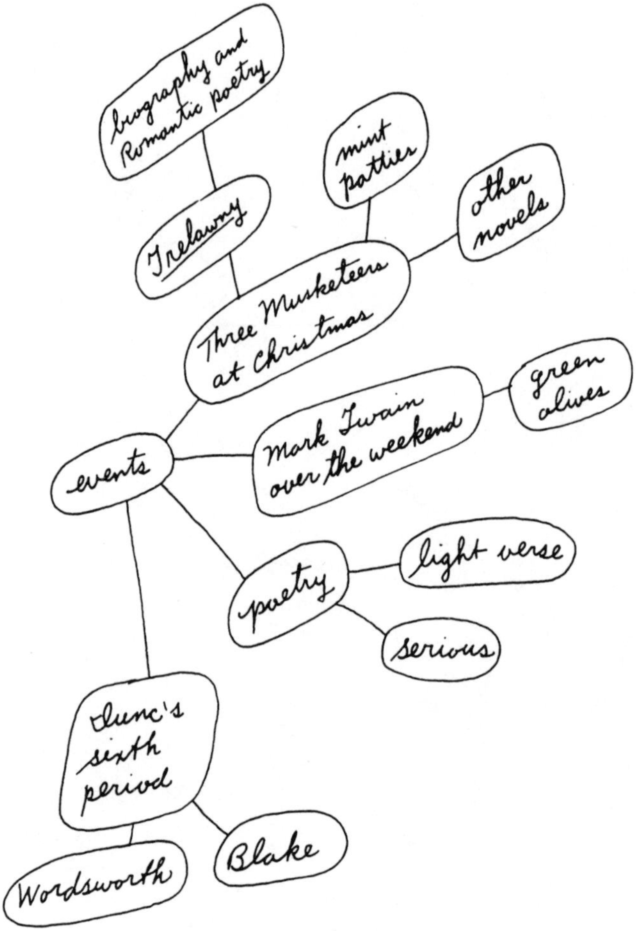

Figure 10.

William Wordsworth and William Blake. Figure 10, the "events" node of my cluster, shows the final planning before I started to write.

My cluster did not capture everything that was to go into my essay. In fact, the process of composing the essay generated ideas that I could not have predicted before I started to write. However, the planning and generating stage (often called "prewriting") had now ended, and I was ready to begin composing the essay on my computer.

A Word About Clustering

As a method of generating ideas and beginning to plan the form of a piece of writing, clustering has many advantages over either the formal outline or random notes. The formal outline imposes a rigidity that often hinders the organic process of generating ideas and planning how to use them. With the cluster you can add ideas at any point; formal outlines are never "open" enough to allow the writer to add here, there, and everywhere. In other words, the cluster can grow like a plant, but the formal outline is an inflexible scaffolding.

Unlike random notes, however, the cluster begins to bring order to a writer's wide-ranging thoughts. If you look back at Figure 9, you will discover that the cluster implies an essay with two major parts: "scene" and "events." "Events" has three parts: "*Three Musketeers* at Christmas," "Mark Twain over the weekend," and "poetry." (In fact, I could easily use this cluster as the basis for a formal outline.)

The writer can add to a cluster or rearrange it as the text develops. The cluster serves both as a prompt for putting ideas into a text and as a schematic representation of the writer's plans for the text. The cluster is open-ended and generative. On the basis of almost any of the items in Figure 9, I could have developed another extensive cluster.

The First Draft

In this draft, crossouts are indicated by strikethroughs with hyphens (~~crossouts~~), and inserts are within brackets [insert].

I remember the first time my sons saw my hometown. In the old blue Plymouth, we approached from the west, ~~rolling,~~ ~~chugging,~~ lurching down Highway 40, through the mirage puddles on the hot asphalt, watching the dust devils dance across the sagebrush flats. [The smell of sagebrush was heavy in the air blowing into the car through the open windows—for we didn't have air-conditioning.] We could see the ~~cloud of~~ yellow, sulphurous cloud from the smelter and the giant smokestacks themselves, from perhaps fifty or sixty miles away. A bit nearer, and we could smell the acrid, choking cloud that belched forth from the smokestacks, and we could see the dust beginning to blow on the flat below town as the afternoon wind picked up.

McGill has no outskirts, no suburbs, just sagebrush flats and then town, the sagebrush growing up to the wire fences of the first row of houses. One moment you're in the Great Basin desert, among jack rabbits and rattlesnakes, and the next you're in such civilization as McGill, Nevada, affords.

We drove down Main street. The post office, a gray sandstone pile, had not changed. Goodman-Tidball, General Mercantile and Service Station, was closed and boarded up, as was the Rexall drug store. Cononelos Market was still open, in the two-story, dirty-yellow frame building that had once housed, on the first floor, the J. C. Penney store and, on the second, the Winterowd family. At the south end of Main Street, a Dairy Queen had opened.

And the McGill Club was still in operation. My father had dealt roulette in the Club during the Second World War, when that institution had served as social center for the community—the kids not allowed behind the partition that separated a soda fountain and ice-cream parlor from the roulette and blackjack tables, the bar, the brass spittoons, the mounted deer heads on three walls, all of this amounting to the "real" McGill Club, the heart and soul of the place.

The frame houses of the townsite were as drab as I had remembered, painted shades of brownish yellow, ~~light~~ dirty gray, and stained white. The lawns were still shabby, and the wire fences sagged as badly as they had when I was a boy.

An interesting thing has happened. Searching for a beginning that would interest my readers and get me into my subject, I decided to give an account of the first time my two sons visited my home town. However, I have become so interested in *that* subject that I have lost sight of my goal. I have begun an essay other than the one I intended to write. Therefore, I back up and start over. As you can see, revising may begin early in the writing process.

I remember the yellow, sulphorous smoke that poured from the stacks of the smelter; the dust cloud that ~~enveloped~~ smothered the town every summer afternoon; the drab houses, painted dirty yellow, gray, and white;

Main Street, with its confectionery, ~~gambling hall and saloon,~~ Rexall drug
store, general store, and post office. I can still see the miles of sagebrush
flat desert stretching beyond town and smell the almost-chemical odor of
sagebrush.

[And the McGill Club—my father had dealt roulette there during the
Second World War, when that institution had served as social center for
the community, the kids not allowed behind the partition that separated a
soda fountain and ice-cream parlor from the roulette and blackjack tables,
the bar, the brass spittoons, the mounted deer heads on three walls, all of
this amounting to the "real" McGill Club, the heart and soul of the place].

Notice that I have included the passage (slightly revised) about the
McGill Club from my original beginning. It seems to me that the
Club symbolizes the cultural level of the McGill that I knew, and I
was unwilling to lose this bit of local color. Particularly if you
compose on a computer, it is easy to rearrange, insert, and delete
material.

During my high school years, my home was in McGill, Nevada, a town
owned by Kennecott Copper Corporation and the site of a mill and
smelter to derive copper from the ore mined in Ruth, some twenty miles
south of McGill. Between McGill and Ruth was Ely, a town of perhaps five
thousand, the seat of White Pine County. I attended high school in Ely.

The town I grew up in was not, then, one of the world's great centers of
culture.

The above sentence was unplanned—came as a happy gift from . . .
somewhere. However, it is an excellent way to begin a discussion of
the "cultural" resources available to me in McGill.

For some reason (my father talked about the lowering of the ionosphere),
~~we were able to~~ we could get radio reception only at night. As a result, I
missed all of the legendary radio serials that played on weekdays after
school was out: "Jack Armstrong, All-American Boy," "Renfrew of the
Royal Mounted," and "Little Orphan ~~Annie.~~" Annie," and others. However,
after sundown, the radio became ~~the McGill subst~~ for the residents of
McGill during the 1940's what television is for the American family today:
a source for news and entertainment. My buddies and I listened without
fail to "I Love a Mystery," "The FBI in Peace and War," "The Shadow,"

["The Sixty-Four Dollar Question,"] and "Your Hit Parade." We heard Edward R. Murrow['s wartime] broadcast[s] from London and followed the commentary of Raymond Graham Swing and Gabriel Heater.

~~My point is that~~

~~We weren't so different, then, from the modern~~

~~The radio generation wasn't so~~ different ~~from the television generation.~~ We did a lot of trampling around the sagebrush flats, hunting rabbits, ~~and in the fall~~ either with our single-shot .22's or our bows and arrows; we sat in the Candy Shoppe, sipping our Cokes and feeling our teenage juices either seep or rush through our systems. Some Friday nights one of us was lucky enough to get the family automobile, and we drove to a dance in the high school gymnasium in Ely. (~~The 1941 Plymouth that Don Johnson's father caressed and pampered was so elegant that I have never lost my lust for Chrysler products Because of the 1941 Plymouth that Don Johnson's father caressed and pampered, I still prefer Chrysler products~~ (The classiest auto we had access to was a white 1941 Plymouth, caressed and pampered by Don Johnson's father. I'm still partial to Chrysler products.)

Again, I'm straying. Reliving my past is so intriguing that I begin to write almost by free association. Don Johnson's Plymouth suggests "Dutch" Holland's old Chevy, which leads me to think of Mr. Armstrong's Packard Clipper, the ultimate White Pine County car. I'll let the parenthesis remain, but will reread what I've written so far and then get back on track. I will move on to the second cultural resource in McGill, the library. Writers need to make sure they do not stray from the purpose they have chosen for themselves.

The McGill Public Library was a single room in the Club House, a residence for unmarried male employees at Kennecott Copper—a hulking, three-story, red brick building. How many volumes on those few shelves? I doubt that the total collection was more than, say, ~~five~~ [three] thousand books. I vividly remember the librarian, but can't recall her name. She was not ~~stout~~ [fat], but portly, in a dignified, patrician sort of way. She wore her salt-and-pepper hair in a bun, and she dressed more primly than anyone else in town—navy-blue, tailored suits, white frilly blouses, Red Cross shoes. She should, by all rights, have been a maiden lady, but she was married, to a Kennecott foreman, I think.

The library, open for a couple of hours each weekday evening, did not offer "God's plenty" for a teenager. I vividly remember checking out *The Magic Mountain,* intrigued by the title. Of course, this massive philosophical novel was light years beyond my reach. The librarian had told me as much when I checked the book out, but I would not listen to her. Defeated, I returned *The Magic Mountain* to the library after a couple of frustrated attempts to get myself interested in the book, and the librarian, with great generosity, guided me to *Tales of the South Pacific,* then just out and, I suppose, one of the very few new books purchased by the library. Whereas Thomas Mann had baffled me, I found the Michener tales enchanting, far more satisfying than the movie [musical based on them].

I'm now having chronology problems. In this essay, I wanted to show that my serious, "chronic" reading actually began after certain "events." However, the inventory of cultural resources includes the library, and it is inevitable that I tell about my experiences with the library, which actually came after the "events." In other words, I have a structural problem here. I will solve it by giving the reader a straightforward explanation. Readers expect that they will be able to follow the sequence of ideas in a text, and it is the writer's job to keep the readers oriented.

But I am getting ahead of myself. My serious, "chronic" reading began after a series of events which ~~are the real focus of this essay~~ I will relate in due time.

The McGill Theatre——~~the last picture show~~. ["The Last Picture Show."] The feature started at 7:30 p.m., but the doors opened at 7:00. Christine Constantine, ~~sold the tickets~~, a stunningly beautiful Greek girl, sold the tickets. (Her father had given me a taste of his "peach" wine. It turned out to be retzina, or "pitch" wine.) ~~Yes, she—and her two sisters—made my teenage juices flow~~.

By the time Christine started selling tickets, the first batch of Jolly Time had been popped, and its smell was irresistible. ~~Connie~~ In the lobby, blonde, rosy, well-fed Connie made and vended the popcorn, tinged with the yellow of imitation butter and salted to just the right tang; ~~in the lobby~~ and ~~none~~ no other has ever equalled its crispness, its wholesome aroma~~,~~. ~~the imitation butter that tinged it with yellow, the salt that gave it just the right tang~~.

At Eastertide, Jim, the irascible old projectionist, always played "White Christmas" as prelude music for the half hour from the opening of the doors until the short subjects began; and at Christmas he played, yes, of course, "Easter Parade." At two or three minutes before 7:30, "The Star-Spangled Banner" rang through the auditorium, and we all stood, hands over our hearts.

~~And that pretty much outlines the cultural resources in McGill: radio at night, the library, and the motion picture theater.~~

The movie that I remember most vividly from this, the archetypical small-town motion picture theater, ~~was~~ is "I Walked with A Zombie."

The section on cultural resources is complete. When I wrote the one-sentence paragraph above, I knew that I was ready to move on—to my home. Notice that I deleted a summary paragraph. It seems to me that the reader does not need to be told that I have now finished my catalogue of cultural resources. While the writer is obliged to keep readers oriented, he or she must not insult them by stating the obvious.

There were two scenes for the events that turned me into a compulsive reader: my home and the sixth-period English class of Mr. Glen A Duncan, "Dunc," as everyone called him.

A couple of things have just happened. In the first place, I have reorganized my essay, changing the structure that I had worked out in the clusters. If you will look back at Figure 9, you will discover that I intended, under "scene," to deal with "home" and "school." Another section of the essay, "events," would tell what happened in these scenes. The first sentence of this new paragraph leads me to realize that I am writing a "drama" and must place my "characters" in the scenes and have them play their "parts" in the "plot." In other words, I am, in effect, eliminating the category "scene," consolidating "scene" material with "events." I also had to check back, to determine whether or not I had yet introduced by my readers to Dunc.

We lived, during those years, above the J. C. Penney store on First Street, across from the McGill Club and, ~~next to~~ south of us, Assuras Meat Market, the Oddfellows Hall to the north. We didn't live in a penthouse on Park Avenue, but we resided comfortably in a four-room apartment, with bath, above the J. C. Penney store on First Street, in the very middle of town, the center of action, if you will.

The comparison between our grubby apartment above the J. C. Penney store and a penthouse on Park Avenue gives the essay a wry tone that I like. I'm saying that we were in the center of the culture of McGill, Nevada. The idea for the comparison simply popped into my mind, and I wrote it down. In fact, the idea of both McGill and New York City as cultural centers is wonderfully ironic. (Yet McGill was *my* cultural center.)

~~A coal stove in the kitchen, a coal heater in the living room~~
My bedroom[, a jerry-built attachment to the main structure,] was beyond the reach of the two sources of heat: a coal range in the kitchen and a coal heating stove in the large room that doubled as our parlor (the north half) and my parents' bedroom (the south half). I shared by bedroom with a cocker spaniel and avoided frostbite by huddling under an electric blanket, certainly one of the first ever manufactured. (The cord to the blanket ran up toward the ceiling, where it joined with a socket dangling by [black] electric ~~cords~~ [wires]. I ~~You~~ turned the socket on first and then set the blanket on "high" and shivered for the first half hour after going to bed.)
~~It was Christmas 1943. I was nearly fourteen years old.~~
In this strange aparment above the J. C. Penney store, in a [Nevada] smelter- and mill-town, ~~there took place events that would forever change~~ certain events turned me into a compulsive reader.

The above short paragraph is a transition, introducing the section of my essay that will deal with reading experiences in my home.

It was Christmas, 1943. ~~The Second World War was raging in the Pacific, Africa, and Europe.~~ Almost every day there was news of someone from White Pine County dying on ~~alien soil~~ [a Pacific island or in Africa]. Mr. Maw, who ran a gas station in Ely, was never right after he received word of his son's death ~~threatening~~ [and threatened] to incinerate any Japanese who came to his station. "Where's Davie?" he would say to his old dog, and the dog would search frantically about the premises of the service station, [looking for the ~~son~~ [boy] who would never return].

That Christmas—a somber time in American history—my parents gave me two books: *The Three Musketeers,* by Alexander Dumas, and *Trelawny,* by Margaret Arms:rong. The night of the 26th of December Mother and Father were away, and I climbed into their bed, in the well-heated bedroom-living room, and began to read *The Three Musketeers,* the marvelous swashbuckling of Parthos, Athos, and Arimas, and their noble friend D'Artagnan. ~~Beside me was a box of chocolate mint patties~~ [Beside me was a box of chocolate mint patties left] ~~Left~~ over from Christmas, ~~was a~~ and as I read, I sucked on these delicacies.

This was the first time that I had been completely immersed in a book, so deeply taken that time was not a dimension of the experience: just the soft bed in the warm room, with the drama of the tale unfolding and the mint patties melting in my mouth, on a bitterly cold winter night in Nevada.

I still have the book. *The Three Musketeers.* Great Illustrated Classics. Published in the United States of America, 1941 by Dodd, Mead & Company, Inc. A handsome gray book, with dark blue design and gold lettering. [The price, in pencil, is still on the flyleaf: $2.50.]

> Without paying any attention to the sword, Milady endeavoured to clamber onto the bed to strike him, and she did not stop until she felt the sharp point at her throat. She then tried to seize the weapon in her hands, but D'Artagnan eluded her grasp; and presenting the point sometimes to her eyes, sometimes to her bosom, slipped out of the bed, endeavouring to retreat by the door leading into Kitty's room.

The Three Musketeers ~~and their friend D'Artagnan (and the alluring Milady) were first bosom friends in reading~~ was, then, the first book that had completely captured me, that had given me the almost mystic experience of total immersion, and from that time on, I lived an extremely "bookish" life. Sitting in our kitchen, next to the coal stove (to provide warmth in the late night hours), I read Maugham's *Of Human Bondage;* the Horatio Hornblower sea tales; *Tap Roots,* [a Civil War epic after the manner of *Gone with the Wind,*] by (as I recall) James Street; *David Copperfield, Oliver Twist,* and *Great Expectations;* and a whole string of cowboy stories, which have no individuality for me now.

During that Christmas season of 1943, I also read the other gift book, *Trelawny,* by Margaret Armstrong: bound in crimson cloth with gold lettering, published by the Macmillan Company in 1940 [and sold for $3.50]. "There are no imaginary characters, events, or conversations in this book. It is fact, not fiction. The narrative is based on Trelawny's writings, corrected and amplified from reliable sources."

Trelawny, friend of Byron and Shelley, was himself as romantic and swashbuckling as D'Artagnan.

> Now and then a man is born with a surname that fits him so well it might have been chosen for him by poet or a painter. Edward Trelawny was one of those fortunate persons. There is a wild flavor in *Trelawny* that would lend a touch of romance to the most commonplace family; and that the Trelawnys never were. They were courageous, adventurous, full of vitality, eccentric, unreliable, prone to extremes; never, to judge from the family records, commonplace.

As I look back, I think that *The Three Musketeers* and *Trelawny* were just the right books for the right person at the right time. They were guaranteed to provide escape from the [squalid] ~~horrid~~ camp in which I lived. In any case, they hooked me. *Trelawny*[,] ~~was~~ the first biography I had ever read, ~~and~~ created for me a lifelong interest in that genre.

Another decision. My essay is extending far beyond the limits that I had envisioned for it. Thus, I will limit my subject to reading at home and will deal with three "events": my Christmas with *The Three Musketeers* and *Trelawny,* a weekend with my father and Mark Twain, and the poetry that the family read aloud. This decision necessitates overhauling the beginning of the essay. You will see the results of this work in the final draft of the essay, which I will include in the chapter.

The second [noteworthy] event in the development of my passion for reading came when my mother left town for a weekend, to attend a convention of the Congress of Industrial Organizations, the CIO, of which she was an officer. Father and I were left to our resources, which turned out to be unconventionally delightful and intensely literary.

Father and I went to the Cononelos market and bought two huge jars of green olives, a stack of salami, a loaf of bread, some cheese, undoubtedly potato chips, and other ready edibles. ~~Father pulled two easy~~ Father arranged a small table between two easy chairs, with a floor lamp just behind the table. On the table, he put a bowl of green olives, potato chips, salami, bread, mustard, and I'm sure, raw onion. Then from somewhere he produced *The Favorite Works of Mark Twain,* DeLuxe Edition, Garden City Publishing Co., Inc., 1939—1178 pages in all.

Dad and I would have a weekend of reading.

I don't remember what Dad read on that marvelous weekend, but I had four complete books (in one volume) to choose from: *Life on the Missis-*

sippi, The Adventures of Tom Sawyer, The Adventures of Huckleberry Finn, and *A Connecticut Yankee in King Arthur's Court,* not to mention sixteen other shorter works: ~~excerpts stories and selections from novels~~ stories, excerpts from books, and sketches. At Dad's suggestion, I started with *Tom Sawyer* and then went on to *A Connecticut Yankee,* which Dad particularly liked.

The result of this experience was inevitable. I became an ardent Twainite, and I still am one. (In my opinion, *Life on the Mississippi* and the *Autobiobraphy* are his masterpieces.)

My third experience with reading at home—in the apartment above the J. C. Penney store—was not so much one event as an ongoing series of experiences. My father had an eclectic love for poetry, and we read a good deal of verse, particularly on Sunday mornings before the gigantic brunch that my mother always prepared ([grapefruit,] fresh side pork or pork loin, baking powder biscuits, gravy, eggs, pastries, coffee).

Dad, a skeptic, took great glee in *The First Mortgage,* a doggerel verse telling of the Bible story, by a poet named Cook:

Sometime, and somewhere out in space,
God felt it was the proper place
To make a world, as he did claim,
To bring some honor to his name.

And we read, I think, every word written by Robert Service:

Men of the High North, the wild sky is blazing,
    Islands of opal float on silver seas;
Swift splendors kindle, barbaric, amazing;
    Pale ports of amber, golden argosies.
Ringed all around us the proud peaks are glowing;
    Fierce chiefs in council, their wigwam the sky;
Far, far below us the big Yukon flowing,
    Like threaded quicksilver, gleams to the eye.
            —"Men of the High North"

Dad loved to declaim verse from *The Pious Friends and Drunken Companions* (The Macaulay Company, 1936):

As I walked out in the streets of Laredo,
As I walked in Laredo one day,
I spied a poor cowboy wrapped up in white linen,
Wrapped up in white linen and cold as the clay.

Dad enjoyed both Dorothy Parker (*Enough Rope*) and Shelley. But I don't remember ever hearing him read the American classics: Longfellow,

Emerson, Whittier, Dickinson. His taste, with few exceptions, was definitely for the comic and ribald, [though I think probably Dad quoted from his elegantly bound copy of the *Rubaiyat of Omar Khayyam* (translated, of course, by Edward Fitzgerald) more often than from any other poet or book. His favorite stanza:

> Some for the Glories of This World; and some
> Sigh for the Prophet's Paradise to come;
>   Ah, take the Cash, and let the Credit go,
> Nor heed the rumble of the distant Drum!]

Though purists might deplore my father's taste for florid or ribald verse, nonetheless poetry became a part of my experience; from my early teens onward, I did not view it as something strange, exotic, with hidden meanings, accessible only to the few. No, poetry (whether written by T. S. Eliot or Robert Service) was to be enjoyed. ~~and, as a matter of fact, in those long gone years, I began to write poetry~~

~~If there~~

What lesson is to be learned from this account of ~~how one young person~~ reading in one home? As I look back on my experiences, I realize that, above all, reading was woven into the fabric of our lives; books were the center of both special occasions and our quotidian existence. They were very much like food: every meal was not an elaborate Sunday brunch, nor was every experience of reading a major occasion. Nonetheless, as we ate three meals a day, so we read books (and magazines, for there was no proper daily newspaper) every day. ~~If, when I was in my early teens, someone had~~

~~I look now at the stack of books that have been part of my life since the~~

The other day my grandson, barely two years old and yet already bookish, was foraging in my library. He pulled Robert Service's *Ballads of a Cheechako* off the shelf and presented it to me to "read" to him. There were no pictures, so he lost interest immediately. But, as I held him close, I said, "You're just a bit too young for that now, Chris, but someday. . . ." And I'm sure that someday Chris and I will read together the books that my father shared with me.

The conclusion—which I must admit I like—came to me, in the form of my grandson, who did exactly what I had said in the above paragraph. And someday, I'm sure, I will share with him the books that my father brought me to.

The Final Draft

Becoming a Reader

I remember the yellow, sulphurous smoke that poured from the stacks of the smelter; the dust cloud that smothered the town every summer afternoon; the drab houses, painted dirty yellow, gray, and white; and Main Street, with its confectionery, Rexall drug store, general store, and post office. I can still see the miles of desert stretching beyond town and smell the almost chemical odor of sagebrush.

And the McGill Club—my father had dealt roulette there during the Second World War, when that institution had served as social center for the community, the kids not allowed behind the partition that separated a soda fountain and ice-cream parlor from the roulette and blackjack tables, the bar, the brass spittoons, the mounted deer heads on three walls, all of this amounting to the "real" McGill Club, the heart and soul of the place.

During the 1940's, my home was in McGill, Nevada, a town owned by Kennecott Copper Corporation and the site of a mill and smelter to derive copper from the ore mined in Ruth, some twenty miles south of McGill. Between McGill and Ruth was Ely, a town of perhaps five-thousand, the seat of White Pine County. I attended high school in Ely.

The town I grew up in was not, then, one of the world's great centers of culture. We had radio (but only after sundown), a motion picture theater, and a small library—and that is the sum total of our cultural resources.

For some reason (my father talked about the lowering of the ionosphere), we could get radio reception only at night. As a result, I missed all the legendary radio serials that played on weekday afternoons: "Jack Armstrong, All-American Boy," "Renfrew of the Royal Mounted," "Little Orphan Annie," and others. However, after sundown, the radio became for the residents of McGill what television is for the American family today: a source for news and entertainment. My buddies and I listened without fail to "I Love a Mystery," "The FBI in Peace and War," "The Shadow," "The Sixty-Four Dollar Question," and "Your Hit Parade." We heard Edward R. Murrow's wartime broadcasts from London and followed the commentary of Raymond Graham Swing and Gabriel Heater.

We did a lot of tramping around the sagebush flats, hunting rabbits, either with our single-shot .22's or our bows and arrows; we sat in the Candy Shoppe, sipping our Cokes and feeling our teenage juices either seep or rush through our systems. Some Friday nights one of us was lucky enough to get the family automobile, and we drove to a dance in the high school gymnasium in Ely. (The classiest auto we had access to was a white 1941 Plymouth, caressed and pampered by Don Johnson's father. I'm still partial to Chrysler products.)

The McGill Public Library was a single room in the Club House, a residence for unmarried male employees of Kennecott Copper—a hulking, three-story, red brick building. How many volumes on those few shelves? I doubt that the total collection was more than, say, three thousand books. I vividly remember the librarian, but can't recall her name. She was not fat, but portly, in a dignified, patrician sort of way. She wore her salt-and-pepper hair in a bun, and she dressed more primly than anyone else in town—navy-blue tailored suits, white frilly blouses, Red Cross shoes. She should, by all rights, have been a maiden lady, but she was married, to a Kennecott foreman, I think.

The library, open for a couple of hours each weekday evening, did not offer "God's plenty" for a teenager. I vividly remember checking out *The Magic Mountain,* intrigued by the title. Of course, this massive philosophical novel was light years beyond my reach. The librarian had told me as much when I checked the book out, but I would not listen to her. Defeated, I returned *The Magic Mountain* to the library after a couple of frustrated attempts to get myself interested in the book, and the librarian, with great generosity, guided me to *Tales of the South Pacific,* then just out and, I suppose, one of the very few new books purchased by the library. Whereas Thomas Mann had baffled me, I found the Michener tales enchanting, far more satisfying than the movie musical based on them.

But I am getting ahead of myself. My serious, "chronic" reading began after a series of events which I will relate in due time.

The McGill Theatre—"The Last Picture Show." The feature started at 7:30 p.m., but the doors opened at 7:00. Christine Constantine, a stunningly beautiful Greek girl, sold the tickets. (Her father had given me a taste of his "peach" wine. It turned out to be retzina, or "pitch" wine.) By the time Christine started selling tickets, the first batch of Jolly Time had been popped, and its smell was irresistible. In the lobby, blonde, rosy, well-fed Connie made and vended the popcorn, tinged with the yellow of imitation butter and salted to just the right tang; and no other has ever equalled its crispness and its wholesome aroma. At Eastertide, Jim, the irascible old projectionist, always played "White Christmas" as prelude music for the half hour from the opening of the doors until the short subjects began; and at Christmas he played, yes, of course, "Easter

Parade." At two or three minutes before 7:30, "The Star-Spangled Banner" rang through the auditorium, and we all stood, hands over our hearts.

The movie that I remember most vividly from this, the archetypical small-town motion picture theater, is "I Walked with A Zombie."

So much, then, for "culture" in McGill, Nevada. Yet I did become an omnivorous reader—largely because my father shared his passion for books with me.

We lived, during those years, above the J. C. Penney store on Main Street, across from the McGill Club, the saloon and gambling hall where my father was a croupier. Next door to us, on the south, was Assuras Meat Market, and the Oddfellows Hall was on the north. We didn't live in a penthouse on Park Avenue, but we resided comfortably in a four-room apartment, with bath, above the J. C. Penney store, in the very middle of town—the center of action, if you will.

My bedroom, a jerry-built attachment to the main structure, was beyond the reach of the two sources of heat: a coal range in the kitchen and a coal heating stove in the large room that doubled as our parlor (the north half) and my parents' bedroom (the south half). I shared my bedroom with a cocker spaniel and avoided frostbite by huddling under an electric blanket, certainly one of the first ever manufactured. (The cord to the blanket ran up toward the ceiling, where it joined with a socket dangling by black electric wires. I turned the socket on first and then set the blanket on "high" and shivered for the first half-hour after going to bed.)

It was Christmas, 1943. Almost every day there was news of someone from White Pine County dying on a Pacific island or in Africa. Mr. Maw, who ran a gas station in Ely, was never right after he received word of his son's death and threatened to incinerate any Japanese who came to the station. "Where's Davie?" he would say to his old dog, and the dog would search frantically about the premises of the service station, looking for the boy who would never return.

That Christmas—a somber time in American history—my parents gave me *The Three Musketeers,* by Alexander Dumas, and *Trelawny,* by Margaret Armstrong, two books that my father had enjoyed. The night of the 26th of December Mother and Father were away, and I climbed into their bed, in the well-heated bedroom-living room, and began to read *The Three Musketeers:* the marvelous swashbuckling of Porthos, Athos, Arimas, and their noble friend D'Antagnan. Beside me was a box of chocolate mint patties left over from Christmas, and as I read, I sucked on these delicacies.

This was the first time that I had been completely immersed in a book, so deeply taken that time was not a dimension of the experience: just the soft bed in the warm room, with the drama of the tale unfolding and the mint patties melting in my mouth, on a bitterly cold winter night in Nevada.

I still have the book. *The Three Musketeers,* Great Illustrated Classics. Published in the United States of America, 1941, by Dodd, Mead & Company, Inc. A handsome gray book, with dark blue design and gold lettering. The price, in pencil, is still on the flyleaf: $2.50.

> Without paying any attention to the sword, Milady endeavoured to clamber onto the bed to strike him, and she did not stop until she felt the sharp point at her throat. She then tried to seize the weapon in her hands, but D'Artagnan eluded her grasp; and presenting the point sometimes to her eyes, sometimes to her bosom, slipped out of the bed, endeavouring to retreat by the door leading into Kitty's room.

The Three Musketeers was, then, the first book that had completely captured me, that had given me the almost mystic experience of total immersion, and from that time on, I lived an extremely "bookish" life. Sitting in our kitchen, next to the coal stove (to provide warmth in the late night hours), I read Maugham's *Of Human Bondage;* the Horatio Hornblower sea tales; *Tap Roots,* a Civil War epic after the manner of *Gone with the Wind,* by (as I recall) James Street; *David Copperfield, Oliver Twist,* and *Great Expectations;* a whole string of cowboy stories, which have no individuality for me how.

During that Christmas season of 1943, I also read the other gift book, *Trelawny,* by Margaret Armstrong: bound in crimson cloth with gold lettering, published by the Macmillan Company in 1940 and priced at $3.50. "There are no imaginary characters, events, or conversations in this book. It is fact, not fiction. The narrative is based on Trelawny's writings, corrected and amplified from reliable sources."

Trelawny, friend of Byron and Shelley, was himself as romantic and swashbuckling as D'Artagnan.

> Now and then a man is born with a surname that fits him so well it might have been chosen for him by poet or a painter. Edward Trelawny was one of those fortunate persons. There is a wild flavor in *Trelawny* that would lend a touch of romance to the most commonplace family; and that the Trelawnys never were. They were courageous, adventurous, full of vitality, eccentric, unreliable, prone to extremes; never, to judge from the family records, commonplace.

As I look back, I think that *The Three Musketeers* and *Trelawny* were just the right books for the right person at the right time. They were guaranteed to provide escape from the squalid camp in which I lived. In any case, they hooked me. *Trelawny,* the first biography I had ever read, created for me a lifelong interest in that genre.

The second noteworthy event in the development of my passion for reading came when my mother left town for a weekend, to attend a convention of the Congress of Industrial Organizations, the CIO, of which she was an officer. Father and I were left to our own resources, which turned out to be unconventionally delightful and intensely literary.

Dad and I went to the Cononelos market and bought two huge jars of green olives, a stack of salami, a loaf of bread, some cheese, undoubtedly potato chips, and other ready edibles. Dad arranged a small table between two easy chairs, with a floor lamp just behind the table. On the table, he put a bowl of green olives, potato chips, salami, bread, mustard, and, I'm sure, raw onion. Then from somewhere he produced *The Favorite Works of Mark Twain,* DeLuxe Edition, Garden City Publishing Co., Inc., 1939—1178 pages in all.

Dad and I would have a weekend of reading.

I don't remember what Dad read on that marvelous weekend, but I had four complete books (in one volume) to choose from: *Life on the Mississippi, The Adventures of Tom Sawyer, The Adventures of Huckleberry Finn,* and *A Connecticut Yankee in King Arthur's Court,* not to mention sixteen other shorter works: stories, excerpts from books, and sketches. At Dad's suggestion, I started with *Tom Sawyer* and then went on to *A Connecticut Yankee,* which Dad particularly liked.

The result of this experience was inevitable. I became an ardent Twainite, and I still am one. (In my opinion, *Life on the Mississippi* and the *Autobiography* are his masterpieces.)

My third experience with reading at home—in the apartment above the J. C. Penney store—was not so much one event as an ongoing series of experiences. My father had an eclectic love for poetry, and we read a good deal of verse, particularly on Sunday mornings before the gigantic brunch that my mother always prepared (grapefruit, fresh side of pork or pork loin, baking powder biscuits, gravy, eggs, pastries, coffee).

Dad, a skeptic, took great glee in *The First Mortgage,* a doggerel verse telling of the Bible story, by a poet named Cook:

> Sometime, and somewhere out in space,
> God felt it was the proper place
> To make a world, as he did claim,
> To bring some honor to his name.

And we read, I think, every word written by Robert Service:

Men of the High North, the wild sky is blazing,
    Islands of opal float of silver seas;
Swift splendors kindle, barbaric, amazing;
    Pale ports of amber, golden argosies.
Ringed all around us the proud peaks are glowing;
    Fierce chiefs in council, their wigwam the sky;
Far, far below us the big Yukon flowing,
    Like threaded quicksilver, gleams to the eye.
            —"Men of the High North"

Dad loved to declaim verse from *The Pious Friends and Drunken Companions* (The Macaulay Company, 1936):

As I walked out in the streets of Laredo,
As I walked in Laredo one day,
I spied a poor cowboy wrapped up in white linen,
Wrapped up in white linen and cold as the clay.

Dad enjoyed both Dorothy Parker (*Enough Rope*) and Shelley. But I don't remember ever hearing him read the American classics: Longfellow, Emerson, Whittier, Dickinson. His taste, with few exceptions, was definitely for the comic and ribald, though I think probably Dad quoted from his elegantly bound copy of the *Rubaiyat of Omar Khayyam* (translated, of course, by Edward Fitzgerald) more often than from any other poet or book. His favorite stanza:

Some for the Glories of This World; and some
Sigh for the Prophet's Paradise to come;
    Ah, take the Cash, and let the Credit go,
Nor heed the rumble of the distant Drum!

Though purists might deplore my father's taste for florid or ribald verse, nonetheless poetry became a part of my experience; from my early teens onward, I did not view it as something strange, exotic, with hidden meanings, accessible only to the few. No, poetry (whether written by T. S. Eliot or Robert Service) was to be enjoyed.

What lesson is to be learned from this account of reading in one home? As I look back on my experiences, I realize that, above all, reading was woven into the fabric of our lives; books were the center of both special occasions and our quotidian existence. They were very much like food: every meal was not an elaborate Sunday brunch, nor was every experience of reading a major occasion. Nonetheless, as we ate three meals a day, so we read books (and magazines, for there was no proper daily newspaper) every day.

The other day my grandson, barely two years old and yet already bookish, was foraging in my library. He pulled Robert Service's *Ballads of a Cheechako* off the shelf and presented it to me to "read" to him. There were no pictures, so he lost interest immediately. But as I held him close, I said, "You're just a bit too young for that now Chris, but someday. . . ." And I'm sure that someday Chris and I will read together the books that my father shared with me.

7

To Learn to Write

I live in gratitude to my parents for initiating me—and as early as I begged for it, without keeping me waiting—into knowledge of the word, into reading and spelling, by way of the alphabet. They taught it to me at home in time for me to begin to read before starting to school. I believe the alphabet is no longer considered an essential piece of equipment for traveling through life. In my day it was the keystone to knowledge. You learned the alphabet as you learned to count to ten, as you learned "Now I lay me" and the Lord's Prayer and your father's and mother's name and address and telephone number, all in case you were lost.

My love for the alphabet, which endures, grew out of reciting it but, before that, out of seeing the letters on the page. In my own story books, before I could read them for myself, I fell in love with various winding, enchanted-looking initials drawn by Walter Crane at the heads of fairy tales. In "Once upon a time," an "O" had a rabbit running it as a treadmill, his feet upon flowers. When the day came, years later, for me to see the Book of Kells, all the wizardry of letter, initial, and word swept over me a thousand times over, and the illumination, the gold, seemed a part of the word's beauty and holiness that had been there from the start.

EUDORA WELTY
One Writer's Beginnings

What must writers learn? How can they best acquire this know-how and knowledge? Can writing be taught? If so, how?

These are the questions that this chapter will explore. We will discuss the components of a writer's knowledge and skills, and then we will focus on four groups: grade school children, high school students, adults, and "basic" writers (that is, adolescents or adults whose writing ability is, for some reason, significantly impaired).

The chapter will go on to explain some instructional "scenes" and methods that have proven effective. This discussion is aimed at the writing teacher and at the interested layperson—parent, school board member, principal—who wants a general idea of how writing can best be taught. In effect, the discussion is the application of much of the theory that has come before it.

Learn What?

In a sense, this is the easiest question that we must answer about learning to write. The *how* is much more difficult.

From Aristotle to the latest pronouncements about writing, the totally commonsense notion has been that a writer must generate ideas about her or his topic, structure those ideas, and express them in acceptable language—all within the scope of purpose and audience. Sticking to the classical scheme, we can say that a writer needs to master the art of *invention* (discovering ideas), *form* (structuring those ideas), and *style* (expressing the ideas appropriately). This assumes, of course, that the writer actually has a purpose—something to say, a problem to be explored or solved, information to be communicated.

Invention, arrangement, and style—these categories are worth thinking about, are essential if we are to consider learning to write. The discussion in the sections that are to follow will gain substance from the chapters that have preceded this one.

Invention: Discovering Ideas

Human experience tells us that language is about something. Of course, it can be "about" simply providing 500 words of errorless nothing, or it can be an error-riddled text about a consequential matter. Neither of these options is, of course, acceptable.

Two categories of writing are useful when we think about invention: *professional* and *general*. Professional writing is that of experts in a field writing for other specialists, often in predetermined forms such as the standard scientific report. General writing is that of educated people writing for others like themselves. They are writing about what used to be called the commonplaces, the concerns that all of us share as citizens and human beings. Thus, chemists writing as generalists are quite different from chemists writing as professionals. When they write as chemists, their ideas and materials come from the processes that they have learned to use in their profession.

It is the case, then, that writers must learn techniques for finding significant ideas about their subjects. They must become problem solvers. In this chapter, some of the ways in which writers can learn to be more efficient problem solvers are explained and demonstrated.

Form and Style

Writers also are able to control the form or structure of their developing text so that it is coherent—that is, so that readers can derive the gist and understand how the parts of the whole relate to one another and ultimately to the gist. A reader should be able to construct a branching-tree diagram or organizational chart of a coherent text, showing the main idea and indicating how the suboridinate ideas relate to it.

Style is the kind of language a writer chooses for the text. Depending on the writer's purpose and the audience for the text, diction might be formal ("I shall leave immediately"), informal (I'm going right now"), or slangy ("I'm cutting out of here toot sweet"); ideas might be expressed literally ("The office was very busy") or figuratively ("The office was a beehive"); sentence structure might be elaborate or simple. Good writers are versatile stylists.

Speaking and Writing

Anyone who has tried to read the transcribed recordings of a meeting or a conversation—for instance, the infamous Watergate transcripts—knows that writing is not merely speech written down. We also know that fluent speakers can be impaired writers.

Earlier in this book, we discussed the obvious (but often overlooked) fact that a person can write without inscribing, without creating marks on clay tablets, paper, or a computer display. In general, as all of us sense, writing does differ from speech in some important ways, chief of which is the matter of specificity and detail—what in the jargon is called "contextualization."

When you talk face-to-face with a person, you get all sorts of hints about whether you're giving the hearer what he or she needs, and as a matter of fact, the hearer can interrupt you to ask for more details or can indicate impatience with the minuteness of your account: "Yes, yes, I know that already." The following example shows how this principle worked in an actual conversation recorded by my colleague Elinor Ochs:

(1) Two girls speaking:
    B: Y'have any cla—y'have a class with Billy this term?
    A: Yeah he's in my Abnormal class.
    B: Oh yeah. How?
    A: Abnormal Psych.
    B: Still not married?
    A: (loudly) Oh no, definitely not.[1]

Elinor Ochs makes the important distinction between planned and unplanned discourse—which is in many ways a more useful distinction than that between written and spoken discourse, for writing is characteristically thought out in advance, whereas speech is typically spur-of-the-moment. Even in extemporaneous writing, the process allows planning, since it moves more slowly than speaking.

Planned and Unplanned Discourse

A survey of the features of unplanned spoken discourse gives some idea of the gulf that lies between fluent conversation and fluent writing.[2] First, speakers of unplanned discourse rely on the immediate context, the "scene" in which the discourse is taking place, to convey their meaning. Since they can point to items, the following question would be meaningful in the context of a speaker pointing to an empty fried chicken carton, soiled paper napkins, and a soft-drink can on the floor of a room:

(2) *Pick up that stuff, will you?*

Speakers can also gesture and use facial expressions to help them convey their meanings.

Second, and interestingly, speakers of unplanned discourse use sentence structures that are generally learned early in the process of language acquisition rather than those learned late. For example, children acquire the use of coordinating conjunctions early and the use of subordinating conjunctions somewhat later. In unplanned spoken discourse, one finds more coordination than in written discourse. Telling of a subway incident in which a woman was saved from falling off the platform and into the path of a train, one speaker said this:

(3) So I was walkin' along the edge *and* uh as I said there were these people talkin' *and* this woman lady was describin' somethin' . . .[3]

Third, unplanned spoken discourse tends to be more repetitive than writing, as the following examples demonstrate:[4]

(4) Two girls speaking
    B: This fella I have uh *"fella"* This *man,* he had uh f-who I have for linguistics is
    A: Hm hm
    B: really too much
(5) On skiing over a cliff:
    M: So I sorta rushed myself. And I uh went down this this uh cliff not really a cliff but it was a very sharp incline of the mountain.
(6) *F:* Well we came um we stayed across the street from our house. I used ta live in Florida an' we stayed across the street cuz my mom was in the hospital an' we were really small.

Finally, speakers of unplanned discourse tend to use repetitive formulas that would be painfully obtrusive in writing

(7) *B:* So I went, *ya know,* to class this morning . . . and . . . uh . . . *ya know* we had this quiz.
    A: And you hadn't read the stuff, *right?*
    B: Right . . . and *ya know* M— bases half your grade on the quizzes.

Phatic Discourse: Establishing a Channel of Communication

Another distinction between writing and speaking is important: much spoken discourse is not intended to be highly informative, but is aimed at establishing social and psychological bonds between speaker and audience. Listeners normally expect a good deal of the sort of discourse that linguists call *phatic,* that is, talk intended to establish a "channel of communication," not to convey information. One can think of talk about the weather (or, in Los Angeles, the freeways), which characteristically serves to begin conversations that ultimately will "get down to business."

Learning, Bottom-Up or Top-Down

From the preceding discussion we can conclude that to make the shift from speaking to writing, a person must do the following:

1. Learn to contextualize, not relying on the immediate "scene" or on a listener's ability to signal the need for more information.
2. Use more "mature" sentence structures.
3. Eliminate the repetition that is allowed in speech and is sometimes necessary because a hearer cannot "scan" backward to gain a missed point.
4. Avoid the repetitive formulas of unplanned spoken discourse.

Therefore, it would seem that writing instruction should start with that basic unit of discourse, the sentence. Once students have mastered the written sentence, they are ready to go on to the next largest unit, the paragraph, which is after all nothing but a collection of sentences. And once students have learned to produce coherent paragraphs with a clearly stated topic sentence and adequate supporting sentences, they are ready to take the final step, assembling paragraphs into an essay.

In fact, we might use these phases in instruction and learning to organize a whole secondary-school composition program: freshman year, sentence drill; sophomore year, paragraph practice; junior year, three-paragraph essays; senior year, five-paragraph essays. (The five-paragraph essay is a form much beloved in schools but has no existence in the world outside the English classroom.)

All this sounds perfectly reasonable until we begin to think about the discussions in the second and third chapters of this book. From those discussions we can extrapolate principles that show the "perfectly logical" progression from sentence to paragraph to essay to be perfectly irrational.

Why Bottom-Up Instruction Doesn't Work

Language Acts Begin with a Communicative Intention

The language act begins with a general intention, a purpose, a meaning to express, never, or almost never, with a form to be permeated with meaning. To be basic to the point of banality, we might say that conversations begin with a topic—"What did you think of the Trojan-Baylor game yesterday?"—not with a request for language forms: "Say some sentences for me, will you?"

Response Is to Intention, Not Form

In language situations that fulfill their communicative function, the response is always to intention—to what the speaker or writer is trying to say, not to the form of the utterance or the text. And this point is so important and sticky that we will pursue it a bit.

Here is an anecdote from my recent past. I assigned a paper in my class for teaching majors. The students questioned me a good deal about what I expected (including the inevitable "How long should it be?"), and there was some interesting give-and-take as the class tried to "psych me out" or, less cynically, to form a conception of me as a reader. Ultimately one somewhat older student, a woman who seemed both worldly wise and world weary, said, "What he really wants is some writing so he can pick our sentences apart." I responded, "Aha, Ms. K— has it. She knows her English teachers, all right. You know, just last night at the dinner table I said to my son, 'Let's talk.' He replied, 'What do you want to talk about, Pop?' And I said, 'Oh, it doesn't really matter. I just want to criticize your pronunciation.' "

The point is this: when attention shifts from intended meaning to form of utterance or text, communication ceases; the language transaction is stymied. But the plot gets thicker. Often, the form is so obtrusive that focus inevitably shifts from matter to manner. In one senior English class we were discussing a paper by one of the students. One reader had this to say (not in a snide, cutting way, but lovingly, with the intention of being helpful): "Frankly, the spelling was so bizarre that it ruined the paper for me." We then began to discuss the problem of spelling: how it is a societal norm, how gross misspellings detract from the semantic intention of the writing and suggest to readers that the writer is only marginally literate, hence uneducated, hence unreliable as a source of information and opinion. In other words, spelling is very important in terms of the written language transaction.

And the plot thickens still more. Reponding to "errors" out of context is futile. In writing (or speaking), an error is only an error when it is perceived as a block to the communicative function of the discourse. In the case of writing, some readers are more error sensitive than others, and English teachers are probably the most sensitive of all. But any language form in the abstract is neither good nor bad, right nor wrong.

For teachers (which means anyone attempting to help a writer gain control of the medium), response to errors must always be in terms of their effect on the communicative function of the text. One sister-in-law of an English professor said (very sadly, in my opinion), "I never write to you because I'm afraid you'll see all the errors I make in my writing." In fact, the errors in this person's writing undoubtedly would not count, for her brother-in-law would be interested in her and what she had to tell him, not in its form. She would not be writing her letters in the context of a university or even of a learned community, but as sister-in-law to brother-in-law, and this brother-in-law at least would not be so inhuman as to discount an intelligent woman because she misspelled "geneology."

Response to errors in writing must always be in terms of what the writer is attemping to do, for whom, in what context. In other words, the response is to semantic intention, not to errors per se.

Language Transactions Do Not Build from the Bottom Up

Writers (and speakers) begin with a general intention, the highest-level component, and fit the pieces together so that they accomplish this purpose.

Focusing on Form Reduces Sensitivity to Meaning

The more attention a writer (or speaker) pays to form, the less reserve there is for purpose, for meaning. (The instructional implications of this principle will be the subject of a later section of this chapter.)

All the scholarly evidence, as well as our own experience with language, leads us to the conclusion that instruction must always be top-down. All too often, writing instruction in the schools is characterized by (1) the bottom-to-top approach, which starts with the smallest unit (the word or the sentence) and works up to the whole text (usually a five-paragraph essay); and (2) attention primarily to formal "correctness," not to semantic intention. Of course, students must develop fluency with sentences and must learn to avoid or correct mechanical errors, but only within the context of a communicative purpose.

Writing in the Lower Grades

This section will be largely a series of negatives, of thou-shalt-nots, with a few gems of positive advice interspersed.

Ninth Grade: The Watershed Year

At about ninth grade, according to Jean Piaget, children reach the stage of cognitive development in which they are able to do abstract thinking, what Piaget calls "formal operations." We may or may not subscribe to Piagetian theories of mental development, but we do know that at about fourteen years, children make dramatic changes, moving from childhood toward adulthood. Personal experience convinces me that at about fourteen students are ready to begin writing genuine exposition and true arguments—in other words, to produce the kinds of writing that count in high school, college, and the world. One longitudinal study of 338 children in Oakland, California, from kindergarten through high school revealed that all socioeconomic groups made significant gains in language skills, oral and written, at the ninth-grade level—

a development that I like to call "the Piaget leap."[5] For these and other reasons, I think that ninth grade is a watershed year.

Before Ninth Grade

Before ninth grade, I would argue, the child should be encouraged to write without fear of "error," and heavy emphasis should not be placed on surface form. After all, we want children to *acquire* all the arts and skills of composition, and the schools can be a significant help in this process by providing a scene in which children make attempts to express themselves in writing and receive responses to what they are trying to do, not merely to the surface form of their texts.

In *Growth Through English,* John Dixon captures the spirit of what I'm trying to convey. Children don't gain language ability through dummy runs and drills, but through dialogue and by moving freely between talk and writing. "In ordering and composing situations that in some way symbolize life as we know it, we bring order and composure to our inner selves. When a pupil is steeped in language operation we expect, as he matures, a conceptualizing of his earlier awareness of language, and with this perhaps new insight into himself (as creator of his own world)."[6]

Some genres of writing are useful and even necessary in high school, in college, and in the world: researched documents, editorials, scientific reports, business letters, personal essays, summaries, critiques, and many more. The word *genre,* is important. The classic detective story is a genre, as is the modern romance novel, and so are the sonnet and the Elizabethan tragedy. It would be impossible for us to undertake the writing of an exemplar of any of these genres without first immersing ourselves in others of its kind. In other words, one learns to write detective stories in large part by reading such stories and getting a sense of how they work.

Because we gain genre knowledge largely by experience with the genre, not by direct instruction, it makes no sense to ask children to produce writings in a given genre unless they have read fairly extensively in that genre. Thus, we can say that such writing projects as elaborate "research papers" have no place in the early grades and, in my opinion, should be delayed until after ninth grade.

Teachers of younger children should not focus on form, but should provide the developing writers with rich feedback concerning what they are trying to accomplish with their writings—that is, with responses to the writers' semantic intentions.

In short, teachers and parents

1. should not emphasize editing skills before about grade nine, and, in fact, should deemphasize them in the lower grades.
2. should not insist that younger writers begin to produce genres that they might need later, but which are out of their reach at their present stage of development—in fact, teachers and parents should not emphasize forms at all.
3. should create an unthreatening, supportive atmosphere in which children are encouraged to express themselves in writing and know that they will receive sympathetic responses to what they are trying to say in writing.
4. should view writing as a means through which children grow both intellectually and emotionally.

In Secondary School

I will generalize here, taking as my example a high school writing class at the junior or senior level.[7] In primary school the emphasis is (or should be) on writing as an aspect of and aid to development. The child writes to discover self and the world. In secondary school the emphasis shifts a bit, toward the communicative and persuasive functions of language (without losing the personal, expressive uses). Students begin to write expository essays, reports, and research papers. The stories that they write should begin to develop complex plots, and their poems should start to evince more formal control of language. Furthermore, high school students are ready to begin mastering the features of edited standard English.

Edited Standard English

As Chapter 2 points out, there are many dialects of spoken English, some that have prestige and general acceptance and some that stigmatize their users in the context of educated, middle-class society. There is only one prestige dialect in writing, however, which we have called edited standard English. All of us recognize it and even more readily recognize deviations from it. It adheres to certain rules of capitalization, punctuation, spelling, verb agreement, and so on. It is the form of language we see in newspapers, most magazines, and public documents. It does not necessarily constitute good writing, for although its grammar may be impeccable, it often does not make sense, does not fulfill its communicative function. One would never say, "I read a wonderful article on the economy last night. There wasn't a misspelled word, and the author capitalized all of the proper nouns correctly." But if there are misspellings and if the nouns are improperly capitalized, we are likely to discount the article. In other words, it is very important that writers learn to produce edited standard English prose that is relatively free of errors in those particulars which distinguish it from other kinds of English.

When Students Need Help to Write "Correctly"

We know that many students need massive help with such fundamentals as capitalization, not to mention punctuation, verb agreement, and spelling.[8] But the logic of our discussion and studies by scholars[9] lead us to conclude that marking papers for mechanical errors is unproductive; indeed, Lester Perelman, in an unpublished study done at the University of Southern California, reported that such response is actually counterproductive.

This is an extremely important concept for parents, administrators, board members, and other constituencies of public secondary schools. Because the belief that writing teachers should meticulously "correct" student papers is almost universal, teachers are under tremendous pressure to note every error by placing symbols (usually in red ink) in the margins of papers—a futile and perhaps destructive practice.

The arithmetic here is fairly simple. We are endowed with only so much ability to attend. The beam of our attention need not be a laser in its sharp narrowness, but we cannot attend profoundly to what we are trying to communicate and at the same time invest a great deal of concentration in mechanical niceties. The fact that fluent writers can proofread as they go only demonstrates that they must invest little of their attention in correcting errors.

For basic writers who are consciously and painstakingly learning proofreading skills, however, the mental investment in regularizing the text is virtually overwhelming. (I refer back now to the distinction between conscious learning and unconscious acquiring that was the subject of much of the discussion in Chapter 3.) For these beginners much of the writing process is not automatic; they must ponder each mark of punctuation, each verb and its subject, each pronoun and its antecedent. A good analogy is the first few days of transition from a familiar typewriter to a word processor. The writer making the transition must invest attention heavily in manipulating the machine, at the expense of semantic intention. In the process of gaining fluency, the computer user is wise not to attempt serious composing, but rather to copy manuscripts or merely play around.

The problem, obviously, is that students must learn to conceive and write papers that are significant, that say something of interest or importance in a logical, coherent way, but at the same time do not violate the norms of edited standard English. In other words, students must learn the art of composing and the skill of proofreading or editing, two kinds of learning that can be and often are antithetical to one another.

The Workshop and the Laboratory

One way to solve the problem of how to give students both the general ability to compose and the specific skills necessary to produce "correct" edited standard English is this: create two *scenes* for instruction, one in which composing takes place, the other in which editing skills are learned. That is what colleagues and I did in the Huntington Beach Union High School District, with gratifying results.[10]

Roughly characterized, the *writing workshop* is rhetorically charged with values and with the concerns of audience and scene, unsystematic, "messy"; the *laboratory* is arhetorical, systematic, neat.

THE LABORATORY

As to the physical scenes themselves—the places where workshop and editing skills are taught: the laboratory is not a place, but a concept. It is a given kind of instruction for certain goals. Two of the most effective labs in Huntington Beach were extremely simple in their physical details. Lab 1 was a file cabinet on wheels that the teacher—the gifted, energetic, dedicated Catherine McGough—moved from room to room throughout the day. In the cabinet were exercises on photocopied sheets—some adapted from existing sources, some devised by the teacher herself, all fitting a general framework or inventory of skills needed to produce edited standard English.

Lab 2—developed by Joanne Haukland and Christine Rice, both superb teachers—was a separate room. For observers who expected to find an electronic wonderland in a good lab, Lab 2 must have been a terrible disappointment, for its "equipment" was nothing more than a couple of dozen cardboard boxes filled with photocopied exercises and arranged according to an inventory of skills. Offhand, I cannot say how much money was spent on materials and equipment, but obviously the sum was insignificant.

Every writing teacher knows that proofreading skills are a variable among students in a class; some appear to need instruction in everything, while others have problems in limited areas. The separation of the lab from the workshop allows, even demands, the individualization of instruction. The English class model of grammar drill on Monday, discussion of a poem Tuesday, theme assignment on Wednesday, library activities Thursday, and time for elective reading on Friday breaks down. For the lab and the workshop are interactive and flexible.

THE WORKSHOP

Characterizing the workshop and how it interacts with the lab could best be accomplished with a videotape that would demonstrate, not tell about the two. However, a picture of the workshop can be presented. Here is a summary of the kinds of things that go on there:

1. Discussion of topics by the entire class. Exploring problems through brainstorming and other heuristics.
2. Small-group activities of two or three students; for instance, two students reacting to and making suggestions regarding a paper (perhaps a rough draft) produced by a third student.

3. Composing-on-the-board, with volunteers making attempts to solve a given writing problem; for example, getting a paper by one member of the class under way effectively.
4. Discussion of one, two, or three photocopied papers produced by class members.
5. Conferencing, with the teacher circulating about the class to help individual students with writing problems while other members of the class work on their papers.
6. Some proofreading lessons for the entire class, dealing with a limited problem that all have in common.
7. Reformulation exercises, in which the class members make suggestions for improving one of their fellows' papers.
8. Discussion of how a paper should be changed in order to meet audience expectations.
9. Freewriting, letting the words flow at random from the tip of the pen.
10. Journal writing.
11. Publishing activities, in which groups of students or the entire class participate in getting a collection of their writings ready for publication and distribution.
12. Class development of writing assignments, during which students devise topics, define audiences, and delineate situations.

The workshop is a messy place, highly charged, purposive in terms of writing something for someone for some reason. When it becomes obvious that the student's writing must reach an audience that expects edited standard English, the lab assignment becomes meaningful. Because editing skills are put into context, students grasp their importance.

In College

Three of my former students represent college populations in general.[11] There was Kim, with her understatedly expensive wardrobe and impeccably manicured nails. She was majoring in international marketing because she liked people and wanted to travel. Roger, a "faculty brat," was very bright, extremely witty, and a delight. And then there was Mary Ann, a lovely but extremely shy Chicana.

I suspect that Kim was bright, but her intelligence didn't show through the brick wall of conventional decorum she had inherited. She was prompt with her work, courteous, alert in class, and completely dull. She needed shaking out of her five-paragraph-essay value system and modus operandi. Here is a sample of her work early in the semester:

If Change Were Possible, How Would You Change Your Life

After giving serious thought about what I would like to change in my life, I have come to the conclusion that I am very fortunate. I can not think of a major aspect I would like to have different about myself, yet I am not near to saying that I do not want to change at all. There is an intermediate stage that I would call improvement, and I believe that there is room for improvement in everyone.

One part of my personality, which I feel insecure about, does need enhancement: expressing my opinions publicly. Personal expression, I think, is the most important factor in communication and the interchange of thought or opinions is the key to success in marketing and international affairs, both of which I am interested in. In these fields it is necessary to persuade another person to be interested in what you are offering which can only be done by showing confidence and relaying your message well. . . .

Kim's paper reveals few violations of the norms of edited standard English. In that respect, it is quite prim and proper. But one could hardly say that it is engaging, either as the explanation of original ideas or as the expression of personal aspirations and viewpoints.

In some ways, Roger was as much of a problem student as Kim: he wanted more and more challenges, and he kept me busy keeping him productively busy. For him, reading, thinking, discussing, and writing were already a way of life. Here is a sample of Roger's work at the beginning of the semester:

What you are reading right now on the few pages in front of you is the end product of an idiosyncratic writing process. Not long ago, the author began writing the words in front of you, hoping that through a descriptive, unorthodox essay he could bring you, perhaps, to revelation of the method in his composing.

You notice first that the author has written this short essay in the third person. It is important that an author be conscious of himself and be able to envision himself as someone else would, noticing his little peculiarities, as it is for him to survey the world and its people. The writer, in order to relate his own experience to an audience, must understand himself so that he may compare and contrast himself with the readers, identifying himself with them while at the same time enlightening them as to his individuality and unique knowledge. The author in this essay is, in short, attempting in front of an audience to critically analyze an aspect of his life. He is, for a change, observing himself.

Mary Ann was the perfect case study of the bright, willing student who enters higher education with massive language problems. Her writing for my class was totally engaging, but in mechanics would have been completely unacceptable to the educated community. (In my opinion, this community is wrong, but my opinion does not rescue the hundreds of thousands of young people whose language keeps them out of the system.) Here is a sample of Mary Ann's unedited writing:

> If change were possible, how would you change your life? If change were possible, I would save my other half. In December of 1957 a young man and a very lady were to be wed. This young man was determined in his character. He was 23 years old and fresh out of the army. This young man was named Ramon _____. This lady was kind-hearted in her character. She had just turned 16 years by 3 months. This young was named Mary_____, and soon to be our mom.
>
> Ramon and Mary were married the 28 to december of 1957. Two years were to pass and they would start thier family. Mary was to give birth in the beginning of the year 1959. It was February 4, 1959, 4 o'clock in the morning and Mary would give birth to a pair of bouncing baby girls, only to know that one was to die.
>
> The first girl was healthy as can be. Her name was Jessie. the second girl had a hole in her heart, and doomed. Her name was Mary Ann. Mary Ann was to die in four months because of her heart. Four months passed and both girls were living. At the sixth month, Jessie's Heart would stop. This is the life I want to save. My other half.

Varieties of Writing

I encourage students to do the kinds of writing that were discussed in the previous chapter: explanatory writing, the "how" of complex problems and the "why" of opinions; exploratory writing, the tentative outlining of problems and display of ambivalence; and argument, the setting forth of "conclusive" research, scientific evidence, and/or irrefutable logic. And then there is the *journal*. Almost all writing is a public performance intended for an audience, and performances are always tinged with anxiety and threat—that's what makes them exiciting. Imagine the utter boredom of an art form consisting only of masterpieces. That's why, upon occasion (I am assured by my infallible intuition), Placido Domingo sings in the bathtub: for the sheer joy of singing, even as you or I might do. The journal is singing in the bathtub: always a complete success, never threatening.

Writing as Problem Solving

The focus in grade school is on the personal development of the writer. As long as growth is taking place, form and genre are not of particular concern. At about ninth grade, the focus shifts toward public writing, toward texts that explain, argue, and persuade. When the writer enters college, he or she should be ready to use writing as an instrument of problem solving. I begin each semester by asking students to write about some problematic aspect of the university: the physical plant, the administration, the curriculum, whatever. In explaining how to go about this assignment, I use the cafeteria as a case in point, for it is a truth universally acknowledged that all cafeterias in institutions of higher education are problematic. Indeed, when I ask the class if the cafeteria is a problem, I get virtually total agreement that it is: the food isn't good, the prices are too high, the place smells, and so on.

Well, then, we have an opportunity to investigate in detail, to do a report that we can submit to the proper authorities, and thus perhaps bring about change. But how does one go about investigating the cafeteria? Here are some suggestions that I give the class and that we discuss in some detail.[12]

1. First, we want to record as many features of the cafeteria as possible, preferably on a sheet of paper or index cards. "What sort of data would you want to obtain?" I ask, and I get answers such as the following: dimensions, brightness of lighting, seating capacity, noise level, patronage during various hours, odors, costs, decor, utensils, and number of employees.

2. Now I suggest that the intestigators have a mountain of more or less unrelated data, which is a good entry to the subject, but

which must somehow be systematized. So I ask the students to think about the cafeteria as a system with interrelated parts. They begin to analyze the relationship of the kitchens to the serving lines, the location of the cash registers, the layout of the serving area, and so on. What had been a montage of features becomes a blueprint or diagram, with an emphasis on relationships.

3. A blueprint is, after all, static, and a cafeteria is a dynamic operating unit. So I now suggest that we set the place in motion and begin to think about traffic flows (the time it takes to get through the lines, which is easily determined with a stopwatch), the movement of the food from the kitchen to serving line to trays, and the movement of trays from the clean stack to their final destination in the washer. In short, we now have a third perspective on our subject, and as usual we record our data and impressions in detailed notes.

4. A fourth perspective is based on contrast: how does the subject (in this case, the cafeteria) contrast with other items in its class (namely, eating establishments)? The students can compare cafeteria prices and quantities with those of McDonald's; they can compare the cafeteria with fine restaurants and greasy spoons and with cafeterias in other institutions. The variation between the subject and other similar items in its class will be either favorable or unfavorable.

5. The fifth perspective requires students to look at what might, for lack of a better term, be called distribution. The cafeteria, a system in itself, is part of multiple larger systems. Because it is part of the physical plant and layout of the university, its location may be an important consideration. It is also part of the financial structure of the university, and we need to determine its economics— whether it breaks even, makes money, or loses money. And it is also part of the administrative structure of the university: someone is head person at the cafeteria, and he or she reports to someone else, and so on.

Once the students have considered all five of these angles for a week or so—gathering information, letting ideas germinate, re-thinking tentative conclusions—they can begin to ask themselves the question that will lead ultimately to a piece of writing: "On the basis of my current knowledge, what changes would I recommend?" Having gathered ideas and data for several days, each student is ready to present the background that will make his or her recommendations telling.

Responding to Writing

Feedback, response—this is the single most important help that writing students can receive! Therefore, I arrange several kinds of response situations and spend about one-third of all class time with them: small-group discussions, conferences, and entire-class discussions. I reproduce four or five of each group of papers I receive and use these for class discussions.

However, before students feel right about submitting their work to the scrutiny of the entire class in open discussion, an air of trust and confidence must be established. Witty and cynical instructors will poison the atmosphere to such an extent that discussion can never to a comfortable, effective learning situation. The atmosphere in a writing class must be tolerant and loving, not brittle.

Creativity and Writing as Problem Solving

It is a truism, but nonetheless, life is a series of problems—decisions that must be made, difficulties that must be unravelled, choices, snarled personal relationships, puzzles. This being the case—every day being a series of problems, one after the other—it is paradoxical that so few people think about the nature of problems.

Writing is not only a means of conveying information; it is also an important way of understanding and solving problems. Therefore, when a person (child, teenager, or adult) learns to write, he or she is also learning to become a better problem solver.

In a problem situation, things just don't add up; there is *dissonance.* Often we sense problems before we fully understand them: we are uncomfortable with the way our careers are going, but don't quite know why; we can't seem to get along with the boss and don't understand the reason; we are torn between two courses of action and thus can't move one way or the other until we make up our minds; two political candidates appeal to us, but we must choose one to vote for.

In *Conceptual Blockbusting* James L. Adams says this:

> Few people like problems. Hence the natural tendency in problem-solving is to pick the first solution that comes to mind and run with it.

Figure 11. Volkswagen Art.
(*Source:* From Sidney J. Parnes, *Creative Behavior Workbook*
[New York: Charles Scribner's Sons, 1967].)

The disadvantage of this approach is that you may run either off a cliff or into a worse problem than you started with. A better strategy in solving problems is to select the most attractive path from many ideas or concepts.[13]

But to discover many ideas or concepts, you must become a skilled asker of questions. And you must overcome *blocks*. Everyone has heard of, and most of us have experienced, writer's block: the inability to get started on a piece of writing. Writer's block is just one aspect of a larger set of problems that might be called "blocks to creative thinking." In *Conceptual Blockbusting,* Adams discusses four kinds of blocks: perceptual, emotional, cultural and environmental, and intellectual and expressive.

It is quite possible to look at something without seeing it at all. This is a *perceptual block.* For example, unless clued in, most people will look at Figure 11 without seeing a Volkswagen. But if they encounter a middle-aged woman, conservatively dressed and carrying several books under her arm as she walks across a college campus, all they see is a professor, though the woman may in fact be a student or, for that matter, the local narcotics peddler.

Two causes of perceptual blocks are stereotyping and inability to see a problem from various angles. For example, if you have trouble solving the following problem, you are caught by a stereotype. (The solution is in the paragraph following the statement of the problem, but don't look at that until you make an effort to provide your own solution.)

> **(8)** A young man is badly injured in an automobile accident. Brought by paramedics to the emergency room of the hospital, he is examined by a physician who decides that he needs immediate brain surgery. The ER physician calls a neurosurgeon who, upon examining the young man, says, "I can't operate on him. He's my son." That statement was true, yet the ER physician knew that the neurosurgeon was not the boy's father.[14]

If it took you any time at all to explain this seeming contradiction, you should blush and, as penance, deny yourself dessert at supper tonight, for you have allowed yourself to be caught by stereotyped thinking. You have assumed that all neurosurgeons are male. Obviously, in this case the surgeon was the boy's mother.

Here, adapted from a book entitled *Creative Growth Games,*[15] is another problem. How many solutions can you devise?

> **(9)** A handsome young prince fell in love with the daughter of an ugly, selfish queen, who, being a widow, wanted the young man for herself. The queen promised the young man riches and power if he would marry her, but the prince wanted only the daughter. Of course, the selfish queen would not give her consent to that marriage.
>
> One day as the three were walking in the garden, the queen proposed that they decide the matter by chance. The queen would put both a diamond and a ruby in an empty jewelry box, and the princess, blindfolded, would choose one of the gems. If she chose the ruby, the prince would marry the queen; if she chose the diamond, he would marry her.
>
> The queen ordered a servant to bring an empty jewelry box, and when it arrived, she carefully took objects from her pocket and put

them into the box. The sharp-eyed prince, however, was able to see that the queen had slipped two rubies into the box, not a diamond and a ruby. She then blindfolded the princess and ordered her to choose one of the stones.

If you were the prince, how would you solve the problem created by the queen's dishonesty?

If you are unable to "walk around" this problem and view it from various angles, you can offer only two solutions: refuse to make the choice, thus entering into a confrontation with the queen, or draw the ruby and live with the tragic consequences. However, this kind of "head-on" approach might not be the best solution. Suppose, for instance, that the princess were to say, "Madam, I ask that you draw a stone from the box. The one that remains in the box will determine my fate." Since the queen will draw a ruby, the other stone, by her own avowal, must be a diamond.

An interesting example of the inability to see beyond the normal and accepted is illustrated by the following puzzle, which is easy to solve for a person who breaks out of steretyped thinking.[16]

With no more than four straight lines, and without raising your pen or pencil from the paper, draw a line through each of the nine dots.

$$0 \qquad 0 \qquad 0$$

$$0 \qquad 0 \qquad 0$$

$$0 \qquad 0 \qquad 0$$

Adams gives a number of solutions to this problem, but the most obvious one is shown at the end of this chapter.

To help overcome perceptual blocks that stand between you and the solutions to problems, you can ask yourself the following questions:

1. *Am I thinking in stereotypes?* We must put things and concepts into mental categories. That seems to be the way the mind works. However, as we sort out and categorize, we run the risk of stereotyping.
2. *Have I really isolated the problem?* In a complex system one fault may create havoc. Everyone who has worked with com-

puters knows that this is *the* essential question. Until you isolate
the exact problem, you can do nothing to make the program
work.

3. *Have I viewed the problem from all possible angles?* In your
   mind, picture someone buying an automobile. She walks around
   it, gets inside, takes a test drive, opens the trunk and hood, and
   perhaps even looks at the underside. Now picture someone thinking about a problem, always from the same point of view, not
   "walking around it," not trying to take it apart, getting only one
   angle of vision. In problem solving, you need to be flexible in
   adopting angles of vision.

Because of emotional blocks, we are afraid to take risks even
when there will be minimal consequences or none at all. Of course,
all creative work is to some extent perilous. Creating new things
often means the old thing or idea will be abolished; thus, creativity
has a destructive aspect. Because creative thinking disrupts old
patterns (which are often stereotypes), it frequently creates temporary chaos, and some people simply cannot tolerate anything that
is not orderly. (One is reminded of the bachelor uncle who spends
so much time grooming, pressing his clothes, and shining shoes
that he is unable to go out; or the woman who will not drive her
new car because it might become dirty or even get scratched.)

Another emotional block to creative problem solving is the ten-
dency to judge prematurely. Before you start throwing ideas out as
impractical, you should generate many alternatives. Giving thumbs-
up or thumbs-down too early in the process of solving problems is
likely to stop you dead in your search for ideas. A leading researcher
in creativity, D. N. Perkins, has this to say about judging ideas:

> Experiments suggest that just how you are critical makes a big differ-
> ence. In one investigation, some people were instructed to free-wheel,
> forget about quality, and devise as many solutions as possible. Others
> were to give only high-quality solutions. It was found that the first
> group produced more high-quality solutions, albeit with a lower aver-
> age quality. So in this case the emphasis on quality impeded perfor-
> mance. However, in another study people were instructed not just to
> strive for quality but to try to meet specified standards. In a problem of
> inventing plot titles, they were asked to produce an "imaginative, cre-
> ative, or unusual title for this plot." With even this slight clarification of
> standards, the results were quite different. Those given the standards

produced a larger number of superior solutions, with a higher average quality of solution as well.[17]

The old advice to "sleep on it" applies to emotional blocks. Some people can't distance themselves from a problem for any length of time, but worry about it continually and frustratingly. It seems that letting a problem "incubate" in the subconscious is often productive. In one of the most famous instances of creative problem solving, the French mathematician Henri Poincaré had a flash of insight after a period of incubation. He had been working on the Fuchsian functions, and

> just at this time I left Caen, where I was then living, to go on a geologic excursion. . . . The changes of travel made me forget my mathematical work. Having reached Coutances, we entered an omnibus to go some place or other. At the moment when I put my foot on the step the idea came to me, without anything in my former thoughts seeming to have paved the way for it, that the transformations I had used to define the Fuchsian functions were identical with those of non-Euclidean geometry. I did not verify the idea; I should not have had time, as upon taking my seat in the omnibus, I went on with a conversation already commenced, but I felt a perfect certainty. On my return to Caen, for conscience's sake I verified the result at my leisure.[18]

This account is fairly typical: after a period of incubation—during which the solver does not consciously work on the problem—a solution pops up, Eureka! But, of course, this is not to say that if you let a problem incubate, you will automatically experience the Eureka phenomenon.

Answering the questions that follow should help you overcome emotional blocks to creative problem solving:

1. *Am I afraid of taking a risk?* You might systematically list the possible consequences if you fail to solve the problem. Chances are, the real danger (even to your ego) is slight.
2. *Am I unwilling to experience chaos?* In starting to solve your problem, you might upset the order of things, creating disorder, but that should be only a temporary state of affairs.
3. *Am I too judgmental?* If you are too critical of yourself and others, you will stop the flow of ideas.
4. *Do I allow opportunity for incubation?* To be able to do so, you

must start early so that impending deadlines won't eliminate the possibility of letting ideas grow in the subconscious.

Intellectual and expressive blocks would keep you from solving the following problem:[19]

> From her grandmother, a woman inherited four gold chains, each consisting of three links. Wanting to put the chains together to form a necklace, the woman consulted a jeweler, who told her that it would cost ten dollars to open a link, connect it with another link, and solder it shut. "Since I must make four connections, the price will be forty dollars." "On the contrary," replied the woman, "you can do the job for thirty dollars at the rate you have quoted me."

Was the woman right? If so, explain her reasoning.

It is important to use the proper "language" for solving a problem. Consider, for instance, how difficult it would be to do long division without mathematical notation. If you didn't use an alternate language in solving the gold necklace problem, you probably had difficulty. However, had you used a diagram, the solution might have come more readily. Figure 12 demonstrates that the woman was right in telling the jeweler he could make the necklace for thirty dollars instead of forty. The woman saw that by separating the three links of one of the chains, the jeweler could use those individual links to join the three remaining chains.

Generally speaking, problems come in two varieties: those we must deal with in natural language and those best solved with alternate languages such as mathematics or diagrams. If you are blocked because your skill at mathematics or writing is inadequate, you have a learning task ahead of you, but it is certain that many people with perfectly adequate "language" skills fail to use them appropriately in problem situations.

The following story illustrates cultural and environmental blocks. An anthropologist studying native Americans in Alaska knew that these people eat blubber and that eventually he would have to do so, but he dreaded the thought. In their culture, blubber was a delicacy, but in his it was not used as food. Finally, at a meal, he was served a white blob. Summoning all his stamina, he took a mouthful, but became nauseated and had to leave the igloo. When he returned, his hostess asked him, "Don't you like dumplings?"

Cultures have their accepted ways and their taboos, and it is

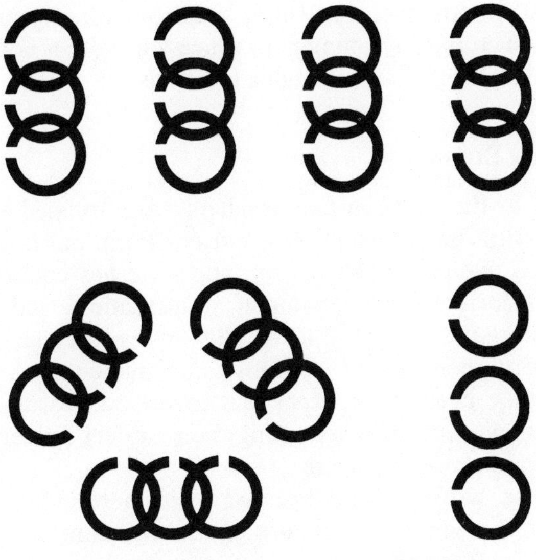

Figure 12. Gold Necklace Puzzle.

difficult to circumvent or change these. For example, in some cultures dogs are eaten, but not in the United States; thus, the suggestion that abandoned pets be used for food would run up against an almost insuperable cultural block. One person seriously suggested that dogs and cats executed at animal shelters could be used as food for other pets, but even this suggestion, as logical as it may seem, brought horrified reactions, including one from a woman who said that she didn't believe dogs were cannibalistic. (The response was this: "They can't read the label of the dog food can to find out what kind of meat it contains.")

It goes without saying that creativity flowers most luxuriantly in a supportive environment: in the laboratory where co-researchers are helpful and nonjudgmental; in the art class where ineptness or failure will not bring ridicule; in the classroom where teacher and students realize that making mistakes is necessary to learning.

As to advice about overcoming cultural and environmental blocks? They are more difficult than other blocks because they are largely beyond our control. You can't do much to change social norms and taboos over the short haul, but often you can get around them. If the environment in which you work is not supportive, you might think about changing locations.

A Hortatory Summary

Too often in the past, writing teachers have stressed form and style almost to the exclusion of invention. Form has often meant the artificial five-paragraph matrix, and style has connoted little more than correctness in grammar, punctuation, and spelling. Undoubtedly students need the ability to write coherent prose and to adapt their style to purpose and audience. Above all, however, they need to be experts at invention, learning to discover the significant ideas regarding their subject matter and becoming skilled problem solvers.

In any case, writing instruction that begins bottom-up, with emphasis on style (sentence structure, diction, grammatical correctness) and form (the paragraph, the five-paragraph essay), is defying both the laws of nature and common sense. People use language to communicate, to solve problems, to express themselves, and for countless other purposes; they do not speak merely to achieve clear pronunciation, and they do not write just to produce correct spellings. Writing instruction should always proceed from the top down: from the writer's purposes and needs.

Before ninth grade, children should be encouraged to write, and correctness in grammar, spelling, and punctuation should not be stressed. Furthermore, in the lower grades children are not cognitively ready to develop elaborate logical arguments or to do complicated research writing.

At about ninth grade children are ready to use language as an instrument of abstract thinking, for what Jean Piaget called "formal operations." Beyond ninth grade, students can begin to compose arguments for and against theses, interpretations of literature, research papers, summaries, and other types of transactional texts. If they have not already acquired the ability to write edited standard English, high school students can begin to learn the rules of grammar and punctuation that prevail in the written dialect.

However, teaching students the skills of grammar, punctuation, and usage should not be confused with instruction in the art of writing, and one way to avoid this confusion is to create two instructional scenes, a workshop in which students attempt to give adequate written expression to their semantic intentions and a laboratory in which students consciously learn to manage the features of edited standard English.

Writing instruction in college should not be radically different from that in high school. However, the emphasis should be moved toward writing as problem solving, writing as an instrument of thought, and writing as a means of accomplishing goals.

From grade school through graduate school, writing should be viewed as an intrinsic part of the individual's personal development and as a means whereby he or she can participate in shaping society.

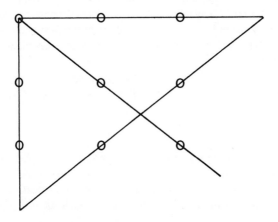

One solution to the problem on page 169.

8

The Student and the Schools

To acquire literacy is more than to psychologically and mechanically dominate reading and writing techniques. It is to dominate these techniques in terms of consciousness; to understand what one reads and to write what one understands; it is to *communicate* graphically. Acquiring literacy does not involve memorizing sentences, words, or syllables—lifeless objects unconnected to an existential universe—but rather an attitude of creation and re-creation, a self-transformation producing a stance of intervention in one's context.

PAULO FRIERE
Education for Critical Consciousness

In this chapter I would like to discuss, first, a philosophy of education for reading and writing and, second, some important differences among students. The philosophy of education will not be abstruse, but will, I think, have some obvious and immediate applications.

Education for Critical Consciousness

I derive my heading, of course, from Paulo Freire, whose book of that title is one of the central statements regarding education in general and literacy in particular.[1] Even the term "critical consciousness" is resonant, suggesting as it does that education should give people the ability to analyze and evaluate their society and their role in that society and thus take charge of their own destinies.

Freire, with good teachers at all levels from kindergarten through graduate school, deplores the "banking concept" of education, in which a teacher pours knowledge into the passive receptacles before him. As Freire says, "Communication gives way to communiqués by the teacher, who makes deposits which the students meekly receive, memorize, and repeat."[2] It is not revolutionary to posit that learning must be active, not passive, and that the teacher and the student must interact, carrying on a dialogue that replaces the lecture-monologue of the banking model of education. However, in the context of Freire's work, this good-natured, sensible position on learning becomes something less familiar and more revolutionary.

Specifically, Freire first leads us to a critical understanding of the difference between what I will call *Kultur* and a redefined "culture." Next, he plunges us into the abyss of indeterminacy, the belief that texts have no single, stable meaning. Both of these moves have profound implications for our schools.

Kultur and Culture[3]

Kultur is a given: stable, immutable, and of unquestioned value. It is what institutions pass on from generation to generation, in the form of canons, collections, and societal norms. Manifestations of Kultur are *Julius Caesar* in the eleventh-grade literature anthology (and that anthology itself); the Getty Museum in Malibu; the Lincoln Center for the Performing Arts. These are "given," donated, conveyed. They are preexistent and for all practical purposes eternal. They also, of course, belong to certain classes in society.

Culture, on the other hand, is always becoming, being made. In Freire's view the cultured person is one who sees herself or himself as a creative agent, not merely a partaker, a donee. Illiterates, who stand in awe of Kultur, are puzzled by it, afraid of it, would discover that what they and their neighbors create—a clay doll, the poetry in a popular song—is also a part of culture, for "culture is all human creation."[4]

Freire, of course, is talking about Brazilian peasants, but substitute "high school senior' or "college freshman" for "illiterate," and the principle is extended—the principle that everyone can be a culture-maker and that culture is not confined to tomes, monuments, concert halls, and museums.

The point, however, is to preserve Kultur by gaining for it the allegiance of critically conscious beings who envision themselves as participants in the same spheres of action as the "masters." One of the most maligned works of Kultur is that wonderful tale *Silas Marner,* long the staple of high school English courses. Culture, in Freire's sense, is not a revolution that would abolish this monument, but a creative, dialectical movement that would incorporate it, with other diverse works both old and new, in a dynamic process of becoming.

"Cultural literacy" (discussed in Chapter 5) is a most important concept at this moment. As E. D. Hirsch, Jr., explains, it is

> that knowledge that enables a writer or reader to know what other writers and readers know within the literate culture. Thus it is not only a knowledge of convention and vocabularies but is also a knowledge *that* this information is widely shared by others. Moreover, since this shared culture is changing at its edges, the content of cultural literacy is also changing. New things become part of it and old things drop away— even while the more permanent central core remains.[5]

I think that Hirsch's argument is unexceptionable. We have seen that we read with our minds, not our eyes; we have seen also that writers achieve their purposes through the means of the knowledge that they share with their readers. Without cultural literacy, there would be no reading or writing, unless, of course, we would take information retrieval to be the sole function of literacy. The question is not whether we should work toward cultural literacy, for literacy *is* cultural, but how we should achieve it.

Problem-Posing Education

Freire would argue that we can achieve cultural literacy only through what he calls "problem-posing education," which comes about when the teacher and the students work together to solve a problem. Thus, problem-posing education eliminates the absolute distinction between teacher and student and "consists in acts of cognition, not transferals of information."[6] This is not to say that the teacher does not "know" more—about *Silas Marner* and George Eliot—than the students, but that the students, in dialogue with the teacher, must generate their own knowledge, a goal that they cannot reach if they deal only with Kultur, which is given to them, and not with culture, which they are creating and which includes their own works. Thus, a writing class that uses the "masters" as examples of what might be accomplished and student texts as paradigms of the failure to reach the ideal of Kultur will only alienate the learners. A literature class that promulgates only Kultur will be equally alienating. A basic reading class that relies only on texts foreign to the students' cultures is bound to fail.

Culture, then, has no hard-and-fast parameters, but is continually created by those who reinterpret what is and was and who contribute their own works to the immediate future. In Freire's words, "Problem-posing education affirms men as being in the process of *becoming*—as unfinished, uncompleted beings in and with a likewise unfinished reality."[7]

Indeterminacy: The Loss of Certainty

The danger in problem-posing education is obvious: all absolute certainty vanishes except the faith that new insight and greater understanding lie just beyond the next question. As Freire says, "To exist, humanly, is to *name* the world, to change it. Once named, the world in its turn reappears to the namers as a problem and requires of them a new *naming*. Men are not built in silence, but in word, in work, in action-reflection."[8]

Reality is objective enough, Freire tells us, but is meaningless without interpretation and is thus multiple, not single. He gives a marvelous example. A "culture group" from the slums of Santiago were discussing the implications of a picture showing a drunk staggering down a street and three young men talking on the corner. The group of participants interpreted the scene thus: "the only one there who is productive and useful to his country is the souse who is returning home after working all day for low wages and who is worried about his family because he can't take care of their needs. . . . He is a decent worker and souse like us."[9]

The starting point for any educational program must be the existential situation, not only because attitude and scene are in some ways synonymous, but because meaning is scene-bound, context-oriented. "Neither language nor thought can exist without a structure to which they refer," says Freire. "In order to communicate effectively, educator and politician must understand the structural conditions in which the thought and language of the people are dialectically framed."[10] Each individual lives in a "thematic universe," a web of interlocking concerns, and it is these "generative themes" that form the basis for Freire's pedagogical method, which I will now outline briefly.

The literacy teacher begins with a *generative* word, such as *favela* (slum), and breaks it into syllables: *fa-ve-la*. These syllables in turn generate phonemic groups: *fa-fe-fi-fo-fu, va-ve,* and so on. However, the word *favela* is not presented visually until the group "discusses the problems of housing, food, clothing, health, and education in a slum . . . and further perceives the slum as a problem situation." Other generative words are presented, and ultimately the group is using its newly acquired knowledge of phonemic combinations to read and then write other words.[11]

The method involves what might be called *technic* (that is, phonemic instruction) and *rhetoric* (that is, the relationship of words to the thematic universe in which the subjects live)—and of the two, rhetoric is by far the most important. Technic makes words, but rhetoric makes meanings.

Problematization

The literacy method leads both to *conscientization* and to *problematization*. Conscientization is the awakening of critical awareness, enabling one to enter into the "eternal dialogue between man and man, between man and his Creator. It is this dialogue which makes of man an historical being."[12]

Problematization is opposed to the banking concept of education, underlying which are the consoling certainties of accepted knowledge and tradition and the belief that behind every situation and text there is *a* meaning. But problem-posing education sucks us into the vortex of indeterminacy, where knowledge is constructed and "truth" ever evolves.

Often, as I jet here and there, I look below me at the clouds and have the strange, irrational illusion that they are solid stuff; falling out of the plane, I would land on the billowy mass and be saved. But then comes the alternate vision of a terrified plunger clawing at vapor as he passes through the cloud mass toward annihilation—which must be something like the feeling that students have when they realize that the apparently solid foundation of determinate meaning is an illusion.

In problem-posing education, students become junior colleagues of the teacher in the quest for knowledge; no longer are they passive listeners, transcribing undigested information in their notebooks. "The role of the problem-posing educator is to create, together with the students, the conditions under which knowledge at the level of *doxa* is superseded by true knowledge at the level of the *logos*."[13]

Students and Literacy

In regard to students, I would like to introduce the following considerations: cognitive style, neurological disorders, the socioeconomics of literacy, English as a second language, and the influence of television on literacy. The purpose of this discussion is to give parents and other constituencies a grasp of some of the most severe and interesting problems in literacy.

Cognitive Style

BRAIN FUNCTION: LEFT HEMISPHERE AND RIGHT HEMISPHERE

Modern work in brain function has caught the imagination of the public, to such an extent that talk about the "dark, intuitive" right hemisphere (RH) and the "logical, orderly" left hemisphere (LH) is common at cocktail parties. In drawing conclusions about brain function and literacy, however, we must be extremely cautious, realizing that in most people the LH is dominant but that in some, RH "rules." On the basis of what we know about the hemispheres, we can then hypothesize that cerebral organization will affect reading and writing.

LH and RH can be characterized by their typical features.[14] The LH is the language hemisphere (usually). LH brains are usually good at sequential thinking, logic, and mathematics; deductive; and good at establishing whole-part relationships. RH brains are good at recognizing gestalts; work with images; good at establishing part-whole relationships; and inductive.

The neurosurgeon and brain researcher J. E. Bogen has coined the most appropriate terms for the funcitoning of LH and RH.

The LH, he says, is *propositional,* and the RH is *appositional.* Bogen somewhat cautiously generalizes that "simultaneous patterns rather than sequential order distinguish appositionality from propositionality."[15]

It is common in writing classes to find two almost diametrically opposed styles. One is well organized, but highly general, never getting down to specific cases or examples. We might call this type of writing propositional, for ideas follow one another in a perfectly logical sequence, and we can perceive the structure of the text. The other is concrete and specific, but chaotic. Often such writing has no apparent central topic, and ideas, images, and examples are put side by side with no apparent sequence or logical connection. Again calling on Bogen's terms, we might call this second type appositional. Whether or not these writing styles come about because of cerebral organization, they correlate amazingly well with what we know about brain function.

Some years ago, I ran across examples of writings by schizophrenics that illustrate my point clearly.[16]

Propositional
The subterfuge and the mistaken planned substitutions for that demanded American action can produce nothing but the general results of negative contention and the impractical results of misplacement, of mistaken purpose and unrighteous position, the impractical service-abilities of unnecessary contradictions. For answers to this dilemma, consult Webster.

Appositional
I hope to be home soon, very soon. I fancy chocolate eclairs, Doenuts. I want some doenuts, I do want some golden syrup or treacle, jam. . . . See the Committee about me coming home for Easter my twenty-fourth birthday. I hope all is well at home, how is Father getting on. Never mind there is hope, heaven will come, time heals all wounds, Rise again Glorious Greece and come to Hindoo Heavens, the Indian Heavens. The Dear old times will come back. We shall see Heaven and Glory yet, come everlasting life. I want a new writing pad of note paper.

"Normal" students write papers that are only a bit less pronounced in the propositionality or appositionality than the two examples just given.

When a teacher asks highly propositional writers to give examples, be specific, and stop generalizing, that teacher is not asking the students to learn a "skill" but actually to change their mode of cognition, and this is clearly a major undertaking. When a teacher tells appositional students to get a topic or thesis and then organize the writing around that thesis, the teacher is suggesting not only that the students restructure their paper, but that they restructure their thought process.

Perhaps the appositionalist needs carefully structured writing assignments that help him or her gain the genre knowledge needed in order to develop a thesis logically. And intense and extensive exposure to the most concrete and imagistic of writing might help the propositionalist. One way of viewing the situation is this: the appositionalist needs the propositionalist's strategies and vice versa.

Field Dependence and Independence

Professor James D. Williams of the University of North Carolina and I did a study of field dependence and independence as they correlate with the writing abilities of students in grades 6, 9, 10, and 12. Field dependence is the ability to decontextualize or, more simply put, to discover a pattern that is embedded in a larger pattern, as in Figure 13. Many of us have seen pictures of a Dalmation embedded in the dappling of a forest. Field dependents find it difficult if not impossible to see the Dalmation. Those who are field dependent cannot readily find one specific geometric figure that is embedded in a larger figure.

As will become obvious, we might as well substitute the term "remedial writer" for "field-dependent writer," because in defining the characteristics of field-dependent writing we are providing a penetrating characterization of remedial or basic writing in general.

On the basis of the Group Embedded Figures Test—a very reliable instrument we administered to some 300 subjects—we found that nearly two-thirds of all secondary students are field dependent and that this cognitive style has consequences for writing (and for reading, although our study did not investigate reading ability). Specifically, a group of trained readers were able, with great reliability, to identify the writing of field-dependent and independent students. Clearly, a large percentage of the remedial students in writing (and reading) classes are field dependent.

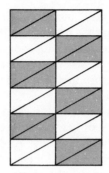

Find simple form "E"

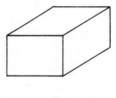

E

Figure 13.

The expository essays of field-dependent students can be characterized as follows:

1. They lack contextualization. That is, the writers do not identify
   their topic explicitly, do not provide background information,
   and do not construct an audience.
2. Their argument is "appositional"; that is, it is characterized by
   a series of claims without warrants or evidence.
3. The writing is both incohesive and incoherent, characterized by
   severe segmentation (that is, each part is discrete, lacks flow,
   and is only generally related to the topic).

4. The exposition collapses into expressive discourse characterized by simple sense impressions.

The characteristics of field-dependent personal-experience narratives are as follows:

1. They are incohesive and incoherent, marked by severe segmentation and lacking flow.
2. The writing is appositional in the sense that the writer remains on one level of abstraction, generally failing to become specific.
3. The writing is imagistic and/or impressionistic, dominated by simple sense impressions.
4. A moral may dominate the conclusion of the response.

The fact that large numbers of students are highly field dependent is interesting, but not the main concern of this discussion. From the work that Williams and I have done, we can map out the needs of a large percentage of secondary student writers, the most compelling of which relate to the following:

1. Contextualization (the ability to develop a topic and to supply appropriate background information for a target audience).
2. The development of arguments (providing both detail and warrants).
3. Cohesion or flow.
4. Coherence (a discernable structure based on a main point).
5. Tone and authorial "distance."
6. Writing mechanics (in most cases).

For each of these features of field-dependent writing, there are steps that educators can take to improve writing instruction. With regard to contextualization, instruction should focus on the gists of readings, encouraging students to find main points and to sum up readings in their own words. Collaterally, students should develop "topics" and discuss what would be needed to make them credible to readers. Exercises in contextualization, then, focus on gists and details that develop these gists. With regard to the development of arguments, students need to learn to supply evidence for assertions and to explain how that evidence applies to the assertions.

Cohesion or flow is really a wide-open question. I hypothesize that cohesion will take care of itself as students become skilled at structuring exposition, narrative, and argument. And presumably work with contextualization and the development of argument will bring about coherence. I have not yet determined whether work with logical forms (e.g., syllogisms and sorites) translates into more coherent writing.

In the following appositional essay, written in one class period by a field-dependent student, the argument becomes a narrative and the writer fails to provide reasons for his thesis that students should not be allowed to chew gum on campus:

> Do you think there should be gum? I don't think there should be gum because the people could do bad things with it.
>
> I don't think there should be gum in schools because if someone was chewing gum in a class and the teacher was trying to explain an assignment and he was chomping away and the teacher said "Spit it outside in the garbage." So the kid goes outside and spits it out and he missed. So he says, "Oops, I missed." And he doesn't want to pick up that slimy piece of gum so he leaves it there.
>
> Then, after the period the teacher walks out of the class for lunch and he steps on the gum. He gets more made [*sic*] and then when you come in after lunch he gives you megga homework and you say, "What's this for," so he gives you more homework. And who wants a mad teacher who gives a lot of homework. Don't chew gum in school. Please!

Next, in contrast, is an in-class essay by a field-independent student. Note how this writer states a thesis and then marshalls arguments in its behalf. (This essay, like the first one, is transcribed just as the student wrote it, with mechanical and spelling errors intact.)

> Upon entering high school students are faced with several decisions of a personal level which they must make. Among these decisions is whether or not to smoke. There is much pressure put upon the adolescences by their peers to "light up" with most parents having the opposite views. Caught in the middle of this heated battle are the schools. A recent proposition made by the schools is to set aside an area for smoking on the schoolgrounds. Does this mean the school is condoning smoking? Yes, to a very large degree it does. If the students are given this area to use for smoking more students will begin "lighting up."

There is no useful reason for such an area, and much to the dismay of many parents this proposition may someday come into affect.

With the awareness of the cancer-causing affects of the cigarettes the schools should be condeming their use. On each package reads a warning label to warn off that person from using the harmful product yet millions of teenagers, and adults alike are still smoking. Doctors warn of serious results from smoking such as lung cancer, deadening of the cilia that line the throat, and several others as well. Yet, still we keep smoking. If areas are set aside in our schools we are leading our children into an addiction from which some may never return. The cons far outweight the pro's in the situation especially those from a medical stand point.

The future of these smoking teenagers is a factor as well. Studies have shown that smoking takes as much as five years off the life of a smoker, and that of those who begun smoking in their teens fewer were able to quit. Some of these students may die of cancer before attaining their goals, and take away the contributions they might have put forth.

Neurological Problems

Without doubt, some literacy problems result from either cerebral "miswiring" or lesions. It is the case that an apparently normal student—one who is bright, alert, a speaker of standard English, having all of the characteristics associated with literacy—may be unable to read or write proficiently because of, for instance, aphasia.

Table 4 gives an overview of the sorts of problems that characterize asphasia. Broca's aphasia, damage to the language areas in the frontal cortex, "impairs the mechanisms for organization and execution of language." Subjects with Broca's aphasia would, for example, use ungrammatical syntax, but would be able to comprehend perfectly well. In contrast, Wernicke's asphasia impairs comprehension. In conduction aphasia, "Damage to the pathways connecting the posterior and anterior areas for speech and language results in relatively intact comprehension and production but poor repetition."[17]

There is every reason to believe that some of the students who, at any level, have trouble acquiring literacy have neurological problems. Hence, we should be extremely cautious in assigning remediation and absolutely fearful about flunking anyone.

TABLE 4. Aphasic Syndromes and Symptomatology

Clinical Syndrome	Locus of Lesion	Speech Output	Written Output	Auditory Compensation	Reading Input
Broca's aphasia	Interior posterior frontal	Phonemic par-aphasias; agrammatic deletions; word order OK; meaning OK	Same as verbal	Limited under-standing of function words; otherwise OK	Same as auditory comprehension
Wernicke's aphasia	Superior mid- and posterior temporal	normal to jargon; word order may be normal to very impaired; meaning may be irrelevant, vague or non-sensical;	Same as verbal	Can distinguish speech from non-speech; auditory compre-hension is mildly to severely impaired	Impaired to degree of auditory comprehension
Conduction aphasia	Parietal operculum; arcuate fasc. and adjacent and deep cortex	Some phonemic paraphasias; word order OK; meaning is appropriate	Same as verbal	Normal to mildly affected	Normal to mildly affected
Isolation of the speech areas	Cortex surrounding F. Sylvius, the peri-Sylvian cortex	Normal if repeating	Severely impaired	Severely impaired but does process speech	Limited to severely impaired; no comprehension
Trans-cortical motor aphasia	Anterior or mesial frontal	Normal if repeating	Usually impaired	Normal range	Normal to limited
Trans-cortical sensory aphasia	Tempero-parietal surrounding F. Sylvius	Normal to jargon; may be very like Wernicke's pt	Usually impaired	Can distinguish syntactic errors but otherwise severely impaired	Usually impaired
Anomic amnestic aphasia	Posterior middle temporal; or, diffuse	Normal except for nouns which may be omitted, substituted or paraphrased	May be similar to speech output	Usually in normal range	Similar to auditory comprehension
Alexia Agraphia	Supra-marginal & Angular gyn	Usually in normal range	Severely impaired	Usually in normal range	Severely impaired
	Note: Alexia may occur without agraphia (lesion of CC and LH's visual cortex)				
Word deafness	Between auditory cortex & superior temporal gyrus	Usually in normal range	Usually in normal range	Hearing is OK but severe impairment of speech comprehension	Usually in normal range

Source: Daniel Bub and Harry A. Whitaker, "Language and Verbal Processes," in *The Brain and Psychology,* ed. M. C. Wittrock (New York: Academic Press, 1980), pp. 214–15.

Spontaneity of Speaking and Writing	Grammatical Words (Functors)	Fluency	Lexical (Content) Words	Repetition
Severely impaired, hesitant with frequent pauses	Usually missing with some errors in usage	Mildly to severely impaired	Usually present	Limited as in speech output
Normal range but often repetitious, stereotyped	Present but often in-appropriate or erroneous	Normal to hyperfluent	indefinite, nonspecific nouns; usually paraphasias and often jargon	Impaired to the degree of auditory comprehension
Mildly impaired to near-normal	Occasionally missing to frequently missing	Mildly to moderately impaired	Usually present	Severely impaired with frequent paraphasias
Severely impaired to absent	Present when repeating	Normal when repeating	Present when repeating	Echolalic with completion and correction or minor errors
Severely impaired	Usually present	Normal when repeating	Present	Normal range
Normal range	Usually present	Normal range	Similar to Wernicke's pt.; indefinite nouns with paraphasias and some jargon	Normal range
Normal range	Usually present	Normal range except blocking on nouns	Nouns usually missing, with occasional circumlocutions	Usually normal range
Speaking is normal; writing is often inhibited	Present in speech output	Normal speech range	Present in speech output	Normal range
Normal range	Present	Normal range	Present	Severely impaired

Socioeconomics and Literacy

One hardly needs a sheaf of statistics to prove that illiteracy corre-
lates with poverty; within a population, a low level of literacy
usually means low socioeconomic status. However, some of the
implications of this fact are well worth thinking about.

The British sociolinguist Basil Bernstein has studied the relationship of social class to language for a number of years. In 1954 he
began to teach in the London City Day College; his pupils were
messenger boys released from their post office duties for one day a
week to attend classes. He found these youths unable to follow or
participate in discussions; obviously, they had language difficulties.

It is important to stress that Bernstein did not and never has
claimed that his students lacked intelligence or were somehow
genetically inferior to their middle-class, literate fellows. In fact,
Berstein's work tended to support the thesis that language deficits,
not lack of intelligence, were reflected in low scores on literacy-
based IQ tests.

Berstein's great contribution was his theory of *codes* related to
social classes. Lower-class people—the messenger boys, for
example—were limited to a "restricted" code, a use of language
that affirms shared values, that is comprehensible and effective
with members of the group, and that relies on a shared sense of
culture and scene for its meaning. The restricted code is, in a
sense, in-group language, and we all use it upon occasion, talking
in ways that would be puzzling to "outsiders." The point that
Bernstein makes is that upper-class people, in general, have access to an "elaborated" code, language use that does not rely on
context or the in-group solidarity of shared values and culture.
This code, Berstein says,

> will facilitate the verbal transmission and elaboration of the individual's
> unique experience. The condition of the listener, unlike that in the case
> of the restricted code, will *not* be taken for granted, as the speaker is
> likely to modify his speech in the light of the special considerations and
> attributes of the listener. . . . If a restricted code facilitates the construc-
> tion and exchange of communalized symbols, then an elaborated code
> facilitates the verbal construction and exchange of individualized or
> personal symbols.[18]

The elaborated code is necessary in writing about any subject for
unknown readers. Elaboration consists, as a matter of fact, largely

in contextualization—that is, supplying the background information that the reader needs in order to grasp the writer's intention and point.

Extrapolating from Bernstein's work, we can speculate about why the lower-class people he studied had not acquired the elaborated code. Notice that the restricted code stays "at home," is comfortable in a familiar environment, and does not aspire to the "larger world." One might say that the restricted code is the language of the neighborhood, if one takes "neighborhood" as a metaphor. The elaborated code transcends the neighborhood and functions in the academy, in places of government, in managerial offices, and in the media. If one does not aspire to leave the "neighborhood"—or, finally, believe that moving outward and "upward" is possible—there is no particular reason to acquire a new code. Thus, the failure in language education reflects the failure of society at large to fulfill its promise that everyone can move upward socially and economically.

In a study of literacy among mill workers in the Piedmont of the Carolinas, Shirley Brice Heath[19] gathered data that supports Bernstein's distinction between restricted and elaborated codes, although we might switch the terminology and, following a suggestion by Richard Fliegel,[20] speak of local and "collegiate" literacy—that is, the sort of literacy that allows one to function in the larger educated community.

In "Trackton," Heath found that people do read, but only a limited range of texts: schoolbooks, Sunday school books, and the Bible. The writing that takes place in "Roadville" consists of brief formulaic letters. As Fliegel argues, the residents of Roadville and Trackton carry the norms of oral culture into their literacy, and we can assume that anyone desiring to move outward and "upward" from the two communities to the orientation associated with literate culture would attempt to gain collegiate literacy, which, as Fliegel says, "regulates the conventions of most expository prose."

Edwin J. Delattre speaks of the *insiders,* who "have the power to learn their way about and to gain access to the meaning and significance of ideas and events. The outsiders are eternally strangers to such meaning."[21] In spite of the elitist overtones of the statement, the fact is that collegiate literacy is absolutely necessary for participation in the world of ideas, but it is of course not necessary to attend college to gain collegiate literacy.

In a sense, the expository essay can stand as the prototypical example of collegiate literacy, and this essay

> has a rhetorical purpose beyond "conveying information"; it attempts to convince the reader that its model of experience or the world is valid. It does not seek to engage the reader in a course of action, however, but rather in a process of reflection, and its means of convincing are accordingly limited to the use of evidence and logical proof and the posture of open-mindedness. These methods are also associated with the liberally educated person, who is meditative, reflective, clear-headed, unbiased, always seeking to understand experience freshly and to find things of interest in the world.[22]

English as a Second Language

The Los Angeles Unified School District is not typical, but in its ethnic mix it is nonetheless an excellent example of the English-as-a-second-language "problem." Of the 574,000 students in the district, 159,260 were in bilingual education programs as of February 1987, and of these, 143,546 were native speakers of Spanish. Regardless of how one feels about legislation now pending to make English the official language of California and other such moves to give one language official and legal status, no one would argue that these youngsters should not, by the most effective means available, master English in order to function effectively in American society. Table 5 is worth pondering, for its reflects not only the language diversity, but also the cultural diversity in one large urban school district.

The issue is not *whether* students should be able to speak, read, and write English, but *how* best to give them that ability. In the following discussion, I rely heavily on the work of my colleague Stephen Krashen, who states the issue succinctly: "We teach language best when we use it for what it was designed for: communication."[23] In other words, we should begin with a heavy quotient of skepticism about drills and dry runs.

In the third chapter we distinguished between unconscious acquisition of language and conscious drill. Acquisition comes about when the learner—whether a child gaining a first language or an adult gaining a second language—is immersed in a language environment, hearing the language spoken, attempting to make himself or

TABLE 5. Primary Languages among Students with Limited English Proficiency in the Los Angeles Unified School District

Language	Elementary	Secondary	Special Education	Total
Afghan	8	30	1	39
Afrikaans	2			2
American Indian				
Cherokee	1			1
Hopi	1			1
Navajo	2			2
Amharic	14	20		34
Arabic	193	116	13	322
Armenian	438	362	41	841
Assyrian	28	20	2	50
Basque		3		3
Bengali	14	4		18
Bulgarian	6	5		11
Burmese	12	10		22
Ceylonese	4	2		6
Chinese				
Cantonese	1,607	772	36	2,415
Mandarin	134	136	4	274
Taiwanese	57	59	5	121
Toishanese	46	20		66
Other Chinese	310	186	15	511
Creole	3	21	1	25
Croatian	6	3	2	11
Czech	10	7		17
Danish	1	2		3
Dutch		2		2
Farsi	519	453	27	999
Finnish	3		1	4
French	50	28	5	83
German	19	13	2	34
Greek	18	5		23
Guamanian	2			2
Gujarati	3	32	2	37
Haitian Creole		2		2
Hawaiian	3			3
Hebrew	229	173	5	407
Hindi	59	28	7	94
Hmong	6			6
Hungarian	41	13	2	56
Ibo		2		2
Icelandic	1	1		2
Indonesian	34	22	1	57
Italian	32	16	11	59

TABLE 5. (Continued)

Language	Elementary	Secondary	Special Education	Total
Japanese	63	92	11	166
Javanese	2			2
Khmer	624	331	12	967
Korean	1,745	1,206	38	2,989
Kurdish	2			2
Lao	61	51	4	116
Latvian	1			1
Lithuanian	1		1	2
Malay	14	2	1	17
Melanesian	6	2		8
Nepali	1			1
Norwegian	6			6
Punjabi	39	26	1	66
Pashto	10	10		20
Philippine				
Ilocano	31	12	2	45
Pilipino	868	491	48	1,407
Visayan	9	5		14
Polish	47	17		64
Portuguese	33	29		62
Romanian	61	31	4	96
Romany	2	1		3
Russian	70	36	3	109
Samoan	102	19	2	123
Serbian	3	1		4
Serbo-Croatian	8	3	2	13
Sinhalese	4	4		8
Slovak	3	1		4
Spanish	108,355	31,035	4,156	143,546
Swahili		2		2
Swedish	9	2		11
Thai	192	153	4	349
Tibetan	1			1
Tongon	18	9	1	28
Turkish	16	3	1	20
Urdu	56	22	2	80
Vietnamese	1,008	827	42	1,877
Yoruba	4	3		7
Yiddish	1			1
Other	60	22	2	84
Total	117,704	37,035	4,521	159,260

Note: Based on elementary, secondary, and special education bilingual program surveys (forms 20, 21, and 23), February 1987.
Source: Los Angeles *Times,* 10 February 1988, part 1, p. 3.

herself understood in it, and receiving feedback to these attempts. A useful simplification is input–output–feedback, with no conscious learning of rules or paradigms. On the basis of the language experience, the learner develops a reservoir of competence.

However, one can consciously learn rules to monitor one's output. A simple example is "i before e except after c." We have termed this conscious rule-learning and its attendant practice *drill*. As in learning a first language and learning to write, the problems of second-language learning center around acquisition and drill.

Common sense and our own experience, backed up by convincing research, define the usefulness and limitations of drill knowledge for second-language learners. As we have seen, the two main considerations are time and attention. Language users cannot pay attention both to the meanings they want to convey and the surface forms in which those meanings will be expressed. For example, a person learning German cannot attempt to use definite articles correctly and at the same time carry on a conversation, unless the utterances of the exchange are formulas that she or he has memorized. If, however, the language learner has time, as is the case with most writing, she or he can divert attention from semantic intention to surface form (grammar and sentence structure) to regularize the language.

Before the learner can apply rules, however, she or he must understand them, and it turns out that most grammatical rules are furiously complex. For example, relative clauses are common in language, and the ability to use them is essential for the learner. Here are examples of relative clauses:

The girl *who delivers our newspaper* greeted me.
The girl, *who delivers our newpaper,* greeted me.
The girl *whom I saw* delivers our newspaper.
The girl *that I saw* delivers our newspaper.
The girl *I saw* delivers our newspaper.

To state the rules for just this limited fragment of English grammar is a formidable undertaking, and to learn those rules consciously is an even more herculean enterprise; *acquiring* the necessary rules is much easier and more effective.

Some rule systems are relatively simple and useful to the learner: for example, "in German all nouns are capitalized." This rule solves multiple problems for the learner of written German. In English the rules of capitalization are not very much more complicated and are easily learned. At a slightly more complex level, non-native speakers can, through drill, master "tag questions": . . . am I not? . . . aren't you? . . . isn't he/she/it? . . . aren't we? . . . aren't they? (The French and German equivalents are the invariant forms *n'est ce pas?* and *nicht wahr?*)

It may be that drill in the forms of irregular verbs is also useful to most learners of English as a second language: ring, rang, rung; think, thought, thought; drive, drove, driven. However, it is unreasonable to believe that drill—consciously working with paradigms and learning rules—will carry one very far in gaining a second language.

In Chapter 7, we discussed the relationship between a "writing workshop," in which students had the chance to develop their ideas, and a "skills laboratory," in which they learned some of the rules concerning edited standard English. This split in kinds of instruction seems to be optimal also for second-language learning, and we will talk about that shortly when we turn to instructional scenes. Right now, however, we must turn to what probably seems obvious: the importance of attitude.

The good language learner is motivated and is not defensive. It is virtually a truism in linguistic circles that motivation for language learning is *integrative* or *instrumental,* or both. The learner who is integratively motivated wants to join a language community—to communicate with its members, to talk like they do, to join the society. Thus, people lose their native dialects and acquire new ones, learn the niceties of edited standard English, and acquire second languages. The instrumentally motivated learner has normally a specific reason for learning a language: a physicist wants access to Russian journals in his field, a banker decides to expand her operations to Japan and must speak the language to do so, a student must pass a foreign language test as a requirement for an advanced degree.

Undoubtedly there are some people who learn second and third languages merely for the pleasure of doing do, but by and large, people gain languages other than those they were born to for integrative or instrumental reasons. Furthermore, without those reasons, people are not very successful at learning second lan-

guages, for in this instance attitude is more important than aptitude.[24] This takes us back to the beginning of this chapter, where
we discussed language learning in its sociopolitical terms. If the
130,500 Spanish-speaking students in the schools of Los Angeles
do not value the educated Anglo culture into which mastery of
English—spoken and written—would admit them, they lack integrative motivation; and if they distrust the promises of economic
advancement through language skills, they have little motivation
for learning. Thus, we can see that the problems of English as a
second language are not strictly school-related, but actually stem
from the larger society in which the school is located. In the business of language instruction and learning, the stick is useless, and
the carrot cannot be plastic; it must be real, juicy, and fresh from
the garden.

If students *want* to learn a second language (or second dialect), a
school class can be useful. In the first palce, learners need comprehensible input. In conversation they must understand, at least partially, what is being saaid, and when they begin to read in the second
language, they cannot start with the most abstruse books. (I remember the usefulness and pleasure of reading comic strips in my college
French class.) Furthermore, students can begin, through drill, to
learn some useful rules that they can apply, particularly in writing.

The point is simply that the second-language class should be an
acquisition environment in which the students are motivated and
have teachers who focus almost always on semantic intention, not
surface form. The students need to receive plenty of comprehensible input (written or spoken), have ample chance to attempt to
express their meanings (in writing or speech), and be unafraid to
make the errors through which they can learn.

Television and Literacy

Estimates of the amount of time youngsters spend watching television vary, but A. C. Nielsen surveys for 1986 report the following
number of viewing hours and minutes per week: teenage females,
20:33; teenage males, 22:38; children 2–5 years old, 28:06; children 6–11 years old, 23:31.[25] In any case, children, teenagers, and
adults devote much of their life to the tube, and every hour in front
of the TV is time that could be spent in conversation, with a

book—or on the tennis court, in the swimming pool, on the slopes, or at the beach, for that matter.

The skills needed to process information from a television drama or newscast and from a book are radically different. Presumably it is much easier to learn to "read" the screen than a page. However, if we think about "higher level" processes in reading, the differences between tube and page begin to disappear.

In a most illuminating essay, Gavriel Salomon discusses "Television Literacy and Television vs. Literacy."[26] Let us assume, he says, that

> the comprehension of tv entails three sequential phases: (1) mentally recoding (or deciphering) a coded message into a parallel mental representation (for example, identifying objects in a picture or reading the sounds of printed letters and generating a meaningful word from them); (2) chunking or integrating these components into meaningful units; and (3) elaborating the material to make inferences, new attributions, new associations, new questions, and so on.[27]

The first phase would require radically different skills for "decoding" images on the screen and graphemes on a page. "Rice and Houston observe that prior to mastering the first phase of tv comprehension, young children are very attentive to salient features—e.g., fast pace, sudden changes in tempo, camera techniques—without putting such features into a context"[28]—very much as young children are aware of the page design, colors, and so on, without being able to extract meaning from the print.

In the second phase, children begin to "chunk"—i.e, to see significant parts as they relate to wholes. In this phase, youngsters begin to acquire the genre knowledge that enables them to follow a story, to integrate images, but this ability, Salomon surmises, has little to do with television per se and much to do with general cognitive development.

The third phase might be called "critical reading," which "is influenced not by the symbolic nature of the original message but by such factors as content, the task to be performed on it, one's expectations, previous knowledge, and mastery of general elaboration skills."[29]

Intelligent reading and intelligent viewing apparently demand the same kinds of mental abilities. Furthermore, television has no corner on the trash market, as investigation of the news rack in any supermarket will verify. Salomon argues that the uncritical, sponge-like absorption of television programming is a matter of habit, not the necessary result of viewing. Students can be taught to apply critical thinking to television and that such practice will benefit their reading and writing.

> There seems to be no reason to fear that tv skills, cultivated by the continuous practice of televiewing, will interfere with the development of skills needed for reading and writing. There is more reason to be concerned that more general abilities are not being practiced while watching tv. Thus there is a growing need to tutor and coach youngsters to invest more (rather than less) mental effort in tv by applying to its programs the same general skills we urge them to apply to print material. By so doing, we can help them to perceive tv as less "shallow" and thus witness the cultivation of skills that, as Tidhar's research shows, are transferable to non-tv domains.[30]

Evaluating Reading and Writing Programs

What should one expect to find in a reading or writing class? What sorts of activities are likely to be productive, and which ones are probably ineffective or counterproductive?

The following questions, which evolved from the eight chapters of this book, are a guide to evaluating reading and writing instruction. The answer to each of the questions should be "yes."

Attitudes Toward Literacy

1. Does the definition of literacy, whether stated or tacit, include the use of reading and writing for (a) the "practical" purpose of surviving or even flourishing in the American socioeconomic system; (b) intellectual and cultural development; and (c) personal expression, pleasure, and growth as a feeling, caring human?

The definition of literacy or the attitude toward literacy that prevails in an institution ultimately will determine the opportunities for reading and writing provided to students. A minimalist definition (e.g., the ability to read everyday documents such as business letters and to do everyday writing tasks such as filling out forms) will shift resources and energy away from more ambitious goals for students. A practical definition (e.g., the ability to use reading and writing in the competitive world of business) will shift emphasis away from literacy as a source of pleasure and personal growth.

2. Do those involved with the learner respect his or her culture and try to understand it?

Paulo Freire distinguishes between the educator as extension agent, bringing culture and knowledge to the primitives but remaining aloof from their culture, and the communicator, who enters into a respectful and loving dialogue with those he would try to educate.

3. Do those involved with the learner respect his or her native (spoken) dialect?

To repudiate or belittle a student's dialect is to condemn his or her family and culture. When students are ready to become members of the culture represented by school, they will change their dialects, but until that time, insistence that they talk differently is futile and alientating.

4. Do teachers view texts as systems of cues that allow readers to (re)construct meanings, not as repositories of one determinate and invariant meaning?

The view that one meaning is buried in the text and can be dug out by the diligent reader leads to authoritarianism on the part of the teacher and demoralization of the students, who become convinced that they can never be as successful in finding meanings as the teacher. The view that readers use texts to (re)construct meaning makes interpretation a social process, in which one reader enters into dialogue with others to reach agreement on an interpretation of the text.

Learning

5. Can the program of the class be characterized as one that encourages acquisition rather than drill?

Instruction in reading based on acquisition would emphasize pleasure reading and reading for meaning; there would be much discussion of texts. Instruction in writing would be characterized by a great deal of feedback: peer group discussions of the student writings, individual and group conferences with the instructor, written comments from the instructor. The focus would be on the semantic intention that the writer is attempting to convey to readers. Very little drill would take place.

6. Do teachers generally respond to semantic intention, not to form?

A reading teacher would ask, "What do you think the author of this text wanted it to do? What semantic intention do you think the author was attempting to convey?" In light of these master questions, matters of form gain meaning. Discussions of form, including organization and error, are always in the context of what the author of the text apparently wants to accomplish.

Reading

7. Does instruction emphasize reading for meaning, making all other goals subsidiary to this one?

We read for meaning, not for sounds (phonics) and not to learn to read. Any text designed only to teach subskills such as phonics or intended merely to give students practice in reading will, by and large, defeat its own purpose. Thus, many grade-school reading texts are suspect, as their purpose is not to inform or entertain but to teach skills. In high school and college, texts that are chosen simply to acquaint students with forms (e.g., the research paper, the familiar essay, the report) are likely to be ineffective.

8. Do teachers use phonics and whole-word recognition sparingly and wisely, not as extensive drills?

9. In grade school particularly, do teachers emphasize reading as its own reward, not as a means to gain extrinsic rewards such as candy, money, or grades?

10. Particularly in high school and college, does instruction emphasize critical reading?

11. Is the program flexible, unbound by a rigid syllabus based on a concept of the cultural heritage or cultural literacy?

Through reading, students gain access to literate cultures. However, particularly in grade school and high school, a reading program that is rigidly structured around a set of "great books" is likely to be a failure. Students must perceive themselves as participants in the culture-making process, not as passive recipients of a predetermined cultural agenda.

12. Does the program offer plenty of remedial help—without ghettoizing remedial students?

Insofar as possible, remedial students should be "mainstreamed," gaining remedial help with the regular class. Of course, such a procedure demands great flexibility in the program and a reasonably favorable teacher-student ratio.

Writing

13. Does instruction focus on semantic intention, not on error—on content, not form?

The master question that teachers ask, especially in high school and college, is this: "What do you want this writing to *do?* What semantic intention are you trying to convey?" If form detracts from the writer's purpose, then a discussion of formal matters is meaningful.

14. Particularly in high school, but also in college, are students given the opportunity to do a wide variety of writing, ranging from personal, expressive texts to public forms such as reports?

Various sorts of writing—a short story, a personal essay, a report on a field trip, an argument in favor of some cause—create different problems for the writer, in subject matter, organization, audience, and so on. Encouraging students to write in various genres with a wide range of purposes gives them versatility and lets them experience the whole spectrum of uses for writing.

15. At all levels, is instruction permeated with the sense of audience, of writing a text for some reader or group of readers other than the teacher?

Writing a variety of kinds of texts for a whole range of purposes foregrounds the problems of audience. A letter to the school newspaper is aimed at fellow students; a proposal for some improvement in facilities or curriculum is aimed at the institution's administration; a letter to the editor of the local newspaper is intended for a generally educated audience. Writing classes in which the only reader is the teacher cheat students of perhaps the most valuable lesson in writing: adjusting the text so that it will "get through" to the intended readers.

16. At all levels, is drill minimal?

17. Does the program include individualized remedial instruction?

Remedial instruction in writing is pretty much limited to "mechanics" (punctuation, verb agreement, pronoun reference, etc.). Such instruction should be given on an individualized basis and should be sharply differentiated from the kinds of activities that go on in the writing classroom, where students learn to discover and develop ideas, to organize their ideas effectively, to make their texts interesting for the intended readers, and so on.

18. Are the writings of the students frequently published?

Publication includes photostats of a piece of writing, copies to be given to each member of the class and to serve as the basis for discussion; pieces assembled into class magazines or anthologies; writings printed in school and local newspapers; and writings intended for given publications even though they are not accepted or perhaps even submitted.

19. Do students receive rich responses to their writings?

Students learn to write not through rules and drills but through producing texts and receiving responses to the apparent purposes (semantic intentions) of those texts. Some forms of response are (a) class discussions of given student writings, (b) small-group discussions among peers, (c) individual conferences with the instructor, group conferences with the instructor, and (d) written comments on the text by the instructor.

Coda: The Paradoxes of Literacy

The first paradox is that everyone is an expert on literacy. One person believes passionately that he learned to read through phonics drills in the first grade, and another has the unshakable faith that grammar lessons in high school were the necessary basis for her ability to write. A large percentage of literate people tacitly hold that the potential for reading is virtually a genetic endowment of all human beings, but that the ability to write in any broad sense is an inborn gift like perfect pitch, not to be developed by the unchosen even through years of studying grammar. This universal expertise creates sundry problems for professionals concerned with reading and writing, for the laity claim authority and hence the moral and intellectual right to determine how reading and writing will be taught and to whom and when.

One evening a few years ago when my wife and I were at dinner with friends, a couple who are both graduates of the most prestigious universities and who are omnivorous readers and excellent writers, the conversation got around to literacy. The woman averred that she had not really known how to write until she studied French in college: to learn French grammar, she was forced to learn English grammar, and through that study she achieved the ability to write. A comment on this representative anecdote makes the obvious more so: my friend equated writing effectively only with the ability to produce edited standard English, and she unwittingly expressed her belief that one learns grammar only through conscious study and drill. Our conversation that night did nothing to shake her beliefs, and they are not, of course, absolutely wrong. For most readers, lapses from the norms of edited standard English undermine the effectiveness of a text, and, as we have seen, certain of the "grammatical" or mechanical features of that written "dialect" can be learned consciously through drill.

The second paradox, closely related to the first, is the assumption that reading and writing are unrelated to thinking. A school board member once said to me and a group of my colleagues, "Teach the children to write, but leave their minds alone!" If reading and writing were simply skills—the proper eye movement, the ability to make the sound-letter connection, orthography, punctuation—we could teach children to read and write without disturbing their minds, but an insistent motif of this book has been the idea that literacy affects minds along multiple axes. The ability to read and write enables a person to think in ways that are impossible without literacy and also inevitably brings about changes in values and attitudes. Teachers of reading and writing cannot leave their students' minds alone.

The third paradox is the belief that literacy can be isolated from culture. Study after study has shown—and common sense should affirm—that literate homes create literate children and that literate societies create literate homes. It would seem, then, that both literacy and illiteracy are self-perpetuating. Literacy comes about when societies change as they did in Cuba and Nicaragua or when individuals gain the will to change their cultures. The challenge in our capitalistic democracy is convincing the have-nots, who in general are the illiterate or marginally literate, that the American dream is real, attainable, and worthwhile. A drive through the slums of any American city is enough to convince reasonable people that we have been largely unsuccessful in the pedagogy of the oppressed. Are we asking the literacy have-nots to cooperate in the unending process of recreating culture, or are we extending Kultur to them?

All literacy is cultural, and to attain literacy, one must be a maker of culture, not merely a partaker of Kultur.

Notes

1. The Consequences of Literacy

1. From Carlo Cipolla, *Literacy and Development in the West* (Harmondsworth, G. B.: Pelican, 1969), quoted in John Oxenham, *Literacy: Writing, Reading and Social Organisation* (London: Routledge and Kegan Paul, 1980), p. 68.
2. Selden Ramsay, *Education,* "Fifth Report of the National Council on Educational Research" (Washington, D.C.: NIE, fiscal years 1978–79), p. 32.
3. Ramsay, p. 32.
4. Defender, "St. Maarten's Jaycee Bryson Elected 'Jaycee of the World,' " Windward Islands *Newsday* 4, 491 (November 24, 1980), 12.
5. Ramsay, p. 32.
6. Oxenham, pp. 6–18.
7. I. J. Gelb, *A Study of Writing* (Chicago: University of Chicago Press, 1963), p. 140
8. Richard Fliegel, "The Codes of Literacy," unpublished Ph.D. thesis, University of Southern California, 1986.
9. Fliegel, pp. 103–4.
10. J. R. Clammer, *Literacy and Social Change* (Leiden, The Netherlands: E. J. Brill, 1976), p. 67, quoted in Sylvia Scribner and Michael Cole, *The Psychology of Literacy* (Cambridge, Mass.: Harvard University Press, 1981), p. 3.
11. E. A. Havelock, *Preface to Plato* (Cambridge, Mass.: Harvard University Press, 1963).
12. J. Goody and I. Watt, "The Consequences of Literacy," in *Literacy in Traditional Societies,* ed. J. Goody (New York: Cambridge University Press, 1968).
13. Jack Goody, *The Domestication of the Savage Mind* (Cambridge: Cambridge University Press, 1977), p. 12.
14. Goody, p. 13.
15. Scribner and Cole, p. 31.
16. Scribner and Cole, p. 242.
17. Walter J. Ong, S.J. *The Presence of the Word* (New Haven: Yale University Press, 1967).
18. Walter J. Ong, S.J., *Interfaces of the Word* (Ithaca: Cornell University Press, 1977), p. 18.
19. Ong, *Interfaces,* p. 18.

20. Goody, p. 28.
21. The following discussion is adapted from W. Ross Winterrowd, *Composition/ Rhetoric: A Synthesis* (Carbondale: Southern Illinois University Press, 1986), pp. 84–89.
22. Jonathan Culler, *Structuralist Poetics: Structuralism, Linguistics, and the Study of Literature* (Ithaca: Cornell University Press, 1975), p. 32
23. Jacques Derrida, *Writing and Difference,* trans. Alan Bass (Chicago: University of Chicago Press, 1976), p. 11.
24. Jacques Derrida, *Of Grammatology,* trans. Gayatri Chakravorty Spivak (Baltimore: Johns Hopkins University Press, 1974), p. 18.
25. Kenneth Burke, *The Philosophy of Literary Form,* rev. ed. (New York: Vintage, 1957), pp. 95–96.

2. How Language Works: Some Basic Concepts

1. Patrick Hartwell, "Grammar, Grammars, and the Teaching of Grammar," *College English* 47, 2 (Feb. 1985), 105–27.
2. John Simon, *Paradigms Lost* (New York: Clarkson N. Potter, 1980), p. xiv.
3. Patricia C. Nichols, "Creoles of the USA," *Language in the USA,* ed. Charles A. Ferguson and Shirley Brice Heath (Cambridge: Cambridge University Press, 1981), p. 82. To capture the "flavor" of the example, I have used my own spellings, not Labov's.
4. See Charles Fillmore, "The Case for Case," in *Universals in Linguistic Theory,* ed. Emmon Bach and Robert T. Harms (New York: Holt, Rinehart and Winston, 1968).
5. See J. L. Austin, *How to Do Things with Words* (Oxford: Oxford University Press, 1962), and John R. Searle, *Speech Acts: An Essay in the Philosophy of Language* (Cambridge: Cambridge University Press, 1975).
6. Quoted in Robert Pattison, *On Literacy* (New York: Oxford University Press, 1982), p. 14.
7. Quoted in Peter Farb, *Word Play* (New York: Bantam, 1975), pp. 109–10.
8. See William Labov, *The Study of Nonstandard English* (Urbana, Ill.: National Council of Teachers of English, 1970), pp. 51–56.
9. See H. P. Grice, William James Lectures, Harvard Universtiy, published in part as "Logic in Conversation," in *Syntax and Semantics,* ed. P. Cole and J. L. Morgan, vol. 3: *Speech Acts* (New York: Seminar Press, 1975).
10. Woody Allen, "Spring Bulletin," in *Getting Even* (New York: Random House, 1971), pp. 58–59.
11. James Boyd White, "The Invisible Discourse of the Law: Reflections on Legal Literacy and General Education," in *Literacy for Life,* ed. Richard W. Bailey and Robin Melanie Fosheim (New York: The Modern Language Association of America, 1983).
12. Adapted from W. Ross Winterrowd, *Composition/Rhetoric: A Synthesis* (Carbondale: Southern Illinois University Press, 1986), pp. 74–76.
13. Labov, p. 27.

3. Learning: First Language, Second Language

1. Adapted from Herbert H. Clark and Eve V. Clark, *Psychology and Language* (New York: Harcourt Brace Jovanovich, 1977), pp. 295–96.
2. See Roger Brown, *A First Language: The Early Stages* (Cambridge, Mass.: Harvard University Press, 1973).
3. This is John Searle's classification, cited in Clark and Clark, p. 88.
4. Courtney B. Cazden, *Child, Language, and Education* (New York: Holt, Rinehart and Winston, 1972), p. 78.
5. Clark and Clark, pp. 322–26.
6. Regarding monitor theory, see Stephen D. Krashen, *Second Language Acquisition and Second Language Learning* (New York: Pergamon Press, 1981).

4. To Read

1. Deborah Tannen, "Oral and Literate Strategies in Spoken and Written Discourse," in *Literacy for Life,* ed. Richard W. Bailey and Robin Melanie Fosheim (New York: The Modern Language Association of America, 1983), p. 79.
2. Lewis Thomas, "Clever Animals," in *Late Night Thoughts on Listening to Mahler's Ninth Symphony* (New York: Bantam, 1984), p. 35.
3. Kenneth S. Goodman, "Reading: A Psycholinguistic Guessing Game," *Journal of the Reading Specialist* 6 (1967), 126–35.
4. Beverly McLoughland, "Creature," *Language Arts* 63, 5 (Sept. 1986), 481.
5. See Kenneth Burke, *A Grammar of Motives* (Berkeley and Los Angeles: University of California Press, 1969).
6. See, for example, Glenda L. Bissex, *GNYS AT WRK: A Child Learns to Write and Read* (Cambridge, Mass.: Harvard University Press, 1980); Don Holdaway, *The Foundations of Literacy* (Sydney, Australia: Ashton Scholastic, 1979), and Denny Taylor, *Family Literacy* (Exeter, N.H.: Heinemann Educational Books, 1983).
7. Bambi B. Schieffelin and Marilyn Cochran-Smith, "Learning to Read Culturally: Literacy Before Schooling," in *Awakening to Literacy,* ed. Hillel Goelman, Antoinette Oberg, and Frank Smith (Exeter, N.H.: Heinemann Educational Books, 1984).
8. Suzanne B. K. Scollon and Ron Scollon, "}RUN TRILOGY: Can Tommy Read?," in Goelman et al.
9. From W. Ross Winterowd, *Composition/Rhetoric: A Synthesis* (Carbondale: Southern Illinois University Press, 1986), pp. 70–71.
10. Insup Taylor and M. Martin Taylor, *The Psychology of Reading* (New York: Academic Press, 1983), pp. 121–39.
11. Adapted from Winterowd, *Composition/Rhetoric: A Synthesis,* pp. 50–51.
12. The following discussion of the cue system is adapted from my essay "The Three R's: Reading, Reading, and Rhetoric," in *Rhetoric and Change,* ed. William E. Tanner and J. Dean Bishop (Mesquite, Tex.: Ide House, 1982). The concept of the cue system derives from Kenneth S. Goodman, "Psy-

cholinguistic Universals in the Reading Process, in *Psycholinguistics and Reading,* ed. Frank Smith (New York: Holt, Rinehart and Winston, 1973).

13. Derrida's most central work is *Of Grammatology,* trans. Gayatri Chakravorty Spivak (Baltimore: Johns Hopkins University Press, 1974).

14. E. D. Hirsch, Jr., *Validity in Interpretation* (New Haven: Yale University Press, 1973).

15. Stanley Fish, *Is There a Text in This Class?* (Cambridge, Mass.: Harvard University Press, 1980).

16. Teun A. van Dijk, *Macrostructures: An Interdisciplinary Study of Global Structure in Discourse, Interaction, and Cognition* (Hillsdale, N.J.: Lawrence Erlbaum, 1980).

17. Paul Fussell, *Class* (New York: Ballantine, 1983), p. 5.

18. M. A. K. Halliday and Ruqaiya Hasan, *Cohesion in English* (Bath, G. B.: Longman, 1976).

19. Robert M. Gordon, "The Readability of an Unreadable Text," *The English Journal* 69, 3 (March 1980), 60–61.

20. Edgar Dale and Jeanne S. Chall, "A Formula for Predicting Readability," *Educational Research Bulletin* 27 (1948), 37–54, and Edward Fry, "A Readability Formula That Saves Time," *Journal of Reading* 11 (1968), 513–16, 575–81.

21. Adapted from W. Ross Winterowd, *The Contemporary Writer* (New York: Harcourt Brace Jovanovich, 1981), pp. 467–68.

22. Adapted from Winterowd, *Composition/Rhetoric: A Synthesis,* pp. 61–63.

5. To Learn to Read

1. Ralph W. Tyler, "Testing Writing: Procedures Vary with Purposes," in *Literacy for Life,* ed. Richard W. Bailey and Robin Melanie Fosheim (New York: The Modern Language Association of America, 1983), p. 198.

2. Paul A. Strassman, "Information Systems and Literacy," in Bailey and Fosheim, p. 116.

3. Glenda L. Bissex, *GNYS AT WRK: A Child Learns to Write and Read* (Cambridge, Mass.: Harvard University Press, 1980), pp. 3–33.

4. Insup Taylor and M. Martin Taylor, *The Psychology of Reading* (New York: Academic Press, 1983), pp. 353–55.

5. Carol Chomsky, "Write Now, Read Later," *Childhood Education* 47 (1971), 296–99, cited in Courtney B. Cazden, *Child, Language, and Education* (New York: Holt, Rinehart and Winston, 1972), p. 82.

6. E. W. Williams, "Teaching a Toddler to Teach Herself to Read," unpublished MA thesis, University of Texas at El Paso, 1980, cited in Taylor and Taylor, p. 355.

7. Taylor and Taylor, p. 385.

8. Taylor and Taylor, p. 396.

9. Frank Smith, *Understanding Reading,* 3rd ed. (New York: Holt, Rinehart and Winston, 1982), p. 188.

10. Taylor and Taylor, p. 399.

11. Taylor and Taylor, p. 400.
12. M. Rutter and W. Yule, "The Concept of Specific Reading Retardation," *Journal of Child Psychology and Psychiatry* 16 (1975), 181–97.
13. E. D. Hirsch, Jr., "Reading, Writing, and Cultural Literacy," in *Composition and Literature: Bridging the Gap,* ed. Winifred Bryan Horner (Chicago: Universtiy of Chicago Press, 1983), p. 146.
14. E. D. Hirsch, Jr., *Cultural Literacy* (Boston: Houghton Mifflin, 1988), p. 5
15. Hirsch, *Cultural Literacy,* pp. 127–33.
16. Hirsch, *Cultural Literacy,* p. 146.
17. Paulo Freire, *Pedagogy of the Oppressed,* trans. Myra Bergman Ramos (New York: Continuum, 1981), p. 67.
18. Hirsch, *Cultural Literacy,* p. 19.
19. Paulo Freire, *Education for Critical Consciousness* (New York: Continuum, 1982), p. 48.
20. Freire, *Education,* p. 49.

6. To Write

1. S. Pianko, "A Description of the Composing Process of College Freshman Writers," *Research in the Teaching of English* 13 (1979), 5–22.
2. L. Flower, "Writer-Based Prose: A Cognitive Basis for Problems in Writing," *College English* 41 (1979), 19–37.
3. David E. Simon, *IBM BASIC From the Ground Up* (Rochelle Park, N.J.: Hayden, 1983), pp. 63–64.
4. *IBM BASIC,* 2nd ed. (Boca Raton, Fla.: IBM, 1982), pp. 4–113.
5. *The World Almanac and Book of Facts 1988* (New York: Pharos Books, 1988), p. 175.
6. Quoted in James Boswell, *The Life of Samuel Johnson,* vol. 2 (London: J. M. Dent and Company, 1906), pp. 146–48.
7. Richard Lanham, *Literacy and the Survival of Humanism* (New Haven: Yale University Press, 1983), p. 8.
8. For an excellent, brief summary of empirical research on composition, see Stephen D. Krashen, *Writing: Research, Theory, and Applications* (New York: Pergamon Institute of English, 1984).
9. S. Wall and A. Petrovsky, "Freshman Writers and Revision: Results from a Survey," *Journal of Basic Writing* 3 (1981), 109–22.
10. Pianko, "A Description."
11. S. Perl, "The Composing Process of Unskilled College Writers," *Research in the Teaching of English* 13 (1979), 317–39.
12. Brian Cambourne, "Oral and Written Relationships: A Reading Perspective," in *Exploring Speaking/Writing Relationships,* ed. Barry M. Kroll and Roberta J. Vann (Urbana, Ill.: National Council of Teachers of English, 1981), pp. 91–92. Emphasis mine.
13. Mina P. Shaughnessy, *Errors and Expectations: A Guide for the Teacher of Basic Writing* (New York: Oxford University Press, 1977), p. 19.
14. Shaughnessy, p. 45.

15. Shaughnessy, p. 190.
16. Shaughnessy, pp. 7–8.
17. W. Ross Winterowd, "Composing: A Case Study," in *The Contemporary Writer,* 3rd ed. (Orlando, Fla.: Harcourt Brace Jovanovich, 1989), pp. 28–58.

7. To Learn to Write

1. Adapted from Elinor O[chs] Keenan, "Why Look at Unplanned and Planned Discourse," in *Discourse Across Time and Space,* Southern California Occasional Papers in Linguistics No. 5, ed. Elinor O[chs] Keenan and Tina L. Bennett (Los Angeles: University of Southern California, 1977), p. 17.
2. Keenan, pp. 16–38.
3. Keenan, p. 25.
4. Adapted from Keenan, p. 28.
5. Walter Loban, *Language Development: Kindergarten Through Grade Twelve* (Urbana, Ill.: National Council of Teachers of English, 1976).
6. John Dixon, *Growth through English* (Oxford: Oxford University Press for the National Association for the Teaching of English, 1967), p. 13.
7. Adapted from W. Ross Winterowd, *Composition/Rhetoric: A Synthesis* (Carbondale: Southern Illinois University Press, 1986), pp. 93–113.
8. For a classic study of the problem, see Mina P. Shaughnessy, *Errors and Expectations: A Guide for the Teacher of Basic Writing* (New York: Oxford University Press, 1977).
9. See George R. Hillocks, Jr., "The Interaction of Instruction, Teacher Comment, and Revision in the Composing Process," *Research in the Teaching of English* 16, 3 (1982), 261–78.
10. The discussion of the writing workshop and skills laboratory is adapted from W. Ross Winterowd, "Developing a Compostion Program," in *Reinventing the Rhetorical Tradition,* ed. Aviva Freedman and Ian Pringle (Conway, Ak.: L&S Books for the Canadian Council of Teachers of English, 1980).
11. Adapted from W. Ross Winterowd, *Composition/Rhetoric: A Synthesis,* pp. 98–113.
12. The following set of question is adapted from Richard Young, Alton L. Becker, and Kenneth L. Pike, *Rhetoric: Discovery and Change* (New York: Harcourt Brace Jovanovich, 1970), *passim.*
13. James L. Adams, *Conceptual Blockbusting: A Guide to Better Ideas,* 2nd ed. (New York: W. W. Norton, 1979), p. 11.
14. Adapted from Eugene Raudsepp with George P. Hough, Jr., *Creative Growth Games* (New York: Harcourt Brace Jovanovich, 1977), p. 26.
15. Raudsepp, pp. 27–28.
16. Adams, pp. 24–31.
17. D. N. Perkins, *The Mind's Best Work* (Cambridge, Mass.: Harvard University Press, 1981), p. 139.
18. Quoted in Brewster Ghiselin, ed., *The Creative Process* (New York: Mentor, 1952), p. 37.
19. Raudsepp, pp. 44–45.

8. The Student and the Schools

1. Paulo Freire, *Education for Critical Consciousness,* (New York: Continuum, 1982).

2. Freire, *Education,* p. 75.

3. Adapted from W. Ross Winterowd, "Literacy: *Kultur* and Culture," *Language Arts* 64 (1987), 869–74.

4. Paulo Freire, "Education as the Practice of Freedom," in *Education,* p. 47.

5. E. D. Hirsch, Jr., "Reading, Writing, and Cultural Literacy," in *Composition and Literature: Bridging the Gap,* ed. Winifred Bryan Horner (Chicago: University of Chicago Press, 1983), p. 146.

6. Paulo Freire, *Pedagogy of the Oppressed,* trans. Myra Bergman Ramos (New York: Continuum, 1981), p. 67.

7. Freire, *Pedagogy,* p. 72.

8. Freire, *Pedagogy,* p. 76. The following discussion is adapted from my essay "Black Holes, Indeterminacy, and Paulo Freire," *Rhetoric Review* 2, 1 (1983), 28–36.

9. Freire, *Pedagogy,* p. 111.

10. Freire, *Pedagogy,* pp. 85–86.

11. Freire, *Education,* p. 82.

12. Freire, *Education,* pp. 17–18.

13. Freire, *Pedagogy,* p. 68.

14. See, for example, Robert D. Nebes, "Man's So-Called 'Minor' Hemisphere," *UCLA Educator* 17 (Spring 1975), 9–12, and A. R. Luria, *The Working Brain: An Introduction to Neuropsychology* (New York: Basic Books, 1973). An excellent, brief overview is Jerre Levy, "Cerebral Asymmetry and the Psychology of Man," in *The Brain and Psychology,* ed. M. C. Wittrock (New York: Academic Press, 1980).

15. J. E. Bogen, "Some Educational Aspects of Hemispheric Specialization," *UCLA Educator* 17 (Spring 1975), 27. An expanded version of this issue of the *UCLA Educator* is available: M. C. Wittrock et al., *The Human Brain* (Englewood Cliffs, N. J.: Prentice-Hall, 1977).

16. Brendan A. Maher, "The Shattered Language of Schizophrenia," *Psychology Today* 2 (Nov. 1968), 30–33.

17. Daniel Bub and Harry A. Whitaker, "Language and Verbal Processess," in Wittrock, *The Brain and Psychology,* pp. 211–12.

18. Basil Bernstein, "A Sociolinguistic Approach to Social Learning," in *Penguin Survey of the Social Sciences,* ed. J. Gould (New York: Penguin, 1965). Reprinted in Basil Bernstein, *Theoretical Studies towards a Sociology of Language,* vol. 1 of *Class, Codes, and Control,* 3 vols. (London: Routledge and Kegan Paul, 1975), p. 128.

19. Shirley Brice Heath, *Ways With Words: Language, Life, and Work in Communities and Classrooms* (Cambridge: Cambridge University Press, 1983).

20. Richard Fliegel, "The Codes of Literacy," unpublished Ph.D. thesis, University of Southern California, 1986.

21. Edwin J. Delattre, "The Insiders," in *Literacy for Life,* ed. Richard W. Bailey

and Robin Melanie Fosheim (New York: The Modern Language Assocation of America, 1983), p. 52

22. George L. Dillon, *Constructing Texts* (Bloomington: Indiana University Press, 1981), p. 23.

23. Stephen D. Krashen, *Second Language Acquisition and Second Language Learning* (New York: Pergamon Press, 1981), p. 11.

24. Stephen D. Krashen, "Attitude and Aptitude in Second Language Acquisition and Learning," in *Second Language Acquistion and Second Language Learning.*

25. *The World Almanac and Book of Facts 1988* (New York: Pharos Books, 1988), p. 361.

26. Gavriel Salomon, "Television Literacy and Television vs. Literacy," in Bailey and Fosheim.

27. Salomon, p. 69

28. Salomon, p. 70.

29. Salomon, p. 70.

30. Salomon, p. 76.

Works Cited

Adams, James L. *Conceptual Blockbusting: A Guide to Better Ideas.* Second ed. New York: W. W. Norton, 1979.

Allen, Woody. "Spring Bulletin." *Getting Even.* New York: Random House, 1971.

Austin, J. L. *How to Do Things with Words.* Oxford: Oxford University Press, 1962.

Bailey, Richard W., and Robin Melanie Fosheim, eds. *Literacy for Life.* New York: The Modern Language Association of America, 1983.

Barthes, Roland. "From Work to Text." *Textual Strategies: Perspectives in Post-Structuralist Criticism.* Ed. Josué Harari. Ithaca: Cornell University Press, 1979.

Bernstein, Basil. "A Sociolinguistic Approach to Social Learning." *Penguin Survey of the Social Sciences.* Ed. J. Gould. London: Penguin, 1965.
———. *Theoretical Studies towards a Sociology of Language.* Vol. 1. *Class, Codes, and Control.* Three vols. London: Routledge and Kegan Paul, 1975.

Bissex, Glenda L. *GNYS AT WRK: A Child Learns to Write and Read.* Cambridge, Mass.: Harvard University Press, 1980.

Bloom, Allan. *The Closing of the American Mind.* New York: Simon and Schuster, 1987.

Bogen, J. E. "Some Educational Aspects of Hemispheric Specialization." *UCLA Educator* 17 (Spring 1975), 27.

Borges, Jorge Luis. "The Library of Babel." *Ficciones.* New York: Grove Press, 1962.

Boswell, James. *The Life of Samuel Johnson.* Two vols. London: J. M. Dent and Company, 1906.

Brown, Roger, *A First Language: The Early Stages.* Cambridge, Mass.: Harvard University Press, 1973.

Bub, Daniel, and Harry A. Whitaker. "Language and Verbal Processes." *The Brain and Psychology.* Ed. M. C. Wittrock. New York: Academic Press, 1980.

Burke, Kenneth. *A Grammar of Motives*. Berkeley and Los Angeles: University of California Press, 1969.

———. *The Philosophy of Literary Form*. Rev. ed. New York: Vintage, 1957.

———. *A Rhetoric of Motives*. Berkeley: University of California Press, 1969.

Cambourne, Brian. "Oral and Written Relationships: A Reading Perspective." *Exploring Speaking/Writing Relationships*. Ed. Barry M. Kroll and Roberta J. Vann. Urbanna, Ill.: National Council of Teachers of English, 1981.

Cazden, Courtney, B. *Child, Language, and Education*. New York: Holt, Rinehart and Winston, 1972.

Chomsky, Carol. "Write Now, Read Later." *Childhood Education* 47 (1971), 296–99.

Cipolla, Carlo. *Literacy and Development in the West*. Harmondsworth, G.B.: Pelican, 1969.

Clammer, J. R. *Literacy and Social Change*. Leiden, The Netherlands: E. J. Brill, 1976.

Clark, Herbert H., and Eve V. Clark. *Psychology and Language*. New York: Harcourt Brace Jovanovich, 1977.

Cleaver, Eldridge. *Soul on Ice*. New York: Dell, 1968.

Culler, Jonathan. *Structuralist Poetics: Structuralism, Linguistics, and the Study of Literature*. Ithaca: Cornell University Press, 1975.

Dale, Edgar, and Jeanne S. Chall. "A Formula for Predicting Readability." *Educational Research Bulletin* 27 (1948), 37–54.

Defender, "St. Maarten's Jaycee Bryson elected 'Jaycee of the World.' " Windward Islands *Newsday* 4, 491 (November 24, 1980), 12.

Delattre, Edwin J. "The Insiders." *Literacy for Life*. Ed. Richard W. Bailey and Robin Melanie Fosheim. New York: The Modern Language Association of America, 1983.

Derrida, Jacques. *Of Grammatology*. Trans. Gayatri Chakravorty Spivak. Baltimore: John Hopkins University Press, 1974.

———. *Writing and Difference*. Trans. Alan Bass. Chicago: University of Chicago Press, 1976.

Dillon, George L. *Constructing Texts*. Bloomington: Indiana University Press, 1981.

Dixon, John. *Growth through English*. Oxford: Oxford University Press for the National Association for the Teaching of English, 1967.

Farb, Peter. *Word Play*. New York: Bantam, 1975.

Fillmore, Charles. "The Case for Case." *Universals in Linguistic Theory*. Ed. Emmon Bach and Robert T. Harms. New York: Holt, Rinehart and Winston, 1968.

Fish, Stanley. *Is There a Text in This Class?* Cambridge, Mass.: Harvard University Press, 1980.

Fliegel, Richard. "The Codes of Literacy." Dissertation, University of Southern California, 1986.

Flower, L[inda]. "Writer-Based Prose: A Cognitive Basis for Problems in Writing." *College English* 41 (1979), 19–37.

Freedman, Aviva, and Ian Pringle, eds. *Reinventing the Rhetorical Tradition.* Conway, Ark.: L&S Books for the Canadian Council of Teachers of English, 1980.

Freire, Paulo. *Education for Critical Consciousness.* New York: Continuum, 1982.

———. *Pedagogy of the Oppressed.* Trans. Myra Bergman Ramos. New York: Continuum, 1981.

Fry, Edward. "A Readability Formula That Saves Time." *Journal of Reading* 11 (1968), 513–16, 575–81.

Fussell, Paul. *Class.* New York: Ballantine, 1983.

Gelb, I. J. *A Study of Writing.* Chicago: University of Chicago Press, 1963.

Ghiselin, Brewster, ed. *The Creative Process.* New York: Mentor, 1952.

Goelman, Hillel, Antoinette Oberg, and Frank Smith, eds. *Awakening to Literacy.* Exeter, N.H.: Heinemann Educational Books, 1984.

Goodman, Kenneth, S. "Psycholinguistic Universals in the Reading Process." *Psycholinguistics and Reading.* Ed. Frank Smith. New York: Holt, Rinehart and Winston, 1973.

———. "Reading: A Psycholinguistic Guessing Game." *Journal of the Reading Specialist* 6 (1967), 126–35.

Goody, Jack. *The Domestication of the Savage Mind.* Cambridge: Cambridge University Press, 1977.

———and I[an] Watt. "The Consequences of Literacy." *Literacy in Traditional Societies.* Ed. J. Goody. New York: Cambridge University Press, 1968.

Gordon, Robert M. "The Readability of an Unreadable Text." *The English Journal* 69, 3 (March 1980), 60–61.

Gould, J., ed. *The Penguin Survey of the Social Sciences.* New York: Penguin, 1965.

Grice, H. P. William James Lectures, Harvard University, published in part as "Logic in Conversation." *Syntax and Semantics.* Ed. P. Cole and J. L. Morgan. Vol. 3: *Speech Acts.* New York: Seminar Press, 1975.

Halliday, M. A. K., and Ruqaiya Hasan. *Cohesion in English.* Bath, G.B.: Longman, 1976.

Hartwell, Patrick. "Grammar, Grammars, and the Teaching of Grammar." *College English* 47, 2 (Feb. 1985), 105–27.

Havelock, E. A. *Preface to Plato.* Cambridge, Mass.: Harvard University Press, 1963.

Heath, Shirley Brice. *Ways With Words: Language, Life, and Work in Communities and Classrooms.* Cambridge: Cambridge University Press, 1983.

Hillocks, George R., Jr. "The Interaction of Instruction, Teacher Comment, and Revision in the Composing Process." *Research in the Teaching of English* 16, 3 (1982), 261–78.

Hirsch, E. D., Jr. *Cultural Literacy: What Every American Needs to Know.* Boston: Houghton Mifflin, 1988.

———. "Reading, Writing, and Cultural Literacy." *Composition and Literature: Bridging the Gap.* Ed. Winifred Bryan Horner. Chicago: University of Chicago Press, 1983.

———. *Validity in Interpretation.* New Haven: Yale University Press, 1973.

Holdaway, Don. *The Foundations of Literacy.* Sydney, Australia: Ashton Scholastic, 1979.

IBM BASIC. Second ed. Boca Raton, Fla.: IBM, 1982.

Jakobson, Roman. "Linguistics and Poetics." *Style in Language.* Ed. Thomas A. Sebeok. Cambridge, Mass.: MIT Press, 1960.

Keenan, Elinor O[chs]. "Why Look at Unplanned and Planned Discourse." *Discourse Across Time and Space.* Southern California Occasional Papers in Linguistics No. 5. Ed. Elinor O[chs] Keenan and Tina L. Bennet. Los Angeles: University of Southern California, 1977.

Krashen, Stephen D. *Second Language Acquisition and Second Language Learning.* New York: Pergamon Press, 1981.

———. *Writing: Research, Theory, and Applications.* New York: Pergamon Institute of English, 1984.

Kroll, Barry M., and Roberta J. Vann, eds. *Exploring Speaking/Writing Relationships.* Urbana, Ill.: National Council of Teachers of English, 1981.

Labov, William. *The Study of Nonstandard English.* Urbana, Ill.: National Council of Teachers of English, 1970.

Lanham, Richard. *Literacy and the Survival of Humanism.* New Haven: Yale University Press, 1983.

Lévi-Strauss, Claude. *Tristes Tropiques.* New York: Washington Square Press, 1977.

Levy, Jerre. "Cerebral Asymmetry and the Psychology of Man." *The Brain and Psychology.* Ed. M. C. Wittrock. New York: Academic Press, 1980.

Loban, Walter. *Language Development: Kindergarten Through Grade*

Twelve. Urbana, Ill.: National Council of Teachers of English, 1976.

Luria, A. R. *The Working Brain: An Introduction to Neuropsychology*. New York: Basic Books, 1973.

Maher, Brendan A. "The Shattered Language of Schizophrenia." *Psychology Today* 2 (Nov. 1968), 30–33.

McLoughland, Beverly. "Creature." *Language Arts* 63, 5 (Sept. 1986), 481.

Nebes, Robert D. "Man's So-Called 'Minor' Hemisphere." *UCLA Educator* 17 (Spring 1975), 9–12.

Nichols, Patricia C. "Creoles of the USA." *Language in the USA*. Ed. Charles A. Ferguson and Shirley Brice Heath. Cambridge: Cambridge University Press, 1981.

Ochs, Elinor. See Keenan, Elinor O[chs].

Ong, Walter J., S.J. *Interfaces of the Word*. Ithaca: Cornell University Press, 1977.

———. *The Presence of the Word*. New Haven: Yale University Press, 1967.

Oxenham, John. *Literacy: Writing, Reading and Social Organisation*. London: Routledge and Kegan Paul, 1980.

Parnes, Sidney J. *Creative Behavior Workbook*. New York: Charles Scribner's Sons, 1967.

Pattison, Robert. *On Literacy*. New York: Oxford University Press, 1982.

Perkins, D. N. *The Mind's Best Work*. Cambridge, Mass.: Harvard University Press, 1981.

Perl, S[ondra]. "The Composing Process of Unskilled College Writers." *Research in the Teaching of English* 13 (1979), 317–39.

Pianko, S[haron]. "A Description of the Composing Process of College Freshman Writers." *Research in the Teaching of English* 13 (1979), 5–22.

Ramsay, Selden. *Education*. "Fifth Report of the National Council on Educational Research." Washington, D.C.: NIE, fiscal years 1978–79.

Raudsepp, Eugene, with George P. Hough, Jr. *Creative Growth Games*. New York: Harcourt Brace Jovanovich, 1977.

Rutter, M., and W. Yule. "The Concept of Specific Reading Retardation." *Journal of Child Psychology and Pyschiatry* 16 (1975), 181–97.

Salomon, Gavriel. "Television Literacy and Television vs. Literacy." *Literacy for Life*. Ed. Richard W. Bailey and Robin Melanie Fosheim. New York: The Modern Language Association of America, 1983.

Schieffelin, Bambi B., and Marilyn Cochran-Smith. "Learning to Read Culturally: Literacy Before Schooling." *Awakening to Literacy*.

Ed. Hillel Goelman, Antoinette Oberg, and Frank Smith. Exeter, N.H.: Heinemann Educational Books, 1984.

Scollon, Suzanne B. K., and Ron Scollon. "}RUN TRILOGY: Can Tommy Read?" *Awakening to Literacy*. Ed. Hillel Goelman, Antoinette Oberg, and Frank Smith. Exeter, N.H.: Heinemann Educational Books, 1984.

Scribner, Sylvia, and Michael Cole. *The Psychology of Literacy*. Cambridge, Mass.: Harvard University Press, 1981.

Searle, John R. *Speech Acts: An Essay in the Philosophy of Language*. Cambridge: Cambridge University Press, 1975.

Shaughnessy, Mina P. *Errors and Expectations: A Guide for the Teacher of Basic Writing*. New York: Oxford University Press, 1977.

Simon, David E. *IBM BASIC From the Ground Up*. Rochelle Park, N.J.: Hayden, 1983.

Simon, John. *Paradigms Lost*. New York: Clarkson N. Potter, 1980.

Smith, Frank. *Understanding Reading*. Third ed. New York: Holt, Rinehart and Winston, 1982.

Smith, Frank, ed. *Psycholinguistics and Reading*. New York: Holt, Rinehart and Winston, 1973.

Strassmann, Paul A. "Information Systems and Literacy." *Literacy for Life*. Ed. Richard W. Bailey and Robin Melanie Fosheim. New York: The Modern Language Association of America, 1983.

Tannen, Deborah. "Oral and Literate Strategies in Spoken and Written Discourse." *Literacy for Life*. Ed. Richard W. Bailey and Robin Melanie Fosheim. New York: The Modern Language Association of America, 1983.

Tanner, William E., and J. Dean Bishop. *Rhetoric and Change*. Mesquite, Tex.: Ide House, 1982.

Taylor, Denny. *Family Literacy*. Exeter, N.H.: Heinemann Educational Books, 1983.

Taylor, Insup, and M. Martin Taylor. *The Psychology of Reading*. New York: Academic Press, 1983.

Thomas, Lewis. "Clever Animals." *Late Night Thoughts on Listening to Mahler's Ninth Symphony*. New York: Bantam, 1984.

Tyler, Ralph W. "Testing Writing: Procedures Vary with Purposes." *Literacy for Life*. Ed. Richard W. Bailey and Robin Melanie Fosheim. New York: The Modern Language Association of America, 1983.

van Dijk, Teun a. *Macrostructures: An Interdisciplinary Study of Global Structure in Discourse, Interaction, and Cognition*. Hillsdale, N.J.: Lawrence Erlbaum, 1980.

Wall, S., and A. Petrovsky. "Freshman Writers and Revision: Results from a Survey." *Journal of Basic Writing* 3 (1981), 109–22.

Welty, Eudora. *One Writer's Beginnings*. Cambridge, Mass.: Harvard University Press, 1983, 1984.

White, James Boyd. "The Invisible Discourse of the Law: Relfections on Legal Literacy and General Education." *Literacy for Life*. Ed. Richard W. Bailey and Robin Melanie Fosheim. New York: The Modern Language Association of America, 1983.

Williams, E. W. "Teaching a Toddler to Teach Herself to Read." MA thesis. University of Texas at El Paso, 1980.

Winterowd, W. Ross. "Black Holes, Indeterminacy, and Paulo Freire." *Rhetoric Review* 2, 1 (1983), 28–36.

———. "Composing: A Case Study." *The Contemporary Writer*. Third ed. Orlando, Fla.: Harcourt Brace Jovanovich, 1989.

———. *Composition/Rhetoric: A Synthesis*. Carbondale: Southern Illinois University Press, 1986.

———. *The Contemporary Writer*. New York: Harcourt Brace Jovanovich, 1981.

———. "Developing a Composition Program." *Reinventing the Rhetorical Tradition*. Ed. Aviva Freedman and Ian Pringle. Conway, Ark.: L&S Books for the Canadian Council of Teachers of English, 1980.

———. "Literacy: *Kultur* and Culture." *Language Arts* 64 (1987), 869–74.

———. "The Three R's: Reading, Reading, and Rhetoric." *Rhetoric and Change*. Ed. William E. Tanner and J. Dean Bishop. Mesquite, Tex.: Ide House, 1982.

Wittrock, M. C., ed. *The Brain and Psychology*. New York: Academic Press, 1980.

———, et al. *The Human Brain*. Englewood Cliffs, N.J.: Prentice-Hall, 1977.

The World Almanac and Book of Facts 1988. New York: Pharos, 1988.

Young, Richard, Alton L. Becker, and Kenneth L. Pike. *Rhetoric: Discovery and Change*. New York: Harcourt Brace Jovanovich, 1970.

Index

221